Linkages in South African Economic Development

Forschungsergebnisse der Wirtschaftsuniversität Wien

WIRTSCHAFTS
UNIVERSITÄT
WIEN VIENNA
UNIVERSITY OF
ECONOMICS
AND BUSINESS

Band 41

PETER LANG
Frankfurt am Main · Berlin · Bern · Bruxelles · New York · Oxford · Wien

OLIVER SCHWANK

Linkages in South African Economic Development

Industrialisation without Diversification?

PETER LANG
Internationaler Verlag der Wissenschaften

Bibliographic Information published by the Deutsche Nationalbibliothek
The Deutsche Nationalbibliothek lists this publication in the Deutsche Nationalbibliografie; detailed bibliographic data is available in the internet at http://dnb.d-nb.de.

Cover design:
Atelier Platen according to a design of
Werner Weißhappl.

University logo of the Vienna University of Economics and Business Administration.
Printed with kindly permission of the University.

Sponsored by the Vienna University of Economics and Business Administration.

ISSN 1613-3056
ISBN 978-3-631-58701-0

www.peterlang.de

Contents

List of Abbreviations

ANC African National Congress

AsgiSA Accelerated and Shared Growth Initiative South Africa

BTI Board of Trade and Industry

CES Constant Elasticity of Substitution

COSATU Congress of South African Trade Unions

CP Core-Periphery

DTI Department of Trade and Industry

GEAR Growth, Employment and Redistribution

GEIS General Export Incentive Scheme

IDC Industrial Development Corporation

ISP Industrial Strategy Project

KAP Key Action Plan

MEC Minerals Energy Complex

MERG Macroeconomic Research Group

MIDP Motor Industry Development Programme

NEG New Economic Geography

NIC Newly Industrializing Countries

NIPF National Industrial Policy Framework

NP National Party

RDP Reconstruction and Development Programme

SACP South African Communist Party

SADC Southern African Development Community

SARB South African Reserve Bank

SOE State-Owned Enterprise

SVAR Structural Vector Autoregression

VL Vertical Linkages

Preface

The fact that an Austrian student writes his dissertation on South Africa probably requires some sort of explanation if not justification. I was focusing on questions of development economics in my graduate program and I did have a general interest in Africa then, but still my interest in and my passion for South Africa is mostly explained by a two year stay in the country after having obtained my masters degree in Vienna. While I was not working or studying in the field of economics, it was nevertheless impossible not to notice the daunting social and economic challenges South Africa was facing more than a decade after the end of apartheid. So when I returned to Austria and to university I knew that I would try to research one of these in my dissertation.

Writing a dissertation is not a small matter, and while doing so I have accrued debts to countless people around me. I want to thank all of them, particularly those I forget to mention below.

First and foremost I would like to thank my parents for supporting me throughout my studies and up until today—their support seems no less important now then it was many years ago when I started my academic career. Much to their regret, Sr. Pallotti from the Mariannhill Missionary Sisters enabled me to spend two wonderful years in South Africa to work as a teacher and to discover a most fascinating country. Although it is now three- and a half years that I returned to Austria, continued and close contact to some very special people there has kept the object of my scientific endeavors close to my heart as well. They are Ronita Mahilall, Shaku Reddy, Sibongile Dlamini and Thandeka Mchunu.

In my time at the Institute of International Economics and Development at the Vienna University of Economics I have profited from a healthy balance of academic guidance and academic freedom, from fruitful discussion and a friendly and motivating work climate. For this, Ingrid Kubin, Joachim Becker and my other colleagues at the Institute are responsible.

Lastly, I want to thank my friends in Vienna for their understanding of mood swings that were caused by the very document you are holding in your hands right now. Unfortunately, I cannot in good faith promise betterment on this account. And thank you Osa, you were closest to the ups and downs, and you endured them with a truly unique and admirable patience.

Chapter 1

Introduction

1.1 Motivation

A myriad of serious and pressing problems confront the South African economy. The current account is firmly in deficit, the country still relies on its natural resources—and thus sectors that are very volatile—for a large part of its foreign exchange earnings, growth is less dynamic than policy makers aim for and, last but certainly not least, up to forty percent (depending on the definition) of the working age population are without a job. This is not only an enormous waste of resources and a social tragedy in itself but also lies at the bottom of a whole range of other problems—including poverty, inequality, and rampant crime.

All of these problems can be explained at least partly by the peculiar structure of the South African economy—an economy that has grown around a strong and dominant mining sector. With regards to the external dimension, the current account deficit widens whenever the economy grows because the manufacturing sector is still inward-oriented and a net consumer of foreign exchange. This historical orientation towards the domestic market is possible only because mineral exports financed an import substitution industrialisation path. Unemployment rose to such levels due to massive job losses in mining, agriculture and manufacturing ever since the 1980s. Without touching on the (hotly debated) reasons for this decline here, it is safe to state that job losses in the first two sectors were to be expected due to a structural shift of the economy away from primary activities. The third, manufacturing, could have and should have provided job opportunities on a much higher scale (Hirsch, 2005, 122ff.). It did not, despite the strong industrial base South Africa profits from ever since the discovery of diamonds, gold and a host of other immensely valuable mineral resources. So I turn my attention to the industrial sector, its particular features and structure, weaknesses and potentials for growth.

1.2 Statement of the Problem—A Rapprochement

South Africa can be characterized as a minerals economy (Altman, 2001, 692). It is by far the richest economy in Sub Saharan Africa and it owes this position to its mineral wealth. The discovery of diamonds and gold in the late 19th century sparked a massive inflow of mainly British capital, accompanied by high numbers of skilled white workers (Marais, 2001, 8). The economy was built up around the mining sector and many of the structural features characterizing South Africa today can be traced back to the 'mineral revolution' of the 1870s. Here it suffices to mention the capital intensive industrial development South Africa was experiencing since then. Due to their depth, the exploitation of the mines was a very capital intensive undertaking, requiring expensive exploration operations and elaborate and energy-intensive physical and chemical processes (Feinstein, 2005, 201). This led to an early consolidation of the industry and at the same time these backward linkages fostered growth in coal mining and electricity generation, chemicals (explosives) and a range of other industries (Feinstein, 2005, 107f.). The South African state reinforced these developments by establishing state-owned corporations such as Sasol (petrochemicals), Eskom (electricity) and Iscor (steel) and by joint ventures with the private sector. State investment and support up until the late 20th century was mostly concentrated in capital intensive sectors—where skilled and highly paid white workers would find jobs (Black, 1991, 159ff.).

The evolution of the South African economy around the mining sector led Fine and Rustomjee (1996) to the coining of the term 'Minerals-Energy Complex' or MEC. By MEC they mean the mining sector and the tightly integrated sectors that grew around it: "Coal, gold, diamond and other mining activities; electricity; non-metallic mineral products; iron and steel basic industries; non-ferrous metals basic industries; and fertilisers, pesticides, synthetic resins, plastics, other chemicals, basic chemicals and petroleum." (Fine and Rustomjee, 1996, 79). In conventional statistics, most of the economic activities mentioned above are subsumed under manufacturing, yet this is misleading. Take the smelting and refining of ore as an example: it is tightly integrated with mining itself in terms of technology and the production process and organisationally. More activity in this sector therefore should not be perceived as diversification of the economy away from mining. When these characteristics are taken into account and manufacturing is defined narrowly (excluding MEC activities), then it becomes apparent that the manufacturing sector was stagnating at around 15% to 17% of GDP between 1960 and 1990, while the MEC remained the core of the economy—despite a smaller contribution of mining per se (Fine and Rustomjee, 1996, 81).

One of the problems is that the MEC is capital intensive which leads to a 'paradoxical' production structure in a country with abundant supply of unskilled labour. The trend continued in the 1990s. "Low rates of growth in the labour intensive sectors have combined with overall rising capital intensity resulting in consistent declines in manufacturing employment." (Kaplan, 2003, 10)

So the crucial question is how to diversify out of this capital intensive core of the economy, using its strengths, the acquired skills and knowledge and the potential linkages to downstream sectors, and to steer industrial development towards a more diversified, dynamic and labour absorbing path.

It is a question that was asked by the incoming ANC government in 1994, yet then economic priorities were clearly on macroeconomic stabilization. And it is a question that resurfaces now, with the macroeconomic fundamentals in place and both the scientific community and the government shifting attention to questions of sectoral composition and microeconomic reform within the broad field of industrial policy (see for example Naidoo, 2006).

1.3 State of the Field

The recurring theme is 'linkages': they played a crucial role in South Africa's economic development, where mining activities created backward linkages to providing industries such as chemicals and forward linkages to industrial buyers of their output, so called downstream industries. And they were and are central in industrial policy discussions.

Linkages in Development Economics

In economic theory, the concept of linkages is an old one which came to prominence thanks to the rise of development economics after World War Two. Before that, German economist Friedrich List stressed the importance of productive capabilities that are built up in the development process, and how the pursuit of certain industrial activities calls forth production and is productivity enhancing in other sectors of the economy (List, 1950). After 1945, the concept of linkages was at the very core of the nascent discipline of development economics. Rosenstein-Rodan argued for a "large scale planned industrialization" (Rosenstein-Rodan, 1943, 205) in order to enable the exploitation of complementarity of industries. Myrdal (1957), rather than perceiving the economy as a system that tends toward a stable equilibrium, introduced the notion of a vicious (or virtuous) circle where exogenous shocks lead to a self-reinforcing process of cumulative causation. Albert O. Hirschman then went on to explicitly define backward and forward linkages, the former inducing local production of inputs once demand for these inputs reaches a critical scale, the latter providing inputs locally for downstream producers (Hirschman, 1966). He also enriched the concept by stressing two necessary conditions for linkages to work: scale effects—without economies of scale the concept of linkages would be meaningless since every economic activity is linked to many others—and private entrepreneurial or public responsiveness to incentives. Linkages can also be understood as providing investment opportunities and therefore act as guidance for private and state investment (Hirschman, 1981).

Linkages also informed sector specific industrial policy in East Asia where countries such as South Korea and Taiwan deliberately 'got the prices wrong' to steer industrial development (see for example Wade, 1990, Amsden, 2001). These developments have relevance particularly because they are often evoked by policy makers as a role model for South Africa.

To summarize, I would argue that both theoretical and empirical work has shown that linkages play a crucial part in the industrialisation path a country is taking. They provide opportunities for further activities—in the case of a minerals economy such as South Africa these opportunities naturally appear around the resource endowments. This corresponds to the actual development experience of South Africa. Yet linkages alone cannot be relied on to generate investment. Following Hirschman, I understand them more as opportunity still to be exploited by some agent. Usually this role is taken over by private business, but—and this is what can be learned from the East Asian experience—government should and can play a guiding role in the sectoral allocation of investment when the market cannot be relied upon. It should do so by forging a vision of which path the economy is supposed to take (see for example Chang, 1998); and by picking sectors for support that are on the one hand strongly linked to existing activities, and that on the other hand display dynamic potential as described above.

Linkages in the New Economic Geography Literature

Geographical economics tries to explain phenomena of 'second nature', defined as endogenous forces, brought about by human action, that influence and shape the economic landscape and lead to large regional imbalances and clustering of economic activities (Ottaviano and Thisse, 2004, 2565). I will focus on the New Economic Geography (NEG), an area of research started and brought to prominence by authors such as Fujita, Venables and Krugman (the seminal reference being Krugman 1991a).

Before I elaborate on the logic of NEG models, I want to briefly explain how NEG fits into this literature review—in other words how it can be brought together with the linkages argument of development economics. Interestingly, many papers in NEG cite the classics of development economics such as Hirschman and Myrdal. Krugman himself dedicates one whole book (Krugman, 1997) to this cause. He explains how the ideas of development economists and economic geographers—interesting and relevant as they were—failed to influence the mainstream of economic theory. Taking Hirschman's forward and backward linkages as an example, he argues that they only matter if combined with increasing returns to scale in production. Hirschman was aware of this, yet then, economies of scale were difficult to model in a general equilibrium context because they are irreconcilable with perfect competition. When the standards of mathematical rigour rose in the profession, the linkages and related arguments involving complementarities or circularity were pushed to the margins of economic theory (Krugman, 1997, 25ff.). NEG models allow their reintroduction because they assume economies of scale in production and because they add a spatial dimension (transport costs) to the economy—both of which leads to mathematically told stories that do have a close resemblance to arguments in development economics reviewed above.

The logic of NEG models is probably best explained by starting where it all started: with Krugman's first core-periphery (CP) model (Krugman, 1991a). It constitutes an attempt to understand how and why the manufacturing sector within a national economy might come to be locally concentrated in a core of the economy, a core which then provides the rest of the economy or the periphery with its manufactured goods. Krugman assumes that there are two sectors, the agricultural or traditional sector which is characterized by constant returns to scale and perfect competition, and the manufacturing or modern sector which displays increasing returns to scale. Since transport costs are positive in manufacturing, this will inevitably lead to a limited number of manufacturing production sites (while agriculture is evenly spread). Demand comes from farmers, who are dispersed across the country, and from workers in manufacturing. Since the prevailing technology in manufacturing leads to a concentration in production, final demand from manufacturing wages will be equally concentrated—and a pattern of circular causality emerges. Workers (firms) will move to the core because demand is high, and their very move to the core further increases demand in the core.

The actual spatial distribution of manufacturing activity depends on the parameters of the model: if the manufacturing sector is small and transport costs are high, then manufacturers will locate close to where farmers live, leading to a structure of small towns serving local markets. If then, over time, manufacturing increases in importance, transport costs fall and economies of scale become stronger, it is easy to see how "the tie of production to the distribution of land will be broken. [...] Population will start to concentrate and regions to diverge; once started, this process will feed on itself." (Krugman, 1991a, 487)

Since Krugman's initial contribution, a host of different models with similar features and applications have been presented (for an overview and extensive summaries see Fujita et al., 2001; Baldwin et al., 2003). In the context of industrial policy and industrial development, models with vertical linkages (VL) are particularly interesting. The original contributions in this sub-field are from Krugman and Venables (Krugman and Venables, 1995; Venables, 1996). Fujita et al. (2001, chap. 14-16) present text book versions and very recently, Ottaviano and Robert-Nicoud provided a synthesis of VL models (Ottaviano and Robert-Nicoud, 2006).

What the VL models have in common is that the spatial dynamics result not from movement of labour between regions as in the CP model, but from "intersectoral reallocation of factors within the same location" (Ottaviano and Robert-Nicoud, 2006, 114). These models are set in an international context where labour is assumed to be immobile between regions, yet will move according to wage differentials between the traditional and the manufacturing sector within one location. Firstly, this implies that permanent real wage differentials between countries are possible. Secondly, the driving force of agglomeration now is the manufacturing sector itself which not only produces but also consumes manufacturing goods as inputs. It is then possible to redefine linkage effects. If more firms settle in a region, firms in the region profit from a greater variety of inputs—a forward linkage. At the same time, more firms in a region imply a higher demand for manufactures as inputs—a backward linkage. While these linkage effects act as agglomerative force, the rising manufacturing wage level in the core relative to the periphery acts as dispersion force which at some point might incite firms to establish themselves in the periphery.

Krugman and Venables (1995) develop this set up to retell the story of East Asia's rapid economic rise. In a two regions model, transport costs are initially high so manufacturing happens close to consumers in both regions, a manufacturing core and the periphery. When transport costs fall however, the region initially possessing a larger manufacturing sector offers better conditions for firms due to backward and forward linkages and will cause them to resettle and supply the rest of the world from the now established core. At the same time, this development drives up wages in the core. Letting transport costs fall further however will at one point "be sufficient that the lower wage rate in the periphery more than offsets the disadvantage of being remote from markets and suppliers." (Krugman and Venables, 1995, 861). So firms will start to move and create linkages there, triggering a rapid industrialisation process.

Venables (1996) enriches the model by adding a second industrial sector, one being upstream and supplying only the downstream sector, one being downstream, supplying consumers. Puga and Venables (1996, 1999) provide a particularly interesting framework that lends itself to applications on development economies and industrial development. They set up a multi-country and multi-industry framework where each industry is imperfectly competitive and industries are linked by an input-output structure. Starting with an initial core periphery distribution of manufacturing, they then add an exogenous growth process that expresses itself in increased demand for manufactured goods. At first, strong linkage effects let new firms in the core satisfy additional demand, driving up wages and increasing inequality between regions. At a certain wage level, it becomes profitable for firms to forego benefits from linkages in the centre, and take advantage of low wages in the periphery by moving there. They thereby create linkages and trigger a self-sustaining industrialisation process in the periphery—a story reminiscent of old ideas like circular causality and cumulative causation.

To summarize, NEG models provide an analytical framework which allows isolating 'second nature' effects such as linkages that might be partially responsible for agglomeration processes or, in the case of VL models, the evolution of industrial development in peripheral areas.

1.4 Research Question and Purpose of the Study

I started out with a rather vague formulation of the problem under scrutiny in this dissertation: how can South Africa diversify its industrial sector so to be less dependent on mineral exports and to increase labour absorption. By bringing together the different branches of research presented above, I will now try to narrow the research question and to express it in a more precise way.

Development economists stress the importance of linkages in the process of economic growth. They can be seen as investment opportunities provided by an existing activity that incite further economic activity in linked sectors. The strength of linkage effects is evident in South Africa, where today's development trajectory is still defined by its mineral endowment and the MEC that evolved around it. This is problematic because resource-based sectors are by nature volatile, they often lack the dynamism of manufacturing and, particularly in the case of South Africa, not enough jobs are created in these capital intensive sectors. At the same time, South Africa is not competitive on a global level in low skill manufacturing because it is a middle income country with a corresponding cost structure and comparatively high wages. Clearly, these are two sides of the same coin.

I will first try to shed more light on this particular structure of the South African economy and its industrial sector by simulating a NEG model of the VL type with a highly aggregated input-output structure derived from actual South African input-output tables. Following Fine and Rustomjee (1996) the aggregation will distinguish between mining, the tightly linked manufacturing sectors close to primary activities (which together comprise the MEC) and other manufacturing sectors which include labour intensive industries. In order to illustrate the 'stuck in the middle' position of South Africa, I use a three regions framework by adding an advanced region (the core in terms of NEG) and a low wage region. The three regions possess the same technology captured by the input-output structure, but are differently endowed with a sector-specific natural resource that is used in the mining sector. The latter is crucial to cater for South Africa's mineral endowment. Starting from an initial position that is supposed to (albeit crudely) reflect South Africa's current situation, I will then run a simulation similar to the ones done by Puga and Venables (1996, 1999). An exogenous growth process increases world demand for manufacturing. As a result, further agglomeration in the core and—depending on parameter values—dispersion and a resettlement of certain industries in peripheral regions will occur. Technology and initial endowments determine which region ends up with the respective activities. Presumably, labour intensive sectors will continue to evade South Africa while it might attract firms in sectors that are close to the MEC due to linkage effects.

Essentially, the simulation will allow assessing the role of linkages quantitatively and depict how they—in combination with South Africa's resource endowment—might continue to shape its development path.

Due to the high level of aggregation and the stylized form of the model, results obviously have to be taken with a pinch of salt. Additionally, questions of supreme importance in the theory of industrial policy—for example government's role or the institutional set up—are all abstracted from. In order to increase policy relevance, I will conduct a quantitative assessment of linkage strength and a qualitative case study on industrial policy. The econometric work uses a structural vector autoregression approach to assess the extent of influence of one sector's performance on other sectors in the South African economy. Linkages will be explicitly modeled in this framework to test for the propositions arrived at in the simulation. In the case study on industrial policy, the recent changes in industrial policy strategy of the South African government are scrutinized—a more developmental and interventionist industrial policy is supposed to redirect its industrial development towards a more labour-absorbing path. Whether a break from existing patterns of sectoral growth and from existing patterns of economic policy geared towards these historically strong and well-supported sectors is realistic within the current framework will be subject of this case study.

To sum up, the research question can be restated as follows: To what extent do linkage effects define South Africa's industrial development trajectory, and how suitable is current industrial policy to facilitate a change towards a more diversified industrial development?

1.5 Structure of the Dissertation

The dissertation will begin with an exposition of South Africa's industrial sector in chapter Two. For this purpose I will present a brief history of industrial development, with emphasis on the MEC and questions of path dependence and linkage effects. This is accompanied by a presentation of stylized facts corroborating the dominant role of the MEC up until today. The first section is concluded by a brief summation of the past and current policy response to the overall disappointing performance of the industrial sector.

Chapter Three will present economic theory on linkages. The concept is traced back to development economics, related to industrial policy analysis of the Asian miracle and lastly presented in the NEG literature. In this chapter I will also write down in detail the VL model to be used later.

Chapter Four consists of the simulation analysis. The simulation is based on a model taken from the literature. However the model is adapted to suit the South African case and simulation parameters are arrived at by using data from South Africa's industrial structure.

In chapter Five, and in direct reference to the results of the simulation, an empirical assessment of linkage strengths is carried out. The methodology used is a structural vector autoregression.

Chapter Six is a case study on industrial policy. It complements the simulation and econometric work in two ways: it evaluates results on the importance of linkages from a qualitative and sectoral perspective, and it provides an analysis of sector-specific industrial policy measures and their chances of success.

Chapter 2

South African Industrial Development

This dissertation deals with the sectoral development of the South African economy—how linkages and path dependence shape the structure of the economy and to what extent they might influence the future growth path.

Any such project must start with a historical assessment first. If I claim that path dependence is an issue today, obviously it had to have been an issue historically. Depicting the development of the industrial sector over time will provide the basis for my hypothesis—in a way it aims to justify the research question. To this end I will try to show how South Africa's minerals endowment—discovered in the late 19th century—triggered the industrialisation process and has been extremely influential in its peculiarity up until today. The analysis of industrial development will always be complemented by an examination of economic and more narrowly industrial policy. Again, the historical overview will provide the basis for the appraisal of today's industrial policy and future options.

The chapter is structured in three parts. Firstly, the minerals discoveries in 1867 and 1886 transformed the economy and turned South Africa into a modern capitalist economy. The rise of the mining houses and the early phase of industrialisation that followed will be analysed accordingly. This era also witnessed the political consolidation of South Africa, however two world wars and internal power struggles meant turbulent times and resulted in little cohesion in industrial policy. Secondly, the victory of the National Party in the general elections of 1948 heralded a new era for South Africa.

The architects of apartheid remained in power for more than 40 years and governed over both the post-war boom of the South African economy and its steady decline since the mid-1970s. The continuity in the economic development path and, perhaps surprisingly, in industrial policy inconsistencies will be just as important as the break that my structure seems to imply, however. Thirdly, South Africa's democratic era started in 1994. The political opening was accompanied by the opening of the economy—with a decidedly mixed outcome in terms of output and employment performance. Obviously, the overall policy outlook shifted dramatically since, for the first time in South Africa's history, its leaders were accountable to all its citizens. To what extent this informed industrial policy considerations will conclude this chapter. The historical account ends in 2004, very recent developments will be covered in Chapter 6 on industrial policy strategy.

2.1 The Discovery of Minerals and the Rise of Capitalism

There is no definite account of how exactly the first diamond was discovered in South Africa. According to one version, a trader named John O'Reilly found children playing with the precious stone on a Boer farm near the Orange River in 1867. The farmer, unaware of its worth, initially refused to accept money for a pebble and insisted on giving it to O'Reilly for free. Two years later, the same farmer had apparently attained some knowledge on precious stones and sold another, far bigger stone (in fact it was an 80 carat diamond which was later called the "Star of Africa") to local jewellers for more than eleven thousand pounds. Of this stone, the British colonial secretary at the time famously said that it would be "the rock on which the future of South Africa will be built."(Welsh, 2000, 235)

History has of course proved him right. Diamonds and later gold transformed the South African economy and with it its society and politics. From a sparsely populated rentier economy based on extensive agriculture, it turned into a modern capitalist one within half a century, with mining and manufacturing sectors second to none in Africa. The transformation provided the foundations for modern South Africa and in it one can already identify both the strengths and the weaknesses that characterize the South African economy 140 years later. The focus of the present account will of course be on the industrial sector, which partly owes its peculiar structure to the developments in this early period.

Early History

Europeans arrived and settled at the Cape of Good Hope from 1652 onwards. For a long period they remained confined to the Cape peninsula and its surroundings. During the 18th and 19th century, descendants of the Dutch settlers, the Afrikaners or Boers, slowly migrated along the coast to the east and to the interior, engaging in extensive agriculture. These migrations, most famously the Great Trek of the 1830s and 1840s that was sparked by a controversy with the now British authorities in Cape Town, led to constant conflict with African societies. At issue was access to and control over land and more importantly labour—a very scarce good even before the advent of mining (Feinstein, 2005, 34). The economy was thus still dominated by agriculture in the mid-19th century. The trekkers that settled in the interior were subsistence farmers, and the same is true for African societies. Only in the coastal regions were there pockets of agricultural and commercial capitalism. Cape Town profited from its geographical position and the dynamic of the British Empire and became a commercial hub; the Cape Colony and Natal exported some agricultural products, notably wine and sugar (Iliffe, 1999, 90).

Immediate Effects of the Discoveries

The discovery of diamonds and then gold changed the character of the region and its economy. Within two decades mining activities totally dominated the economy, providing close to 60% of exports from the region (Feinstein, 2005, 101). Surely a change of such proportions must have enormous consequences for any region. I will try to briefly describe the most important for South Africa here, focusing on the role of monopoly capital, linkages to the manufacturing industry, and the political consequences, particularly in terms of industrial and labour policy.

Firstly, the discoveries sparked a massive inflow of mainly British capital, and these capital groups quickly established control over the mining industry. Only briefly were independent diggers able to claim their stake in the diamond fields. Because the diamonds mostly lay underground, expensive shafts had to be built, requiring significant capital outlays. Soon

De Beers Consolidated Mines, founded by Cecil Rhodes, had consolidated the digging claims and controlled total diamond output. The monopolistic structure provided a blueprint for the gold industry. After the exhaustion of surface deposits, much of the gold of the Witwatersrand gold fields was not easily accessible, but embedded in small particles in deep lying hard quartz rock. Only large corporations were able to raise sufficient amounts of capital to undertake the expensive and risky deep-level mining (Feinstein, 2005, 99f.). Fine and Rustomjee (1996, 98) show how mineral production was controlled by six mining houses by 1932. Since they were faced with virtually unlimited demand at a fixed price from world markets, they co-operated closely with each other from the beginning. This was particularly obvious in the recruiting of migrant labour from the whole subcontinent, of which I will write more below. Crucially for the South African economy, they soon diversified and extended their activities to downstream mineral processing, the steel and chemicals sector, engineering, other manufacturing sectors and banking. As a result, the South African economy displays to this day exceptionally high levels of ownership concentration and monopolistic and oligopolistic structures in many of its sub-sectors.

Of what nature exactly were the linkages that mining did provide to the rest of the economy? Before the turn of the century, there seemed to have been very few. Profits from mining were repatriated to Britain, and most inputs into mining and even food supplies for miners were imported (Clark, 1994, 16). However, this proved to be too expensive, and slowly manufacturing increased—there were some consumer-goods and food processing industries and heavy industries providing inputs for the gold mines: cement, chemicals (particularly explosives), mechanical repair and coal-based electricity. The parallel construction of a national railway system added demand for coal, electricity and steel. However, in relation to mining and agriculture they remained minuscule: in 1913 their combined contribution to GDP was less than five percent (Feinstein, 2005, 115; see also Iliffe, 1999, 93).

Manufacturing Gains in Importance

The First World War provided a protective stimulus to the local economy, but in many instances local producers could not take advantage due to a lack of capacity—steel can serve as an example here. After the war however, manufacturing continuously gained in importance and an industrialization process worth its name finally set in. This is visible in the continuously

	Agriculture	Mining	Industry
1911	21,5	27,3	5,9
1918	24,2	18	9,7
1928	18,9	15,7	12,4
1938	12,7	18,3	17
1948	16,4	10	23,3

Table 2.1: Share of activity in percent of GDP

Source: Feinstein 2005, 129

rising share of industry in total activity in Table 2.1. Moreover, the rising proportion of manufacturing activity in this period has to be seen in the context of strong overall growth. As a result, total employment in industry increased from 124.000 in 1916 to 668.000 in 1948 (Feinstein, 2005, 122).

In terms of sectoral development, Table 2.2 shows how in 1924, the manufacturing sector was still dominated by basic consumer industries, particularly food and beverages that contributed a third of total manufacturing output. Heavy industry was concentrated in chemicals, and there was notable activity in non-metallic minerals and basic metals too—all of these of course very closely linked to the mining operations. The inter war period and the 1940s then witnessed significant diversification however. Overall, heavy industry gained in importance, mostly driven by the basic metal industries, increasing its share in total manufacturing to almost 50% in 1948/49. Another notable growth sector was transport equipment. Within light industries, the textiles and clothing sector expanded strongly. To a large extent, these developments were driven by the gold-induced boom after 1933 and then the Second World War—another period of protection from global competition. This time South African producers were able to expand production and for the first time introduced large-scale standardized methods of mass production. In terms of employees, the average firm size doubled over the period (Feinstein, 2005, 123ff.).

Economic and Industrial Policy

To what extent was this industrialisation process driven by economic policy? It is undisputed that the creation of jobs in the manufacturing sector became an important and urgent goal in politics in this period. The Union of South

	1924/25	1948/49
Food, beverages and tobacco	32,4	19
Textiles, clothing, leather, footwear	10	15,2
Wood and furniture	6,9	6,4
Paper, printing and publishing	11,2	7,7
Other manufacturing	2,7	3,4
Total light industry	**63,2**	**51,7**
Chemicals and chemical products	12,1	9,5
Pottery, glass, other non-metallic minerals	7	6
Basic metal industries	8,9	17,6
Metal products and machinery	3,3	5
Transport equipment	5,3	7,8
Rubber products	0,2	2,4
Total heavy industry	**36,8**	**48,3**
Total manufacturing	**100**	**100**

Table 2.2: Share of sectoral net value of output in total manufacturing

Source: Feinstein 2005: 116, 126

Africa, in existence since 1910 as a dominion of the British empire, provided voting rights for the white population only and its foremost concern in the inter-war period therefore was the so-called 'poor whites' problem. The increasingly urbanized and often unskilled Afrikaners competed directly for jobs with Africans, and only in manufacturing could there be well-paid employment for them. The mines whose profits were based on the exploitation of cheap African labour could certainly not be counted on in this regard. So the inter-war period saw the introduction of tariffs on manufacturing products to support domestic production and, perhaps more importantly, the foundation of Escom and Iscor, state-owned electricity supply and steel production entities that were supposed to fuel the industrialisation process. These strategic measures are often interpreted as a victory of Afrikaner interests—farmers, local manufacturers and the working class—over imperial interests, i.e. the mining houses. And it is certainly true that mining capital opposed tariffs that would only increase their input and wage costs and that both Escom and Iscor's foundation was accompanied by nationalist rhetoric, promising to support a domestic downstream industrialisation process and not imperial capital (Clark, 1994, 70).

However, careful studies have revealed that industrial policy lacked consistency and was in actual fact trimmed so as not to go against mining interests. First of all, the agricultural sector received strong support as well, even more so than manufacturing in terms of subsidies. Moreover, tariff protection for agriculture increased input costs for local manufacturing and stifled its growth (Fine and Rustomjee, 1996, 128f.). And while tariffs provided an important stimulus for the textiles sector, overall, rates actually remained low in international comparison, and they were "scarcely applied to key sectors such as steel and engineering for fear of raising mining costs." (Iliffe, 1999, 93) The electricity supply commission Escom was in its beginning a regulator for the already existing private producers of electricity which were owned by the mining houses. It was supposed to guarantee access to cheap electricity for downstream manufacturing. Despite the rhetoric, it always cooperated closely with mining corporations and certainly did not favour local interests over those of 'imperial capital'. Its discriminatory pricing policy towards the local railways which were charged a higher price than the miners is exemplary of this (Clark, 1994, 80). A similar argument can be made for Iscor, the state-owned steel corporation established in 1928. Tariffs in this sector were out of the question due to the lobbying power of gold mines and Iscor's position was further aggravated by its mandate to employ expensive white labour. Despite these initial difficulties, Iscor was able to supply the local market by 1940, fuelled in part by the mining boom of the 1930s (Clark, 1994, 101).

Overall, the diversification observed in the economy "even in the absence of a cohesive industrial strategy" (Fine and Rustomjee, 1996, 144) was often due to diversification of the mining companies themselves and activities remained concentrated in sectors closely linked to South Africa's mineral endowment.

Industrial strategy lacked cohesiveness also because it was saddled with more than one goal—additional to growth it was also to provide well-paid jobs for white workers. Both Escom and Iscor were troubled by the requirements to hire a certain percentage of 'civilized labour'. The segregation of the labour market which continued and was even more strictly enforced after the Second World War later turned out to be one of the most damaging legacies of the apartheid era. It was harmful to society at large, obviously, but it also seriously limited the possibilities of manufacturing growth from a very early stage.

While white labour was protected from African competition and its wages inflated by job reservation, cheap African labour was a necessity for the profitability of mines. The system established to fulfil this need was the yearly migration of workers from the so-called 'native reserves' (Terreblanche, 2002, 246). Black South Africans were compound to 8,3% of the land in the 1913 Land Act, thereby eliminating the opportunity to live from subsistence agriculture. At the same time, all efforts were made to prevent permanent urbanisation. Miners returned home every year over Christmas and were supposed to remain rooted in their reserves. While the system suited mining, manufacturing would have profited from a more stable workforce, from a larger pool of semi-skilled and possibly even skilled labour, and last but not least from a bigger domestic market. During the war, economic and political need forced South Africa to employ more Africans in the factories, but the backlash of white voters was severe: they voted the National Party into power in 1948, and set in motion the formation of apartheid.

2.2 Racial Capitalism—The Apartheid Era

The surprise victory of the National Party was the starting point of an incumbency that lasted far longer than anybody would have expected at the time. White South Africans returned it into power repeatedly, and only the first multiracial elections in 1994 brought its reign to an end. The NP governed over the post-war boom that saw extraordinary growth rates in the 1950s and 1960s and made white South Africans one of the richest groups of people world wide, but it could not prevent the decline and crisis of the economy that started in the early 1970s. The economic crisis was triggered by world economic turbulences, but its underlying causes were to be found without a doubt within the country. The economy never recovered, and its slow demise facilitated the end of the apartheid regime and a negotiated transition to democratic rule. When the African National Congress won the elections in 1994, it thus inherited a deeply troubled society and economy. The roots of the economic problems will be outlined below.

2.2.1 Early Years - The Rise and Golden Age of Apartheid

Apartheid was a system of grand racial segregation—of separate development in the euphemistic language of the National Party. Seekings and Nattrass distinguish between three main areas of intervention and racial segrega-

	Agriculture	Mining	Industry	Services	Total
1948-64	2,8	5,8	6,5	4	4,9
1964-73	3,2	0,5	7,6	5,5	4,6

Table 2.3: Annual growth of real domestic product in percent

Source: Feinstein 2005, 147

tion: political, social and labour-market apartheid (Seekings and Nattrass, 2005, 18ff.). In all three areas there are strong continuities with the pre-1948 era. Political apartheid meant the complete disenfranchisement of the black populace and the formation of the pseudo-independent Bantustans. The latter, although never fully functional or internationally recognized, were the logical endpoint of segregation: black South Africans lost South African citizenship and in turn became citizens of one of the Bantustans according to ethnic affiliation. Social apartheid included residential segregation, segregated public amenities and the prohibition of sexual relationships. Residential segregation led to massive forced relocations to 'whiten' the urban areas and remove Africans, Coloureds and Indians to the reserves (later Bantustans) and assigned townships. Influx controls in the cities and pass laws aimed at limiting the number of Africans living in the townships and working in the urban areas. Lastly, labour-market apartheid reinforced the existing colour bar for skilled occupations and introduced the notorious Bantu education system that denied African children a decent education (Seekings and Nattrass, 2005, 18ff.).

Economic Boom

These reforms were met with stiff resistance by blacks, but the extraordinary economic performance and fast rising income for whites in the early post-war years strengthened the hand of government. The South African economy grew at unprecedented pace. Like much of the rest of the world, it experienced a boom that saw an average annual expansion of around 5% in the 1950s and the 1960s. Growth was driven by mining—South Africa profited from world wide economic growth and buoyant commodity prices—and increasingly by industrial production (Table 2.3).

The development of the Orange Free State Goldfields—only postponed to the 1950s due to the war—provided a massive expansionary boost to the economy. As a project of unprecedented scale—by the end of the 1950s, 60 percent of South Africa's total gold output came from the region (Feinstein, 2005, 166)—it required close cooperation between the mining companies, most importantly the Anglo American Corporation, and the state. The latter had to provide huge capital outlays to make the operations viable in an area that completely lacked suitable infrastructure. That included the provision of water, transport infrastructure in the form of railways and electrification through a power station built by Escom (Fine and Rustomjee, 1996, 157). Part of the capital invested in this project came from profits earned in the trade of diamonds that experienced an exceptional increase in demand after the war. Additionally, other minerals increasingly added to total mining output in South Africa. These included, amongst others, coal, copper, iron ore, asbestos and uranium.

Despite these developments in mining, the performance of industry stands out. Average yearly growth rates of more than six percent led the Chairman of the Board of Trade and Industry (BTI) to claim in 1962 that "in no other country has there, within the brief compass of twenty-five years, been a more complete metamorphosis of its economy and a more spectacular development of its industries." (cited in Feinstein, 2005, 173) Expansion was accompanied by structural changes. The economy experienced a further shift away from consumer goods towards intermediate and capital goods (see Table 2.4).

What triggered this boom? Certainly the role of mining and the various linkages of the mining industry to manufacturing need to be highlighted. Heavily investing mining corporations placed massive orders for capital equipment, drove the expansion of the chemical industry and used the resources they amassed themselves to diversify and invest into various sectors of manufacturing. Fine and Rustomjee therefore claim that growth in the Minerals Energy Complex dominated the industrial expansion at the time. As Mineral Energy Complex (MEC) they define the sectors that are closely linked to mining and the minerals endowment in South Africa and that are dominated by the same large corporations that originated in mining. The sectors subsumed under the MEC label are coal, gold and other mining activities, electricity (overwhelmingly based on coal mining in South Africa), non-metallic mineral products, basic metal industries, and the chemicals and plastics sector (Fine and Rustomjee, 1996, 79). A good part of these activities are generally categorized as manufacturing, yet growth in these activities can hardly be interpreted as diversification away from the mining

	1924/25	48/49	75/76
Food, beverages and tobacco	32,4	19	14,1
Textiles, clothing, leather, footwear	10	15,2	10,4
Wood and furniture	6,9	6,4	3,2
Paper, printing and publishing	11,2	7,7	7,7
Other manufacturing	2,7	3,4	3,3
Total light industry	**63,2**	**51,7**	**38,7**
Chemicals and chemical products	**12,1**	**9,5**	11,4
Pottery, glass, non-metallic minerals	7	6	5,3
Basic metal industries	8,9	17,6	13
Metal products and machinery	3,3	5	22,7
Transport equipment	5,3	7,8	7,2
Rubber products	0,2	2,4	1,7
Total heavy industry	**36,8**	**48,3**	**61,3**
Total manufacturing	**100**	**100**	**100**

Table 2.4: Share of sectoral net value of output in total manufacturing

Source: Feinstein 2005: 116, 126, 187

and minerals sector of the economy. In the period after World War Two, evidence for this lopsided growth can be found in the expansion of the chemicals industry which was supported by the state's involvement in founding Sasol (on which more below) and which diversified into fuel-chemicals, synthetic rubber, industrial chemicals, and the production of polymers such as polyethylene, heavily used in the plastics industries. Additionally, investments in the basic metals sector increased South Africa's capacity to produce steel; aluminium was smelted within the country from 1967, and Escom's capacity to produce electricity continuously increased (Fine and Rustomjee, 1996, 157ff.).

However, this assessment has to be reconciled with the pace of growth in the metal products and machinery sector. Fabricated metal products and machinery (including electrical machinery) increased their share in manufacturing output from five percent just after the war to more than twenty percent in 1975 (see Table 2.4)—seemingly a clear indication of increasing maturity of the economy and also a vindication for the optimistic assessment of the BTI Chairman. Yet, two important caveats undermine this argument: firstly, the investment came from mining conglomerates to a large extent (although foreign direct investment did play an important part in the early years too). This would not have been a problem in itself, but in the South African context, it further entrenched extreme concentration in ownership and hampered the long run dynamism in these sectors. The Anglo American Corporation expanded not only into metal products, but also into heavy engineering, chemicals, textiles, brewing, grain milling and paper making—invariably relying on big, capital-intensive plants (Feinstein, 2005, 175). Secondly, even in its heyday, the metal products industry was a net user of foreign exchange (Clark, 1994, 135) and thus not internationally competitive. The domestic orientation in a comparatively small economy implied a low ceiling in terms of growth potential and a foreign-exchange constraint. Both were not of immediate concern during the economic boom but would come back to haunt policy makers in the long run.

Industrial Policy

In continuity to pre-war preferences, economic policy makers pursued a two-pronged strategy: import substitution and public corporations that further expand their reach mostly within the confines of the MEC. The BTI was responsible for the setting of tariffs. The substantial structural transformation and manufacturing growth that is visible in Table 2.4 might be seen as evidence that the import substitution strategy was indeed successful. However, the jury on the BTI's performance is still out. While Black asserts that "as a result of protectionist policies, the first stage of import replacement was well advanced by the late 1950s" (Black, 1991, 159), Fine and Rustomjee are much more skeptical: "Tariff protection was neither all pervading nor was it central to determining the pattern of industrialisation." (Fine and Rustomjee, 1996, 185). In hindsight the BTI admits that tariffs were often granted on an ad hoc basis and that there was a distinct lack of consistent prioritising. If there was consistency, it related to employment creation for white workers—often an implicit or even explicit prerequisite to receive tariff protection for a sector (Seekings and Nattrass, 2005, 141). This certainly contributed to the capital intensity of the manufacturing sector in South Africa—to the advantage of increasingly skilled white workers and to the disadvantage of the large number of unskilled Africans that would have benefited from the expansion of low skill labour intensive industries. It is also undisputed that South Africa failed to push import substitution further up the production chain and that the manufacturing sector remained inward-oriented and internationally uncompetitive—implying that it continued to be a net user of foreign exchange.

The influence of state corporations on the South African growth trajectory is more clear-cut. Their interventions were narrowly targeted and the focus clearly lay on activities within the Minerals Energy Complex. Escom became the major supplier of electricity when it bought the Victoria Falls Power Company, owned by Anglo, in 1948. It completed the electricity grid by 1969 and continuously increased its output. As mentioned above, the overwhelming source of power for Escom was coal. In return, it supplied 70% of its output to the mines and energy-intensive manufacturing, notably to Iscor by 1960—a further indication of the close linkages between electricity and mining. African and rural households did not profit from the availability of cheap electricity as their connection to the grid was deemed too expensive (Clark, 1994, 158). Iscor, the state-owned iron and steel producer, played an even more prominent role as it continuously expanded its activities both upstream and downstream. In its core business, Iscor was able to produce 70 percent of the domestic steel requirement by 1955 (Clark, 1994, 150). By then it also had its own coal plant and was involved in joint-ventures with the private sector in several downstream activities such as the manufacturing of heavy machinery. In addition to Iscor and Escom, state corporations came into being through the Industrial Development Corporation (IDC), established in 1939. Initially, its aim was to support private capital in labour intensive manufacturing such as textiles and food. However, the difficulties it encountered in the textiles sector—stiff competition from cheap imports and permanent labour unrest—might have contributed to its changing of focus. From the 1950s it promoted large-scale investments in capital intensive industries. Most prominent among these are the founding of Sasol (short for the Afrikaans Suid Afrikaanse Steenkool en Olie or South African Coal and Oil) and Foskor in 1950 and 1951 respectively. The latter is involved in the beneficiation of phosphates and the former converts oil to gas and then gas to petrol. The huge investments required to set up Sasol were too risky and big for the private sector so it remained a public corporation. It succeeded in its aim though and was later largely responsible for the development of the petro-chemicals industry in South Africa. The pattern that evolves gives an indication of South Africa's industrialisation strategy: "the use of minerals to produce industrial goods and provide support for skilled white, as opposed to unskilled, black employment [...] based on increasing both capital and energy intensity and hence mechanisation."

(Fine and Rustomjee, 1996, 183) In contrast to the newly industrialising countries of East Asia, South Africa chose not to develop labour-intensive industries but opted instead for capital intensive production—cementing the exclusion of the African population from the modern economy.

One industrial policy initiative that would have run counter to this strategy but that is widely discredited as a complete failure is decentralisation. In 1960, the government formed the Board for the Decentralisation of Industry, aiming to promote industries close to the homelands. Providing jobs close to the reserves, it was hoped, would stem the tide of African urbanisation. However the programme encountered the same difficulties that faced the IDC in its attempt to build up textiles production and never was effective (Fine and Rustomjee, 1996, 191f.).

Weaknesses

Despite the impressive growth rates of the economy and the manufacturing sector, the weaknesses of the latter were visible even at the time. They became glaringly obvious from the 1970s when the economy entered into crisis mode and will be described in depth in the following chapter. It therefore suffices to briefly outline the issues at this stage.

Firstly, investments were concentrated in capital intensive sectors around the Minerals Energy Complex. Whilst a deliberate effort at the time, these choices precipitated the unemployment crisis that surfaced in the 1970s and plagued the economy ever since. Secondly, despite all efforts of import substitution, manufacturing goods had stubbornly high import components because locally produced intermediate and machinery goods were simply too expensive. In the 1960s, imports started to rise again and they changed in structure—they were increasingly composed of intermediate and capital goods (Scheepers, 1982, 22). Thirdly, manufacturing production was mostly oriented towards the domestic economy and failed to penetrate export markets. Given the small size of the economy and the ultra-low wages paid to Africans, this orientation was always going to limit the growth performance of the sector. Fourthly, the education and labour market policies took its toll in the form of an increasingly deficient skills base in the country. At the end of the 1960s a number of industries already complained about a lack of skilled labour—another theme that was to haunt the economy for decades to come.

Together, low productivity, import intensity and poor export performance led to a major foreign-exchange deficit in manufacturing. In 1975, just at the start of the crisis years, manufacturing imports amounted to 5.7 billion Rand, while exports earned a modest 1.8 billion (Feinstein, 2005, 190). South Africa could only afford this massive leakage thanks to the export surplus in mining.

2.2.2 Crisis and Transition

The structural break that the South African economy experienced in 1973/74 is clearly visible in the data. GDP growth slowed markedly, from an average close to or above 5% in the 1960s and early 1970s to just above 2% thereafter (Figure 2.1). GDP per capita actually decreased in the period 1973 to 1994 (Feinstein, 2005, 201). A poor output performance meant that the structural weaknesses just described above came to the fore and caused a major economic and related political crisis in South Africa.

What triggered the economic crisis? International developments, foremost the world economic slow down, the breakdown of the Bretton Woods system of fixed exchange rates and the oil crisis in 1973 certainly played a catalytic role. The immediate impact of these global developments was heightened inflationary pressure, due to rising prices of imported inputs—mainly oil but also machinery. The price index for imported machinery grew 10,8 percent annually between 1970 and 1974 and then 19,7 percent annually until 1980 (Gelb, 1991, 20). Demand for imported machinery was inelastic and price hikes were passed on to consumers, resulting in a sharp rise in inflation. Inflation added to the woes of a working class increasingly hit by unemployment. African workers became more militant and the resulting strikes—starting in Durban and Cape Town and peaking in 1973 and 1974—heralded the end of stable work relations (Marais, 2001, 38).

The liberalisation of the gold price had more mixed consequences, at least in the short run. The mining industry was faced with rising costs in the late 1960s and early 1970s and was thus 'saved' by the end of Bretton Woods: gold rose rapidly in value and allowed mining companies to extract gold from lower grades of ore that were not profitable previously. However relief proved to be temporary only and the long run decline in total gold produced in South Africa could not be halted (Feinstein, 2005, 203ff.). Also, a freely fluctuating gold price meant that the stability of South Africa's export earnings ended once and for all. The Rand fluctuated strongly, and

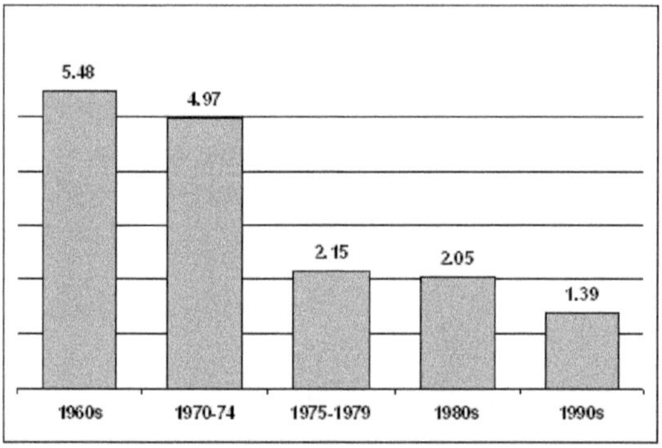

Figure 2.1: Average Annual GDP Growth Rate

the country more closely resembled a traditional commodity exporter. The gold boom of the early 1980s, following the second oil shock, serves as an example: the surge in exports of minerals led to a rapid real appreciation of the currency, damaging export prospects of manufacturing (Feinstein, 2005, 217f.). At the same time, the temporary boom led to massive investments by the private and the public sector, often financed by short-term credit. When the gold price collapsed in 1981, South Africa faced a severe debt crisis and plunged into recession (Gelb, 1991, 26f.).

These external factors represent one side of the coin only, however. Had the South African economy been stronger, it might have been able to absorb these shocks—the East Asian NICs, invariably natural resources importers, were certainly able to. But South Africa was not, and its structural weaknesses were brutally exposed. "It soon became clear that the decline in economic growth was structural rather than temporary, as the production problems in manufacturing (low productivity and import dependence) were made more serious by increasing volatility of mineral exports and of capital flows" (Gelb, 2003, 23).

Internal Factors—Decline in Mining and Manufacturing

The slowdown was felt in all sectors of the economy, yet a look behind the aggregates reveals a more nuanced picture. Primary industries did well in patches, driven by temporary mining booms after 1974 and in the early 1980s

	1974-94	70-74	75-79	80s	90s
Primary Sector	0,5	-2,2	3,04	0,47	-0,06
Secondary Sector	1,4	6,92	2,26	1,53	0,51
Tertiary Sector	2,42	5,19	1,8	2,76	2,37
Total Value Added	1,87	4,14	2,12	2,09	1,61
MEC	1,44	-1,61	3,64	1,47	1,32
Non-MEC Manufacturing	1,22	6,47	3,5	1,02	-0,59

Table 2.5: Real Value Added, Average Annual Growth Rates

Source: Quantec, own calculations

while the secondary sector performed poorly ever after the oil shock. When one distinguishes between non-MEC manufacturing and the performance of the MEC, it becomes obvious that the former faired even worse. Services on the other hand performed relatively strongly and continuously gained in importance (see Table 2.5). On the face of it, it might well be concluded that in this period, South Africa was already—and probably prematurely—entering a phase of de-industrialisation.

I have touched on the changes in global markets that affected the South African gold mining industry above, but to complete the picture, one has to consider the escalating costs that mining companies were facing at home. Two factors were at play: firstly, the average grade of ore steadily decreased. An expected trend in a non-renewable resource, it meant that to produce the same amount of gold, mines had to treat an ever increasing amount of ore, often at deeper levels. Secondly, wages of African miners' wages rose sharply after 1973. Political changes in the greater Southern African region (particularly the independence of Mozambique) meant that workers had to be overwhelmingly sourced within the country, the mining houses wanted to steady their work forces, and lastly workers were more militant and also, since the 1980s, unionised (Feinstein, 2005, 203ff.). Thanks to the rising gold price in the 1970s and early 1980s these developments were long concealed, but after the mid-1980s, the gold price stabilized and profits plummeted, leading to massive lay-offs. To a certain extent, the expansion of coal and platinum mining mitigated the demise of gold, but due to their capital intensity, they could not halt overall job losses in mining.

Looking at the secondary sector, South Africa had a relatively diversified manufacturing sector that accounted for over 23% of GDP (up from 13%

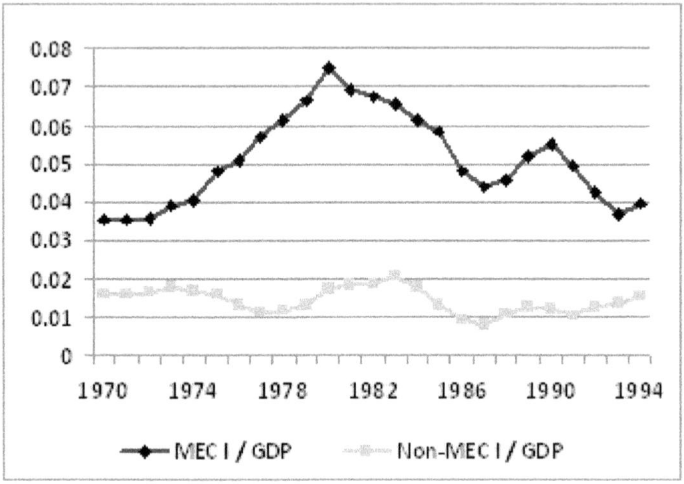

Figure 2.2: Investment as a Share of GDP

in 1946) by 1970. The share in output of food, textiles and clothing was falling while more advanced sectors such as chemicals and transport equipment grew substantially (Black, 1991, 160). Yet even then the weaknesses of the sector were apparent—high import intensity, a lack of international competitiveness, and high capital intensity. The period from 1973 onwards saw an accentuation of these trends.

In terms of sectoral development within secondary industries, the activities within the Minerals Energy Complex outperformed the rest of manufacturing, despite the relative decline of mining. Growth was particularly strong in petroleum products, chemicals and plastics, non-ferrous metals and electricity. The investment pattern reveals an even stronger disparity (Figure 2.2). Non-MEC manufacturing investment lingered at very low levels throughout the period under consideration, while investment in the MEC, particularly in the chemicals and related sectors (but also in mining) grew strongly until the early 1980s.

MEC industries benefited from booming commodity prices in the world markets and enjoyed full support by the South African government (more on this below). Growth was driven by a hefty expansion in coal mining—

directly exported or for the use of Escom, and by the mega-projects Sasol II and Sasol III in chemicals (Fine and Rustomjee, 1996, 168f.). The new Sasol plants dramatically increased its capacity to produce oil from coal—of enormous value for a government faced with an international oil crisis and the threat of economic sanctions—and also allowed it to diversify into the production of industrial chemicals. This was often done in cooperation with the private sector, notably the conglomerates. Apart from electricity and chemicals, the production of non-ferrous metals expanded quickly also as can be seen in Tables 2.6 and 2.7. Aluminium, platinum and titanium smelting operations were invariably carried out by the conglomerates in joint ventures with the IDC or international capital. Fine and Rustomjee (1996, 174) characterise the 1980s as an era of increased interpenetration of the different conglomerates, leading to an erosion of the Afrikaner and 'imperial' origin. At the same time the six emerging groups diversified their activities and controlled large parts of mining, manufacturing and finance, which in turn cemented oligopolistic market conditions in South Africa.

Non-MEC manufacturing developed less dynamically. This is visible in slower output growth and lower investment, but even more so in the poor export performance. The export-output ratio, albeit improving over time, was far lower than for MEC activities, and imports far exceeded exports over the whole period. A brief look at two crucial sectors—the motor and the machine tool industry—serves to illustrate these developments. In 1960, South Africa was the largest developing country producer of cars, leaving countries such as Brazil, Argentina or South Korea behind. However, from 1974 to 1994, transport equipment which is dominated by the motor industry actually contracted in real terms, leading to substantial employment losses. What are the reasons for this decline? The South African automotive industry was historically oriented towards the domestic market. This was possible only because of the unequal income distribution, allowing parts of the population to buy luxury consumption goods at a very early stage of economic development. Due to its inward orientation, it was hit hard by the domestic economic slowdown. Additionally, the local market was too small to achieve scale efficiency, implying low efficiency in production. Another typical characteristic of the industry was its import intensity which did not change until the 1990s, despite the continuous effort of government to reverse this trend. The motor industry remained a significant consumer of foreign exchange (Black, 1991, 163ff.). The story of the machine tool industry is similar in many respects. By the mid-1970s, South Africa had significant local machine tool production, however since then growth slowed down and the sector contracted after 1982 (Kaplan, 1991, 177). It was inward oriented, depending mostly on sales in South Africa and the Southern African region, which both did not develop dynamically. Imports remained high however, and there was very little domestic research and development, leading to poor quality and a failure to penetrate export markets. Kaplan (1991, 185ff.) argues that the reasons for the disappointing outcomes lie in limited government support for producers, a strongly fluctuating exchange rate, and a shortage (and as a result the high cost) of skilled labour.

To summarize developments, secondary industry in South Africa went into crisis mode after 1973 due to a lack of international competitiveness which in turn was caused by low productivity levels. The sector was characterised by a high capital intensity, which was not only due to the sectoral distribution of activities, but also due to government subsidies on capital investment and low interest rates (Kaplan, 1991, 163). The weak growth performance, capital intensity and a lack of competitiveness in the manufacturing sector contributed to two focal points of the crisis of South Africa's economy: the rise of unemployment and the difficulties in the balance of payments (Feinstein, 2005, 224ff.). These economic difficulties in turn fuelled political conflict and led to extreme instability and uncertainty in the 1980s. All three aspects of the crisis will be described below.

The Rise of Unemployment

Due to a lack of consistent and comparable data, it is very difficult to accurately measure the rates of employment and unemployment in South Africa throughout the apartheid era. However, there is little controversy about overall trends: while the country was facing labour shortages during much of its history and the early after-war years, unemployment rose sharply ever after the 1970s and had reached unprecedented levels in the early 1990s when the ANC came to power. I will give a brief summary on the reasons for this turnaround in the labour market below.

From the beginnings of European settlement in the Cape colony, the shortage of labour to farm the land was one of the main worries of white settlers. The advent of the mining industry only exacerbated this problem, and the mining companies set up a system of labour recruitment that covered the Southern African region to find suitable manpower. Growth in manufacturing, particularly during World War Two, provided better-paid

	An. Real Growth [1]	Capital/Labour [1]		Empl/Output [1]		Net Exports [2]		Export/Output [1]	
1 Industry	**1974-94**	**1974**	**1994**	**1974**	**1994**	**1974**	**1994**	**1974**	**1994**
11 Primary, All	**0,50**	**7,27**	**11,10**	**16,44**	**12,40**	**33536**	**51126**	**56,85**	**44,78**
111 Agriculture, Forestry, Fishing	1,56	6,52	5,21	41,49	30,45	665	2479	10,15	9,81
112 Mining and Quarrying	0,14	8,73	26,15	7,55	4,93	32872	48647	73,41	59,25
12 Secondary, All	**1,40**	**9,33**	**14,99**	**5,35**	**4,82**	**-64226**	**-38960**	**10,06**	**15,79**
121 Manufacturing	1,65	8,04	14,82	4,95	3,72	-64044	-39172	13,78	19,46
1210 Food, Beverages, Tobacco	2,33	7,43	11,75	3,92	2,90	1608	1282	13,13	9,09
1211 Textiles, Clothing and Leather	0,82	2,68	2,27	14,62	9,52	-3404	-1116	8,57	18,46
1212 Wood/Paper, Publishing, Print	1,72	6,97	7,69	5,02	3,75	-9813	-1153	10,49	16,72
1213 Petroleum Pr., Chemicals, etc.	5,21	20,85	75,24	3,44	1,71	-10672	-10268	32,56	20,62
12131 Coke, refined Petroleum Prod.	6,07	74,83	40,18	1,81	0,85	-3762	-2755	106,43	22,61
12132 Basic Chemicals	4,31	28,77	79,18	2,13	1,24	-4451	-717	23,24	47,14
12133 Other Chemicals	5,14	12,62	20,88	4,15	1,80	-2000	-6723	4,50	7,91
12134 Rubber Products	2,13	8,84	9,37	6,92	3,85	-233	-727	2,47	10,06
12135 Plastic Products	7,45	3,64	2,60	6,58	3,11	-226	-780	2,49	9,44
1214 Other Non-Metallic Mineral Pr.	0,17	10,16	10,01	7,04	9,71	-769	-667	12,69	10,36
1215 Metals, Metal Products, Machinery, Equipment	-0,55	10,22	14,57	4,32	3,94	-15386	-285	13,08	35,38
12151 Basic Iron and Steel	-0,59	21,89	29,84	4,78	2,96	-1842	12570	19,39	56,27
12152 Basic Non-Ferrous Metals	5,15	18,82	44,10	4,92	2,71	1161	5232	62,24	66,62
12153 Metal Products excl. Machinery	-1,44	3,92	5,47	4,92	5,62	-1362	1306	2,17	12,60
12154 Machinery and Equipment	-1,06	4,86	6,17	3,17	3,72	-13342	-19394	11,57	22,55
1216 Electrical Machinery & Apparatus	2,23	3,66	3,99	8,44	5,66	-2509	-6520	5,64	12,51

Table 2.6: Sectoral Development of the South African economy, 1974-1994

Source: Quantec, own calculations

[a] Per Cent

[b] Million Rand, Constant 2000 Prices

	An. Real Growth [1]	Capital/Labour [1]		Empl/Output [1]		Net Exports [2]		Export/Output [1]	
1 Industry (cont.)	**1974-94**	**1974**	**1994**	**1974**	**1994**	**1974**	**1994**	**1974**	**1994**
1217 Radio, TV, Instruments	3,05	5,48	4,69	4,43	3,02	-4664	-10185	13,80	22,28
1218 Transport Equipment	-0,53	6,20	9,19	2,91	2,92	-15099	-11586	1,61	9,96
1219 Furniture, other Man.	5,193	3,89	2,89	4,44	3,66	-3336	1327	26,48	27,31
122 Electricity, Gas, Water	4,77	118,47	233,7	3,85	1,69	30	260	0,20	0,73
1221 Electricity, Gas, Steam	6,21	93,96	215,8	5,53	1,67	30	260	0,36	0,97
1222 Water Supply	0,61	214,56	286,5	1,76	1,74	0	0	0	0
123 Construction	-1,57	1,30	0,91	6,90	13,54	-212	-49	0,03	0,11
13 Tertiary, All	**2,42**	**19,29**	**19,67**	**9,92**	**9,21**	**-7751**	**-2643**	**3,35**	**3,05**
131 Trade, Catering, Accomodation Services	1,47	5,83	4,54	9,32	12,15	1449	4150	3,50	4,56
132 Transport, Storage, Communication	2,39	44,90	60,57	9,96	5,33	-2373	-1711	12,47	9,28
133 Financial Intermediation, Insurance, Real Estate	2,56	100,85	42,93	2,32	5,43	-3775	-839	3,17	2,34
134 Community, Social, Personal Services	2,93	11,26	14,87	16,31	11,51	-3052	-4243	0,17	0,21
1 All Industries	**1,87**	**13,81**	**16,90**	**8,90**	**7,88**	**-38441**	**9523**	**13,35**	**13,14**
MEC	**1,44**	**15,42**	**40,34**	**6,21**	**3,60**	**20779**	**55774**	**50,44**	**39,59**
Non-MEC Manufacturing	**1,22**	**4,97**	**6,52**	**5,08**	**4,12**	**-51922**	**-46039**	**9,17**	**14,68**

Table 2.7: Sectoral Development of the South African economy, 1974-1994

Source: Quantec, own calculations

[a] Per Cent

[b] Million Rand, Constant 2000 Prices

urban jobs, so that in the early 1960s, mining and agriculture and even parts of manufacturing struggled to recruit workers (Seekings and Nattrass, 2005, 167f.). However, even then, there was urban unemployment, much lamented by the government as idleness and work-shyness of the Natives. This can only be explained by a highly segregated labour market. There is evidence that rural Africans and migrants were actively recruited for low-paid work that urban Africans refused to take up—they were competing in a different labour market, preferring to wait for a better paid job in a different sector (Seekings and Nattrass, 2005, 171).

The segregated labour market also helps to understand why real wages for African workers started to rise from the early 1960s. The increases were first realized in manufacturing, but mining and even agriculture had to follow suit to attract labour (Feinstein, 2005, 231). The strikes that started in Durban in 1972 and that spread throughout the country afterwards allowed African workers to further improve wage and working conditions, albeit from extremely low levels. Since wages of white workers did not increase at the same speed, the racial wage gap became smaller. Moreover, the colour bar that restricted certain professions for whites floated upwards, and skilled Africans increasingly entered qualified positions, notably in the tertiary sector (Feinstein, 2005, 232).

At the same time, unemployment became a visible problem. Because of a lack of official data, several groups of university-based researchers conducted their own surveys, and from the mid-1970s they invariably reported high open unemployment, which at the time still was a new phenomenon (Seekings and Nattrass, 2005, 175).

How can rising wages be reconciled with simultaneously rising unemployment? The most probable explanation is a change in skills requirements for jobs. The biggest employers of unskilled labour, mining and agriculture, both contracted. Additionally, there was technological change favouring skilled labour and mechanisation. Agriculture followed the general trend of higher capital intensity through increased mechanization, and even the mining industry tried to stabilise its workforce, relying less on migrant labour and replacing these unskilled workers by machinery (Feinstein, 2005, 240). Another important reason for the substitution of labour by machinery in mining were the technological changes in extraction related to the deeper-lying ore. The secondary sector was analysed above and also contributed to a steadily decreasing demand for unskilled labour. To make matters worse, the apartheid regime deported unemployed Africans from the cities

	1951	1960	1970	1980	1991	1996
Total Population	13864	17482	22666	29111	37945	42273
Working Age Population	8034	9744	12481	16428	22278	25877
Total Employed	4936	5487	7462	9532	10613	9847
Total Unemployed	196	457	532	713	2331	4882
Unemployment Rate	3,9%	7,3%	6,7%	7%	18%	33,1%

Table 2.8: South African Labour Market (in thousands)

Source: Feinstein, 2005, 274

and supported white farmers to do the same on their farms. This so-called surplus labour was dumped in the homelands, were subsistence farming had long before become unsustainable (Seekings and Nattrass, 2005, 186). The homelands became places of extreme destitution and poverty, and South Africa a place of massive open unemployment.

To conclude, and with all due caution, it is still interesting to look at the time series Feinstein (2005, 274) put together from various sources (see Table 2.8). The data reveal pressure from the supply side in the form of a fast growing population. So when the number of jobs created by the economy virtually stagnated from the 1980s due to slow growth and increasing capital intensity, unemployment rates soared, leaving the incoming government in 1994 with a terribly difficult legacy to deal with.

The Balance of Payments Crisis

The problems in South Africa's balance of payments are also linked to the particular structure of its manufacturing sector as described above and the heavy reliance of its export performance on primary commodities.

Looking at the current account first, imports in the period under scrutiny were dominated by machinery. In 1985, more than half of total expenditure on machinery went to imported machinery (Kahn, 1991, 68). Imports therefore moved pro-cyclically, rising in importance in periods of high growth, and in the case of South Africa, an adjustment of the current account therefore had to come from a depression of investment more than consumption. Current account problems therefore played a large part in the volatility of the economy and motivated the 'stop-and-go' economic policy of the apartheid government in the 1980s (described in more detail below).

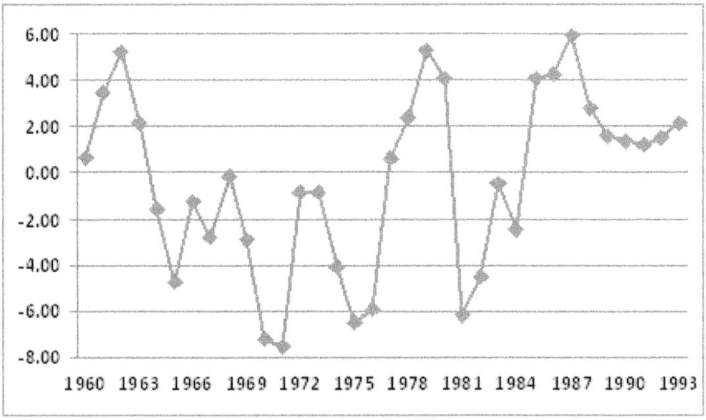

Figure 2.3: Balance of Current Account to GDP

Source: South African Reserve Bank

In terms of exports, the competitiveness problems in the manufacturing sector led to its failure to substantially increase its share in total exports. The bulk of exports continued to be from mining and from those manufacturing sectors that are close to mining—the MEC (see Table 2.6 and 2.7). Given the volatility of commodity prices and their dominance in South Africa's exports, it is easy to see why the current account was indeed vulnerable.

A current account deficit has to be financed by a surplus in the capital account. This was the case until 1977 and then between 1981 and 1984 (see Figure 2.3). The composition of capital inflows in South Africa changed considerably however, moving away from foreign direct investment which dominated until the early 1970s towards private loans. Both the decrease in investment and disinvestment of foreign firms in South Africa and easier access to international finance since the 1970s are responsible for this trend. The increasing importance of loans with ever declining maturity periods in the 1980s implied that the capital account became more susceptible to short-term reversals of flows (Kahn, 1991, 78).

South Africa experienced a capital account shock in 1977 (after the Soweto uprising). The outflow of capital was accompanied by limited access to new loans, rendering deflationary policies and the resulting surplus in the current account the only viable option. Only the sudden increase in the gold price in 1979 provided relief for the strenuous external position of the economy (Kahn, 1991, 66). The second shock in 1985—provoked by the infamous 'rubicon speech' by Prime Minister Botha, which disappointed those hoping for reform in South Africa—hit the country even harder since existing loans were recalled. The adjustment was achieved through deflation which was caused mostly by a slump in private investment and through a depreciation of the Rand. Still the government had to declare a moratorium on all debt repayments to stop the outflow of capital. Financial sanctions against the apartheid regime further limited South Africa's access to foreign exchange, so it had to produce a surplus in the current account. As a result, when growth picked up in 1987, policies to curb investment were set in place immediately (Kahn, 1991, 86). Balance of payments problems therefore severely limited the country's options for economic recovery.

Resistance and Political Crisis

The economic crisis was accompanied by a political crisis of increasing severity. The regime came under pressure from inside the country—through a revived resistance movement—and from the outside, particularly through financial sanctions. The economic policy measures that will be the focus of the next chapter can therefore only be understood in the context of the overall political climate, which I want to touch on very briefly here.

In the 1960s, the heyday of apartheid, resistance to the regime was at an all-time low. The leaders of the ANC were either in prison or in exile after the movement turned to armed struggle. Yet its military capabilities were far too weak to seriously challenging the regime (Marais, 2001, 27f.). The white population enjoyed the fruits of rapid economic growth, leading to a situation of relative political stability.

It was shattered by the strike wave of the early 1970s that was partly caused by rising inflation. The Soweto uprising in 1976, led by students who protested against the use of Afrikaans as medium of instruction, finally put an end to this 'golden era' of apartheid. Apart from inflationary pressures, the biggest economic factor feeding the political crisis certainly was unemployment. Rural destitution forced Africans to seek jobs in the cities, undermining the grand scheme of residential segregation of the races. Permanent urbanisation of large part of the African population was a reality even the regime had to eventually accept, and this group, hit by unemployment, extremely low wages and political oppression, interpreted "the struggle to survive [...] more and more in political terms" (Marais, 2001, 32). In addition to economic woes, the struggle was galvanised by the independence of Southern African neighbour states and the related ideological boost provided by the Black Consciousness Movement. The emergence of the trade unions and the United Democratic Front, a domestic umbrella organisation that brought together thousands of organisations and that had close ties to the exiled ANC, bore testimony to this new wave of mobilisation and resistance.

The regime reacted with a strategy of carrot and stick. The dire situation on the labour markets—skills shortages on the one hand, high unemployment on the other—enticed it to implement reforms from the late 1970s. Minimum wages rose, the colour bar of job reservations was lifted and unions were legalised. Finally, in 1986 influx control was abolished (Seekings and Nattrass, 2005, 148f.). The apartheid government also increased spending on welfare and social services for the African population, particularly in education and urban infrastructure. These reforms reinforced a socio-economic trend that was started by the changing skills requirements in the economy: a stratification of the African population. Its top quintile, urbanised and skilled, was upwardly mobile and netted "almost all the increased income accruing to the African population" (Seekings and Nattrass, 2005, 155). So while interracial inequality slowly abated, intra-racial inequality rose sharply—a development that is usually attributed to the post-1994 regime but that actually started much earlier.

As for the stick, political resistance was brutally repressed to restore stability. Thousands of activists were jailed, or killed by police and covet third forces. The state set up a parallel system of administration, the 'National Security Management System' (Marais, 2001, 47, 55f.) which gave overwhelming power to police and security forces. Often, service and infrastructure upgrading was delivered directly by the same agencies of the security apparatus, combining "repressive force and developmental interventions—often successfully." (Marais, 2001, 58).

While the African National Congress and its allies could not threaten to overthrow the regime militarily, it was clear that the country had reached an impasse. International developments played their role too: economic sanctions, particularly on capital flows aggravated the economic crisis. Then, during the 1980s, the Soviet Union was pulling out of supporting resistance movements all over the world and in Southern Africa. As a result, the

Western powers urged the South African government and the ANC to seek a negotiated settlement (Becker, 1993, 15f.).

Inconsistent Policy Reactions

Economic policy tried to deal with the slowdown in growth in different, partly inconsistent ways. The initial macroeconomic response to the crisis in the early 1970s—an increase in public spending on infrastructure projects—only exacerbated the rise in inflation (Gelb, 1991, 24). Moreover, the Soweto uprising sparked a massive outflow of foreign capital and thereby compelled the regime to adopt a deflationary policy. The budget deficit was reduced from more than 6% of GDP in 1977 to 0.14% of GDP in 1981. "As a result, a cumulative current account surplus of almost R5 billion was generated during 1977–1979 which helped to finance the capital account deficit" (Kahn, 1991, 66). The 'gold boom' from 1979 to 1981—sparked by soaring gold prices—proved to be short-lived. The fall of the gold price in 1981 which was caused by the shift in U.S. monetary policy brought back the balance of payments problems. The NP reacted by tightened monetary and fiscal policy, particularly raising interest rates (Gelb, 1991, 27). The political crisis severely limited South Africa's access to international money markets; therefore the deficit in the current account could only be financed by an increase in domestic savings. These developments climaxed in the debt crisis in 1985 described above. Macroeconomic policy thus remained mainly reactive from the mid-1970s, constrained by the balance of payments problems and mounting expenses on the security apparatus in the face of recession.

However, there was no shortage of more proactive initiatives to reform the country's ailing industrial sector. The changes in the labour regime—a stratification within the African population with more rights for urbanised Africans; and the legalisation of trade unions—aimed at stabilising the work force and ameliorating labour relations. The ultimate goal was to achieve higher productivity through a better trained group of skilled African workers (Marais, 2001, 44). At the same time, there were repeated calls for a more outward-oriented industrial strategy, focusing on manufacturing exports and reducing the reliance on commodities. As Fine and Rustomjee (1996, 186) show however, these efforts went back to the late 1950s, when the Viljoen Commission issued a report calling for higher exports, particularly in targeted sectors such as the motor industry with linkages to the upstream steel and chemical industries. Similar conclusions were reached by the Reynders Commission in the early 1970s and the Kleu report in the early 1980s (Fine and Rustomjee, 1996, 193ff.). All these reports invariably called for a more outward-oriented economy, and increasingly favoured a liberalisation of the trade regime to reduce the anti-export bias created by high levels of protection.

Tariffs were brought down slowly from the 1970s and quantitative restrictions were all but abolished by 1991 (Feinstein, 2005, 218). In addition exports were supported through the General Export Incentive Scheme (GEIS) which paid a tax-free grant to non-raw-materials exports (Hirsch, 2005, 131). These reforms were in line with a broader shift in economic policy towards a more liberal regime, underlined by the privatisation of state-owned companies and attempts to deregulate the economy (Marais, 2001, 105).

Yet, trade liberalisation and export support did not bring about diversification but further reinforced the dominance of the MEC. Partly, such a development was to be expected due to the competitive strength of these sectors. However, industrial policy played its part too. GEIS, despite its contrary intents, disbursed most of its budget to capital intensive firms that would have exported anyway. And the IDC continued to focus on projects within the confines of the MEC, best exemplified by the Mossgas mega-project to exploit South Africa's offshore gas reserves.

For these reasons, Fine and Rustomjee conclude that "[t]he MEC has remained the key component of the economy. [Trough its policies] the apartheid regime has sought to guarantee the interests of the large-scale capitals even as it has released the reins of immediate political power." (Fine and Rustomjee, 1996, 206f.) In other words, there were no consistent and decisive interventions to facilitate a diversification of manufacturing to non-MEC activities. The liberalisation drive towards the end of the 1980s only reinforced long-standing patterns of growth and investment and cemented South Africa's reliance on the MEC and its capital-intensive growth path.

Legacy of Apartheid—a Summary

At the risk of repetition, I want to conclude this chapter with a balance sheet of the economy (see Hirsch, 2005, 27 for a comparable exercise) that was to be taken over by the incoming ANC government in 1994. The focus lies on manufacturing.

The legacy of apartheid was certainly mixed, with some items on the plus side as well. Among these were a well developed infrastructure, particularly in white residential areas; a well-developed and modern financial sector and capital market; pockets of skilled labour and research and science expertise; and an internationally competitive group of firms in the mining and related sectors (Hirsch, 2005, 27). On the downside, the macroeconomic situation was dire. The country was in a prolonged recession, the fiscal deficit was unsustainably high, and so where real interest rates. Manufacturing production was very capital intensive, and in combination with a declining primary sector, this resulted in high unemployment. Additionally most firms were not internationally competitive (with the above mentioned exceptions) but inward-oriented. A large part of the population was disadvantaged by a dismal education system which failed to equip them with adequate skills for a changing labour market. And lastly, large sections of the economy were controlled by a few dominant groups—so that oligopolistic collusion was the rule and smaller and medium companies faced huge obstacles (Joffe et al., 1995, 62).

2.3 Democracy—The First Decade of ANC Rule

The negotiated settlement between the ANC and the government included a liberal-democratic system with universal suffrage, a separation of powers and, on the economic front, a guarantee of property rights and the independence of the Central Bank. The ANC had quietly and quickly dropped its earlier and more radical calls for nationalisation of core industries.

Yet, the crucial question remaining was which macroeconomic and industrial strategy the ANC would adopt to address the country's huge economic problems. At the time, macroeconomic issues took precedence. In line with the policy emphasis of the early years of democracy, I will analyse macroeconomic developments and policy first and come back to industrial development and policy in the second part of this chapter.

2.3.1 The Macro-Economy

The incoming government was first and foremost concerned with stabilising the crisis-ridden economy. The structural crisis outlined above manifested itself in a number of indicators (100f. Marais, 2001, see also Figure 2.4):

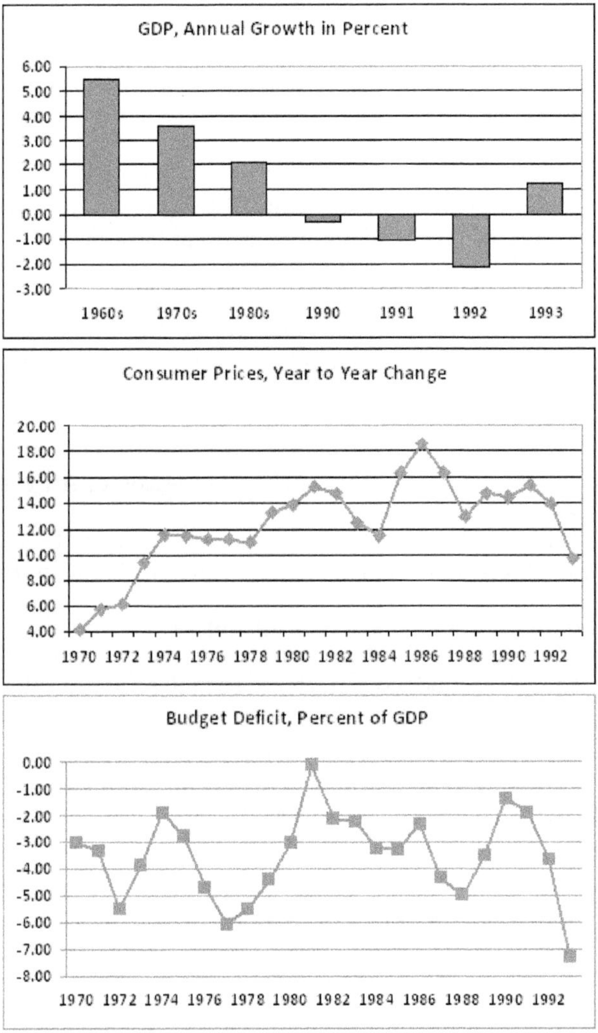

Figure 2.4: Growth, Inflation and Budget Deficit at the Eve of Democracy

Source: South African Reserve Bank

- The feeble GDP growth rate, down from an average 6% p.a. in the 1960s to close to 2% in the 1980s and negative rates in the early 1990s—the very period the negotiations over the shape of transition were happening;

- Declining levels of gross fixed investment, high rates of capital flight and low rates of private investment. Total (public and private) investment as share of GDP fell from more than 25% in the early 1980s to 15% in 1993/1994 (Gelb, 2005, 385);

- Correspondingly low levels of domestic savings (corporate, household and government), down from 25% of GDP in 1982 to just above 16% in 1994 (Gelb, 2005, 388);

- A sharp increase in the fiscal deficit—close to 8% of GDP in 1993—due mostly to increased spending on the suppression of African resistance;

- High levels of inflation—around 15% in the early 1990s, which decreased to single-digit figures in 1994, though, thanks to the recession;

- And chronic balance of payment difficulties.

In order to better understand the eventual strategy adopted by the ANC, it is necessary to look back at the negotiations between the ANC, the apartheid government, business and the unions on South Africa's future. During this process, a number of macroeconomic strategies were developed by the participants. Many of them took the form of 'scenarios' which were supposed to filter realistic and feasible strategies from 'populist' ones (see for example: Le Roux, 1993). Leaving aside some of the smaller differences and details, I will try to present two exemplary strategies—one favoured by the left and best summarised under the header 'Growth through Redistribution' and one favoured by big business and international actors, such as the international financial institutions, here named 'Redistribution through Growth' .

Growth through Redistribution—Social-Democratic Options for the ANC

The following presentation uses comments on two documents published in the early 1990s—the 'Discussion Document on Economic Policy' issued by the party in 1990 and 'Making Democracy Work', a report compiled by a group of international and South African economists (Macroeconomic Research Group, MERG) and published in 1993, to outline the basic ingredients of the strategy (see: Marais, 2001, 124ff., Nattrass, 1994, Gelb, 2005, 367f.).

At the core of the model was—not surprisingly—an active state which intervenes in both the supply and the demand side of the economy. Domestic demand was to be spurred by redistributing income to the poor. The main vehicle to achieve this was a national minimum wage set at "approximately two-thirds of the minimum living level for a household of five" (Nattrass, 1994, 222). This was over double the wage of a full-time farm worker at the time. Assuming that the poor consume wage goods with a relatively high labour and low import content, their spending would be accompanied by a high multiplier, generating income and employment for the very people targeted in the first place. Parallel to this, it was hoped that the introduction of the minimum wage would lead business to develop the skills base of their work force and thereby increase productivity. The state was going to contribute to this by public investment in housing, infrastructure, education and basic health, all to add to the human and social capital of the economy. Moreover, higher productivity would allow South African industry to penetrate export markets over time. This first phase of public investment-led growth was going to re-establish investors' confidence in the potential of the economy, and after a period of an estimated five years private investment would kick in and sustain economic growth.

In terms of supply side activity, additional to the improvement in infrastructure the authors envisaged an unbundling of the big conglomerates and / or state control over new acquisitions and mergers in order to ensure competition. The financial sector was to be restructured, enabling domestic savings to be channeled into productive investment.

In 'Making Democracy Work', the economists involved also tried to address one of the core structural problems of South Africa: the looming foreign exchange shortage particularly in a phase of high and sustained growth (through rising imports in machinery and consumption goods). Avoiding this bottleneck to hamper growth was to be achieved by using the existing capital stock more efficiently—through better qualified and motivated workers and through the restructuring of industry, e.g. by channelling private investment into targeted sectors. Both were crucial regarding the success of the model, and both were equally contentious among economists at the time.

Redistribution through Growth

The alternative model, and the one the ANC chose to adopt to a very large extent in its later policies, was laid out in a number of publications. Here I draw on the growth strategy proposed by big business in South Africa, the South Africa Foundation (1996). Instead of an inward industrialisation strategy, it focused on export-led growth—in remarkable continuity to proposals voiced since the 1950s. Considering the foreign exchange restriction South Africa was facing, economic policy was geared to increase capital inflows (both portfolio and foreign direct investment) and to boost exports. This could be achieved by a broad based liberalisation of the economy. Liberalised capital markets would attract FDI and capital inflows in general; a liberalised trade regime with a gradual abolition of import tariffs and local-input requirements in exports would raise the competitiveness of the manufacturing industry and thereby improve the export performance.

An economic climate conducive to growth was seen as another prerequisite for FDI and local private investment. This included low inflation rates—achieved by an independent central bank, low budget deficits, the privatisation of 'non-essential' state assets and a commitment to moderate wage increases in flexible labour markets. Additional aspects of this strategy that are closer to the first scenario include tax incentives to stimulate private investment, budget spending reforms targeting the poor and increased public investment in social infrastructure, particularly training and skill enhancement of workers.

Choosing Orthodoxy

The former scenario, exemplified in 'Making Democracy Work', drew heavy criticism for a number of its features. First, increased domestic demand through redistributive policies would only spur the growth of labour-intensive industries in South Africa if those goods were not imported from abroad. Judging by the competitiveness problems of these industries in South Africa, this could only be achieved by further protecting them from international competition. At the same time, the planned 'channelling' of private investment hinted at protected capital markets as well. Gelb (2005, 368f.) argues that at that point in history South Africa simply had to open its economy to address the trade and balance of payments problems. Experiencing net capital outflows throughout the late 1980s and sluggish export growth, South

Africa needed to attract foreign capital and boost its export performance to access foreign exchange. There are two underlying assumptions in this argument: foreign direct investment and portfolio investment will only flow when capital markets are liberalised, and exports will become competitive only in an open environment where imports are cheaper.

Secondly, in another contribution, Geld stresses that focusing on the domestic wage goods sector omits addressing issues of profitability and import dependence. "Because the economic crisis was a crisis of production and the supply-side, to be sustainable macroeconomically, a new growth model could not be based simply on the expansion of aggregate demand through income redistribution"(Gelb, 2003, 28). Rather than redistributing consumption, Gelb suggests a redistribution of investment to slowly transform the existing capital structure.

Nattrass (1994, 222f.) in her assessment also targeted the potential foreign exchange shortage. As described above, growth in the MERG-model was compatible with a sustainable foreign exchange position thanks to the more efficient use of existing capital. Nattrass doubted whether the proposed reforms would lead to the desired outcome. Leaving aside less controversial measures such as training, land reform and the promotion of small business, she warned that the increase of the minimum wage might simply lead to shedding of labour instead of an upgrading of skills. Secondly, the intervention of government into the investment decisions of business was more likely to cause capital flight and weaken business confidence then to improve efficiency in capital use.

A probably less substantiated critique was offered in the so-called 'Ikarus scenario' developed within the 'Mont Fleur' scenario exercise. The authors, a group of South African economists, warned that an overambitious government that "embarks on a massive spending spree" (Le Roux, 1993, 14) would cause macroeconomic instability in the form of high deficits, inflation and balance of payments problems. The 'MERG'-report however explicitly rejected such inflationary increases in government spending (Nattrass, 1994, 219).

The latter scenario, 'Redistribution through Growth' was not without its critics however. The focus on an improved export performance and the attraction of foreign capital did formally address the foreign exchange problems South Africa was facing. Yet, there was no mechanism to ensure that private investment would indeed take place (Gelb, 2005, 370). Given the history of South African capital disinvesting and shifting capital abroad, this was indeed a risky strategy. The fiscal straitjacket limited the possibility of public investment, so success depended on local and foreign capital taking advantage of the new, more favourable economic and political environment.

Notwithstanding these doubts, the ANC chose orthodoxy. Whether it decided to drop the 'Growth through Redistribution' approach due to its historical roots as a party of the African middle-class, because it was 'selling-out' its working-class constituency or because of the economic arguments presented above is now a moot point. In one convincing interpretation, Gelb describes the adoption of the export-oriented strategy as one side of an "implicit bargain" that delivered white business' support for the new democratic dispensation in exchange for a racial restructuring of asset ownership (Gelb, 2005, 369). Nevertheless, this choice remained heavily disputed within the ANC and its alliance partners in government, the South African Communist Party and the trade union federation COSATU. In chapter six, I will come back to this conflict and review its recent developments in the realm of industrial policy.

RDP and GEAR

The ANC went into the 1994 election campaign with the 'Reconstruction and Development Programme' (RDP) which became the cornerstone of government economic policy. It was scrapped only two years later though and replaced by GEAR (Growth, Employment and Redistribution) in June 1996 (see Department of Finance 1996). There is disagreement over how different those two documents and the underlying strategies are, but it is undisputed that GEAR is modelled along the 'Redistribution through Growth' line. Its adoption drew heavy criticism from the ANC's leftist alliance partners in government and remains contested up until today.

GEAR promised to lift the South African economy to new heights, pushing the annual growth rate to 6% in 2000 and creating 400 000 jobs a year. "The higher growth path depends in part on attracting foreign direct investment, but also requires a higher domestic saving effort. Greater industrial competitiveness, a tighter fiscal stance, moderation of wage increases, accelerated public investment, efficient service delivery and a major expansion of private investment are integral aspects of the strategy. An exchange rate policy consistent with improved international competitiveness, responsible monetary policies and targeted industrial incentives characterise the new policy environment. A strong export performance underpins the macroeconomic sustainability of the growth path. Private sector employment creation is reinforced by small business promotion, land reform and emergent farmer support, greater labour market flexibility and labour-based public sector infrastructural development projects." (Department of Finance , 1996)

Ten Years into Democracy—Evaluating Macro-Performance in the First Decade

More than a decade later there is ample literature evaluating the performance of the South African economy. The ANC government achieved (a narrowly defined) macroeconomic stabilisation and was widely applauded for that, but many of the problems of the economy remained unresolved. Overshadowing all else was an ever rising unemployment rate of around 40%.

GEAR stressed the importance of a sound macroeconomic environment and defined macroeconomic stability mainly as reduced budget deficits and low inflation. The government certainly achieved the former, so that "[f]iscal policy must be regarded as one of the major successes in the post-apartheid era, in terms of meeting its own objectives" (Gelb, 2005, 373). The budget deficit has been below 3% of GDP ever since 1999 (see Figure 2.5), and total government debt amounts to a managable 36.1% of GDP in early 2005 (South African Reserve Bank, 2005).

One important factor contributing to the decreasing deficit is a much improved and more efficient tax and revenue collection. Tax revenue as a share of GDP is now just below the ceiling of 25% of GDP specified in GEAR (Gelb, 2005, 375). In terms of spending, social services make up close to 60% of government's non-interest expenditure (Department of Finance, 2004, 56). This includes spending on education, social security, health and other social services and is in line with the overall strategic aim of improving service delivery for the poor. Whether increased spending has actually led to better access to housing, water, electricity or grants is an ever-returning issue of political debate (see Marais, 2001, 190). I will return to it in Chapter 6. Public investment remained at low levels in this period however, rising from 3.7% of GDP in 1994 to just below 5% in 2003.

Although the government maintains that fiscal policy was and will remain expansionary, there is a lot of scepticism in the literature. Davies and van Seventer (2004, 147) conclude that the public sector's stance was expansionary, but its effect relatively small. Tight fiscal policy also led to a

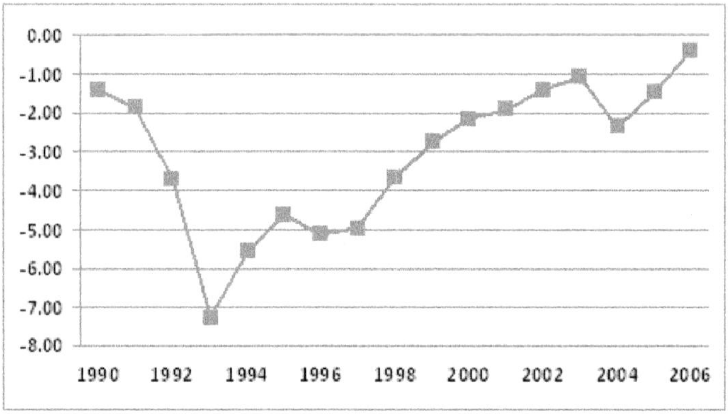

Figure 2.5: Budget Deficit, Percent of GDP

Source: South African Reserve Bank

drop in public sector employment. Close to 150.000 jobs were lost in the public sector in the past ten years (Seidman Makgetla, 2004, 274).

Two decisions taken during and shortly after the transition to democracy shaped the monetary policy regime in post-apartheid South Africa: the independence of the South African Reserve Bank which is now enshrined in the Constitution and the liberalisation of the capital account in March 1995. The sole responsibility of the South African Reserve Bank (SARB) is the achievement and maintenance of price stability. Since 2000, the SARB uses a formal inflation targeting approach. The Ministry of Finance establishes a target range (currently between 3% and 6% of increase of the CPIX). The SARB tries to keep inflation within that range mainly by adapting the repurchase interest rate (Epstein, 2002, 21).

Before the capital account liberalisation, exchange controls and the dual exchange rate (commercial rand and financial rand, the latter applying solely to capital account transactions of non-residents) limited the outflow of capital. The financial rand was abolished in March 1995, and restrictions on residents' foreign investments were gradually removed (Gelb, 2005, 378). In this open environment, the attempt to achieve both low inflation and a stable nominal exchange rate proved to be overambitious. In the wake of

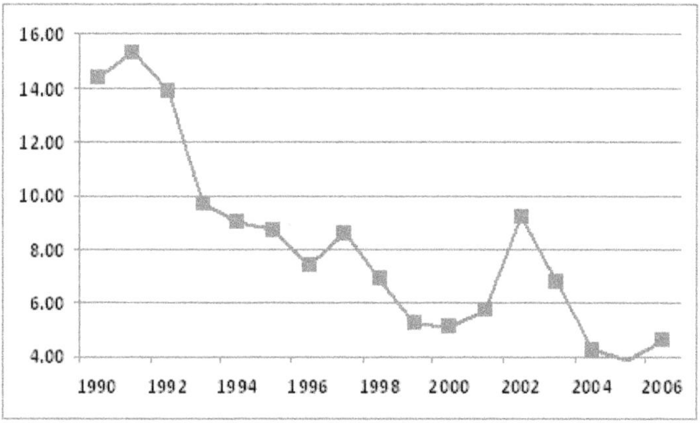

Figure 2.6: Consumer Prices, Year to Year Change

Source: South African Reserve Bank

the Asian crisis in 1998, the SARB gave up its interventions to target the nominal exchange rate and focused solely on price stability.

Inflation did come down and was within the target ranges from 1999 to 2001. In 2002, the depreciation of the Rand led to a temporary rise in inflation, but in 2004 it was back at just above 4% (see Figure 2.6).

High real interest rates were the price to be paid for relative price stability. According to calculations by SARB economists, South Africa's real short term interest rate rose from negative rates in the 1970s and 1980s (-3,2% and -0,8% respectively) to an average 5,6% between 1990 and 2000. These rates are extremely high not only in historical perspective but also in international comparison (Kahn et al. 2002, cited in Epstein 2002, 14). In addition to high repurchasing rates (the main lending rate of the SARB), the opening of the South African capital markets and the perceived risk of investing in South Africa also contributed to high real interest rates.

The impact of high real interest rates is contentious in economic theory. If they lead to higher saving levels and higher savings in turn induce higher investment, then they might contribute to higher growth, but there is little empirical evidence for this. In South Africa another aspect seems more relevant: firms repeatedly claimed in surveys that the high cost of credit is one of the major reasons hindering investment—second only to crime

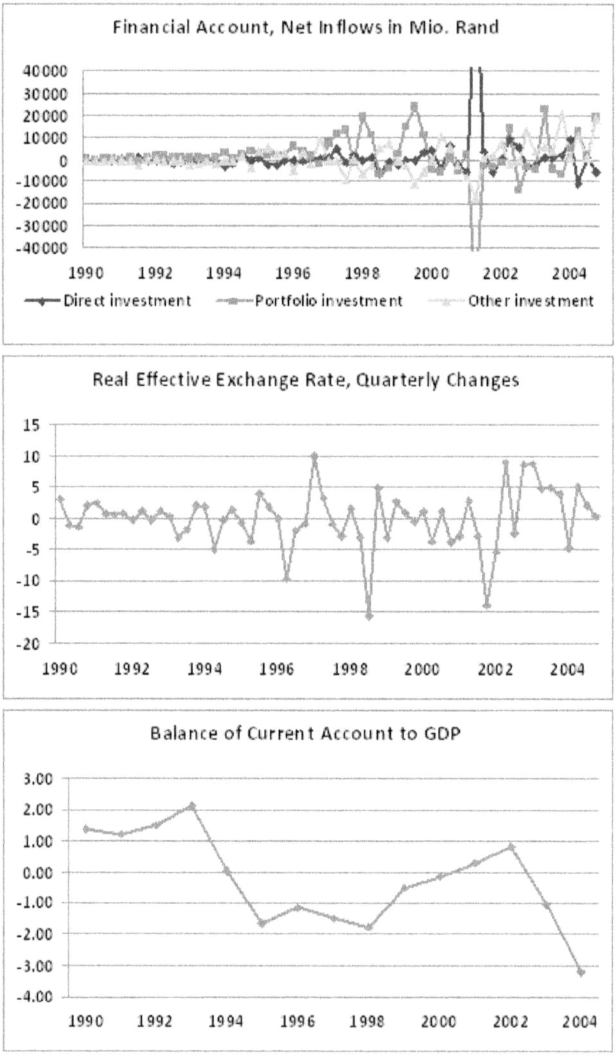

Figure 2.7: Net Inflows, Exchange Rate, Current Account

Source: South African Reserve Bank.
Note: The hikes of direct and portfolio investment in 2001 reflect Anglo's movement of headquarter to London (Seidman Makgetla, 2004, 267)

(Epstein, 2002, 17). Furthermore, the capital account liberalisation led to increased volatility in financial markets. This can be seen in both capital flows and the exchange rate (Figure 2.7).

Capital inflows allowed the Reserve Bank to rebuild its foreign currency reserves by 2004. Importantly, this removed the foreign exchange constraint from the economy and also led to a narrowing of the differential between US and South African yields (Gelb, 2005, 383). Yet, openness has led to extreme volatility in the exchange rate (see Figure 2.7).

This means "inconsistent signals from the exchange rate to producers of tradables, increasing uncertainty and encouraging waiting in production and investment decisions" (Gelb, 2005, 383). The inflow of capital was indeed and direly needed to finance the growing deficit in the current account. Figure 2.7 quite strongly indicates that with economic growth, South Africa still experiences balance of payments problems. The acceleration of growth in the new millennium is reflected in an ever increasing deficit in the current account. Soaring imports were driven mostly by high-value capital goods, but also by imports of (predominantly luxury) consumer goods (South African Reserve Bank, 2005, 31).

Looking back at the targets specified in GEAR, the government only partly achieved what it aimed for. The effects of both a "faster fiscal deficit reduction programme" and a "consistent monetary policy to prevent a resurgence of inflation" (Department of Finance , 1996) can be seen in low inflation and budget deficit numbers. Yet, these are not socioeconomic achievements in their own right, but they are supposed to lead to higher savings, investment and capital inflow—preferably foreign direct investment and thereby contribute to economic growth. I will later show that none of these have come through despite the sound macro-environment. Leaving aside other arguments for now, it is possible that the policies themselves contributed to low investment rates through high real interest rates, a volatile exchange rate and relatively low public investment.

2.3.2 Sectoral and Industrial Development

Industrial development was obviously shaped by the macroeconomic framework conditions. Yet, there were significant sectoral variations, and they corresponded to the pattern observed in previous periods. Sectors close to the country's resource endowment continued their strong performance, while broader manufacturing performed poorly. I will start this section with a de-

	Share of Value Added				Employment 2004	
	1990	1995	2000	2004	Thousand	Share
Agriculture	3,67	2,87	3,27	2,82	1.258	11,04
Mining	9,34	8,9	7,56	7,28	558	4,9
Manufacturing	20,04	19,41	18,98	17,98	1.594	19,99
Electricity	2,57	2,84	2,72	2,36	106	0,93
Construction	3,29	2,81	2,52	2,75	659	5,78
Retail Trade	13,69	13,78	14,64	15,24	2.355	20,67
Transport	7,16	8,12	9,65	10,78	582	5,11
Financial Intermediation	16,42	17,36	18,64	20,34	1.070	9,39
Community Services	23,48	24,29	2,02	20,35	2.158	18,94

Table 2.9: Sectoral Development, an Overview

Source: South African Reserve Bank, Statistics South Africa

scriptive analysis of sectoral performance, then focus on industrial policy initiatives in the decade under scrutiny, and conclude with an assessment of the main problems still facing the economy after a decade of democratic government.

Sectoral Development

A look at the sectoral composition of output and employment confirms structural patterns observed throughout South Africa's modern history (see Table 2.9).

The agricultural sector is comparatively small and highly industrialised. This of course goes back to the Land Act of 1913 which all but destroyed independent black farming (Terreblanche, 2002, 260). The end of apartheid brought an end to heavy subsidies for white farmers and a move towards free markets. This led to increased concentration and further job losses in the sector (Seidman Makgetla, 2004, 274).

Mining's share in output also clearly declined since 1990 but this does not adequately reflect the job losses in the sector. While in 1987 more than 760.000 people worked on the mines, this number was down to just above 402.000 in 2002 (Seidman Makgetla, 2004, 273). A major reason for this development is the relative shift from gold exports to platinum. Platinum mining is far less labour intensive than gold mining.

Turning to manufacturing, the overall performance of the sector remained weak. Its share in the economy further declined and growth rates

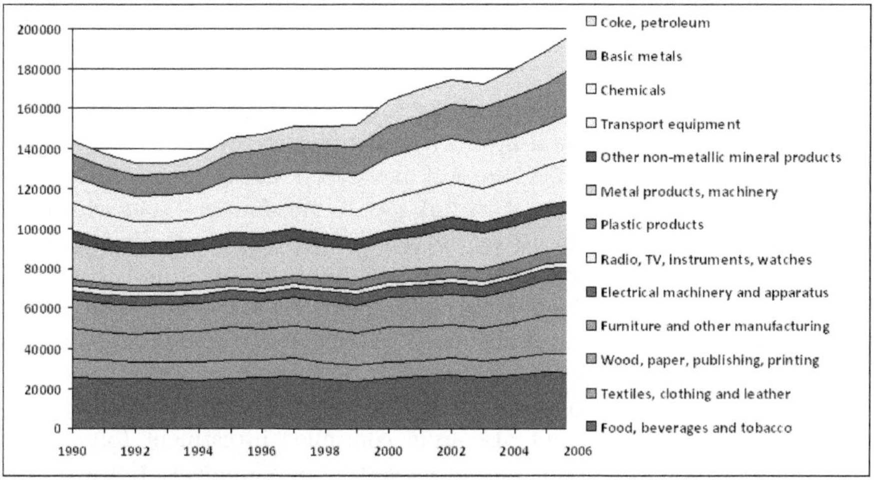

Figure 2.8: Sectoral Value Added, in Constant 2000 Rand

Source: Quantec, own calculations

have been disappointing. In addition, labour intensive branches have grown even slower than the average. This includes food and beverages, textiles, clothing and footwear. "Low rates of growth in the labour intensive sectors have combined with overall rising capital intensity resulting in consistent declines in manufacturing employment" (Kaplan, 2003, 10). Edwards' (2001) decomposition shows that ultra-labour intensive sectors such as wearing apparel and leather products are particularly affected by both weak export performance and growing import penetration. Briefly looking at the rest of the sectors we observe that construction lost in importance, most probably due to the slump in state investment in construction (Seidman Makgetla, 2004, 274) and that services overall become more important.

A more detailed analysis of the manufacturing sector reveals that the MEC concept continues to be relevant for South Africa. In terms of value added, expansion is clearly concentrated in a small number of sectors close to mining—coke and petroleum, basic metals, and chemicals (see Figure 2.8). Overall, MEC sectors grew at 1,92% annually between 1990 and 2006, while non-MEC manufacturing sectors grew significantly less at 1,11% annually (see Table 2.10 and 2.11). The notable exception to this trend is transport equipment. Positive results in this sub-sector are driven by the automotive industry which will be the focus of more detailed attention in the next sub-chapter on industrial policy.

A number of case studies find the following recurring pattern in the chemicals and plastics, metal products and other sectors: While upstream industries located in the MEC are well developed and internationally competitive, downstream sectors with linkages to the former—and which are potentially more labour-intensive—are not developed accordingly (Machaka and Roberts, 2003, Roberts, 2006). In both iron and steel and chemicals, South Africa profits from its mineral endowment. As described above, earlier governments built up these scale-intensive industries through state owned companies (Iscor and Sasol). While each of these was privatised before 1994, they continue to dominate their respective sectors. This dominance results from scale effects but also from continued investment (often with government support) and ongoing technological development. However, the comparative advantage of South Africa's resource endowment is not passed on to downstream producers. Both steel and basic chemicals producers engage in import parity pricing. They charge local customers an import parity price that is just below the one they would have to pay for the imported product. Firms in the metal products and plastics sectors then struggle to become internationally competitive and perform disappointingly in terms of investments and job creation.

In both the metal products and the plastics sector, development was also restricted by the poor overall growth performance of the economy, since most of their output is directed at the intermediate domestic market. In metals, the two main types of products, structural steel and fabricated metals, are inputs in infrastructure related activities and a variety of other industries, and so depend heavily on investment spending of the state and mining companies (Roberts, 2006, 160). Plastic products are also rarely sold to private households, but serve as inputs to various other industries.

Another parallel is export performance. While the upstream products—iron and steel and basic chemicals—are internationally competitive, the downstream sectors are not. Again, this is indicative of a broader pattern in the South African economy, a pattern well known from earlier periods. The export-output ratio of MEC sectors is almost double the ratio of non-MEC sectors (see Table 2.10 and 2.11). Overall, more than 30% of South African exports continue to come from mining itself, particularly gold and platinum. This is down from the early 1990s, where mining still accounted for more

	An. Real Growth [1]	Capital/Labour [1]		Empl/Output [1]		Net Exports [2]		Export/Output [1]	
1 Industry	**90-2006**	**1990**	**2006**	**1990**	**2006**	**1990**	**2006**	**1990**	**2006**
11 Primary, All	**0,21**	**11,15**	**13,53**	**14,25**	**8,78**	**48894**	**53584**	**48,92**	**49,10**
111 Agriculture, Forestry, Fishing	-0,06	5,97	5,79	32,56	19,36	576	9644	4,50	22,56
112 Mining and Quarrying	0,31	21,05	36,00	6,87	3,39	48318	43940	66,82	62,48
12 Secondary, All	**2,10**	**14,82**	**19,39**	**4,79**	**2,40**	**-21073**	**-168789**	**11,75**	**15,34**
121 Manufacturing	1,99	12,89	19,47	3,87	1,91	-21205	-168893	14,49	18,36
1210 Food, Beverages, Tobacco	0,57	9,36	13,96	3,06	1,86	2567	-4430	6,36	6,54
1211 Textiles, Clothing and Leather	0,32	2,44	2,62	10,57	5,74	24	-14906	12,34	8,35
1212 Wood/Paper, Publishing, Print	1,79	7,83	9,62	3,92	2,65	-33	-4608	13,73	9,88
1213 Petroleum Pr., Chemicals, etc.	3,92	63,56	97,30	2,03	0,76	-11764	-21361	14,42	14,86
12131 Coke, refined Petroleum Prod.	5,18	302,63	494,8	1,19	0,30	-5787	-1021	24,27	12,97
12132 Basic Chemicals	2,89	80,60	186,5	1,29	0,44	-658	-3944	24,99	31,03
12133 Other Chemicals	3,62	17,89	25,34	2,20	0,88	-4405	-12133	4,08	7,22
12134 Rubber Products	0,63	8,46	11,88	3,44	2,08	-493	-2113	4,81	15,71
12135 Plastic Products	4,72	3,54	4,75	4,24	1,90	-421	-2149	2,93	5,21
1214 Other Non-Metallic Mineral Pr.	0,44	11,99	16,22	7,74	4,15	-651	-3103	6,23	7,45
1215 Metals, Metal Products, Machinery, Equipment	2,19	10,73	16,08	4,04	2,12	5998	-16455	28,63	38,48
12151 Basic Iron and Steel	4,62	22,33	42,82	3,34	0,74	11770	27786	47,84	49,12
12152 Basic Non-Ferrous Metals	5,29	16,85	78,46	3,95	1,20	6043	2466	76,26	37,22
12153 Metal Products excl. Machinery	0,23	4,52	4,87	5,32	4,13	870	-1806	8,31	14,13
12154 Machinery and Equipment	-0,42	6,30	5,39	3,57	3,57	-12685	-44901	11,79	45,58
1216 Electrical Machinery, Apparatus	1,95	4,17	5,66	6,36	2,07	-4629	-6760	8,25	8,04

Table 2.10: Sectoral Development of the South African economy, 1990-2006

Source: Quantec, own calculations

[a] Per Cent

[b] Million Rand, Constant 2000 Prices

	An. Real Growth [1]	**Capital/Labour [1]**		**Empl/Output [1]**		**Net Exports [2]**		**Export/Output [1]**	
1 Industry (cont.)	**90-2006**	**1990**	**2006**	**1990**	**2006**	**1990**	**2006**	**1990**	**2006**
1217 Radio, TV, Instruments	-0,50	5,19	7,37	2,67	2,06	-5861	-35372	11,65	33,63
1218 Transport Equipment	2,52	7,12	16,44	3,13	1,11	-8404	-55882	5,48	21,77
1219 Furniture, other Man.	1,59	3,10	6,57	2,90	3,15	1548	-8016	19,16	19,11
122 Electricity, Gas, Water	2,16	193,58	258,0	2,50	1,01	183	362	0,57	0,68
1221 Electricity, Gas, Steam	2,37	174,77	240,6	2,59	0,94	183	362	0,75	0,87
1222 Water Supply	0,91	261,53	303,5	2,22	1,24	0	0	0	0
123 Construction	2,71	1,11	2,37	11,42	6,48	-51	-258	0,03	0,05
13 Tertiary, All	**3,37**	**20,03**	**19,49**	**9,46**	**5,88**	**-2424**	**29315**	**2,82**	**4,11**
131 Trade, Catering, Accomodation Services	3,43	4,75	4,52	11,30	8,74	2862	13885	3,50	6,04
132 Transport, Storage, Communication	5,36	50,26	82,22	6,95	1,79	-1184	6435	8,88	8,09
133 Financial Intermediation, Insurance, Real Estate	4,47	55,53	28,91	4,43	4,37	-615	10093	2,49	3,37
134 Community, Social, Personal Services	160	14,27	17,06	12,81	8,17	-3487	-1098	0,21	0,58
1 All Industries	**2,71**	**16,97**	**18,59**	**8,08**	**4,79**	**25396**	**-85890**	**11,76**	**12,08**
MEC	**1,92**	**33,80**	**55,79**	**4,58**	**1,70**	**53899**	**55774**	**39,75**	**32,78**
Non-MEC Manufacturing	**1,11**	**5,86**	**8,64**	**4,21**	**2,43**	**-26039**	**-46039**	**9,89**	**15,49**

Table 2.11: Sectoral Development of the South African economy, 1990-2006

Source: Quantec, own calculations

[a] Per Cent
[b] Million Rand, Constant 2000 Prices

than half of total exports. The share of manufacturing in total exports rose, but interestingly, manufacturing exports became increasingly capital-intensive. "The leaders of the export boom were chemicals, metals, metal products, and machinery. Motor vehicles and paper were also important contributors, while food, clothing, and footwear suffered absolute declines in exports" (Lewis, 2001, 7). Given the large number of unskilled and unemployed workers in South Africa, it "has a 'paradoxical' export structure with a remarkably low and declining share of exports that use unskilled labour, and a relatively high share that use more skilled labour." (Nattrass, 1998, 20).

Imports in general are dominated by manufactured goods. They comprise more than 80% of total imports. While slow growth in the 1990s meant that imports of machinery rose relatively slowly, the imports of labour-intensive manufactured goods were growing sharply (Nattrass, 1998, 20). With growth accelerating in the new millennium, South Africa is again faced with a current account deficit of significant proportions.

Numerous authors tried to assess the overall impact of changes in trade flows on the labour market. Higher import penetration and export growth concentrated in capital-intensive sectors certainly imply that the opening of the economy did not lead to a reduction in unemployment (Edwards, 2001). In fact, South Africa might find itself "being squeezed from both ends of the skills spectrum" (Lewis, 2001, 16). As a middle income country, it has to compete with low-income countries in labour-intensive sectors and developed countries in capital-intensive sectors.

Industrial Policy

South Africa's production structure as a capital intensive biased minerals economy with relatively weak and inward-oriented light manufacturing industries would clearly have an impact on policy choices after 1994. However, an analysis of the development of the South African economy should also take into account the ANC's broader economic strategy. As described above, macroeconomic stabilisation loomed large in policy makers' minds and certainly took precedence over any sector-specific interventions. An 'inward industrialisation' path, geared towards a growing domestic market, and financed domestically by fiscal expansion and / or redistribution of income, was thus never seriously considered. Quite to the contrary, the ANC took early measures to open the economy through tariff reductions in an attempt to foster the global competitiveness of South African firms. Increasing exports from manufacturing would address both unemployment and the chronic balance of payments problems that plagued the economy.

Within this framework, the ANC was faced with the choice between an industrial policy that supported either "smaller businesses and pre-reform uncompetitive labour-absorbing sectors [or] policies designed to exploit existing comparative advantages and bigger projects" (Hirsch, 2005, 122). As a clear and coherent vision is considered vital to industrial policy, it is telling that the actual outcome was more of an "unresolved compromise" (ibid.). Indeed, authors assessing trade and industrial policy in this early phase place emphasis on the liberalisation drive in trade policy. South Africa was a founding member of the WTO in 1995 and implemented a simplified tariff structure and an overall reduction of tariffs. Trade liberalisation was combined with a range of general—i.e. not sector-specific—supply side measures in order to boost international competitiveness and exports. These included export credit guarantees and support in market, innovation, research and development. However, firms do not appear to have frequently taken advantage of these measures and this has limited their effectiveness (Kaplan, 2004, 626).

One notable exception to this pattern is the automotive industry. The Motor Industry Development Programme (MIDP) managed to retain production in South Africa amidst a significant reduction of tariffs, helping producers achieve international competitiveness. Moreover, there are significant linkages to other sectors due to local sourcing incentives (Roberts, 2005, 28). The success of this sector, however, is exceptional and has not been repeated in other sectors where firms place little importance on the Department of Trade and Industry's (DTI) strategies (Kaplan, 2004, 627).

At the same time, there has been well-funded support in MEC sectors. The Strategic Industrial Projects programme, implemented by the DTI between 2002 and 2005, provided tax relief for large investment projects which were mainly concentrated in heavy industry (Roberts, 2005, 25). The same is true for the lending of the Industrial Development Corporation (IDC), South Africa's main development bank and holding company. It has historically supported industries close to mining and continued this pattern throughout the 1990s (ibid.).

Not surprisingly, most assessments attribute limited success to industrial policy. As seen above, South Africa has certainly failed to significantly develop manufacturing capacities outside the MEC and limited pockets such as auto components.

I would like to conclude this review of the first ten years of industrial policy with a self-assessment by Alan Hirsch, the former Chief Director of the DTI: "It is probably fair to say that government is haunted by the nagging feeling that we could have and should be doing more. Surely we know enough to be able to identify some key sectors that can grow faster with effective policies" (Hirsch, 2005, 160). This statement must be understood within the context of a gradual shift in emphasis towards a more interventionist policy that targets sectors explicitly and on a broader basis. This shift will be analysed in Chapter 6.

Taking Stock after Ten Years

Overall, the growth performance of the economy has been disappointing. Given the population growth rate of 2% per year, an average GDP growth rate of 2.77% between 1994 and 2003 (Gelb, 2005, 367) is clearly not enough to address the manifold problems of the economy, particularly high unemployment (Figure 2.9).

Why is South Africa trapped in a low-growth path? Low investment certainly plays a major part in any explanation. Davies and van Seventer (2004) argue that while government saving was consistently lower than government investment, the gap steadily decreasing thanks to the rise in the public savings rate. This attempt of "reversed crowding out" did not bring about the desired increase in private investment though. Instead, the private savings rate fell accordingly (Figure 2.9).

Indeed, low gross savings (14.4% of GDP in 2004) and low gross capital formation (16.5% of GDP in 2004) are identified by most authors as major constraints on growth in South Africa. Overall savings are still far below the levels achieved in the 1980s. One possible explanation is the parallel opening up of the economy. "A downward trend in private sector savings is often observed when financial or trade liberalisation takes place. Prior to liberalisation, limited spending outlets might lead to an artificial propping up of savings." (Davies and van Seventer, 2004, 142).

What other reasons might be responsible for low investment? Fiscal policy is of course dampening public investment which remains below 5% in 2003 (albeit growing slightly since a shift in policy priorities in 2001) (Gelb, 2005, 387) and FDI never reached expected levels. A number of surveys

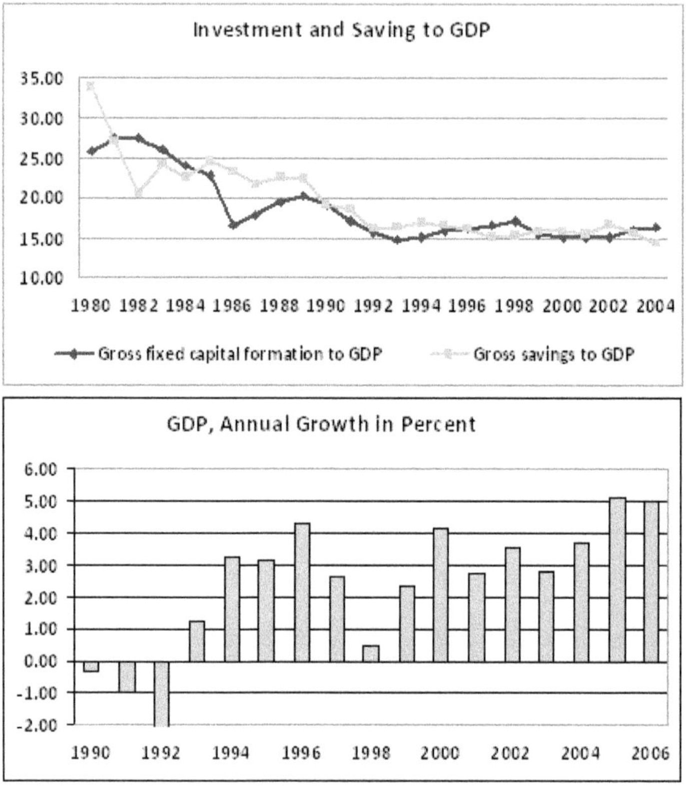

Figure 2.9: Growth, Savings and Investment

Source: South African Reserve Bank

have been conducted to find out more about the restrictions companies make responsible for their low investment. Chief Executive Officers of large (more than 50 employees) manufacturing firms named the following obstacles to their business' growth (cited in Lewis, 2001, 21): crime and theft; cost of capital and credit; volatility of the Rand; impact of labour regulation; corruption and administrative costs; shortage of skilled labour (ordered by importance).

Crime tops the list in another survey conducted by Gelb as well (cited in Epstein, 2002, 18). It seems to be a big obstacle to smaller firms in particular. Second only to crime, the high cost of capital severely constrains investment. As described above, high real interest rates prevail in South Africa due to restrictive monetary policy which focuses on attracting foreign capital inflows. While CEOs rank high interest rates highly, econometric studies do not always support this conclusion. Yet when considering the effect of tight monetary policy and high interest rates on both the cost of capital itself and the amount of retained earnings (after paying interest costs), it is highly significant (ibid., 19).

The volatility of the Rand particularly hits exporters and thus the very core of the growth model. The impact of the other three factors mentioned is less clear. Labour regulations are a highly contested issue and the impact on firms is far from obvious. For now it suffices to note that 30% of firms in the same survey claimed that the new regulations had actually improved labour relations (Lewis, 2001, 23). Bhorat and Cassim (2004, 18) come to the conclusion that "manufacturing firms on the whole do not view the labour legislation environment as a significant constraint on employment expansion". Looking at corruption, only 1% of firms reported that they were asked to pay bribes. Finally, 80% of firms said that it was extremely or moderately hard to find managerial or professional staff.

Authors focusing on industrial development and policy are skeptical about the value of surveys with existing firms however. If one wants to find out about binding constraints for growth, it indeed does not seem appropriate to ask existing firms—they might well reflect the bias in an economy's structural features that prevent diversification and faster growth. In South Africa's case, the development that sticks out is its premature deindustrialisation, or, as Rodrik puts it, "the shrinkage of the non-mineral tradable sector since the early 1990s" (Rodrik, 2006, 3). Non-mineral tradables include the manufacturing sector that performed so disappointingly. This sector uses unskilled labour intensively, and its recovery would provide major relieve on the labour market. Rodrik identifies the structural shift away from manufacturing and tradables as the main cause of the unemployment crisis. He observes three related developments in the last 15 years: there was firstly a substitution process towards skilled labour within industries, secondly, capital intensity within sectors rose, and thirdly, low-skill intensive sectors lost importance (Rodrik, 2006, 10). While the first two are common features of economies opening up to global competition, the third is surprising given South Africa's factor endowment and requires explanation. He finds a strong decline in the relative profitability of manufacturing activities to be its main cause. Although he does not distinguish between MEC and non-MEC sectors, this differentiation would in all likelihood accentuate his analysis, given that the few positive outliers in manufacturing development are almost exclusively in the confines of the MEC.

So why did profitability decline? The opening of the economy and increased import penetration played a role, as did the fluctuating real exchange rate. A large part of the decline remains unexplained in his regression, but I would agree with Rodrik's speculative answer that South Africa is "caught between more advanced countries at the high end and China at the low end" (Rodrik, 2006, 22). Historically strong sectors close to the mineral endowment and those with sufficient policy support (automotive) could avert this trend, but the large majority of manufacturing could not. What this means in terms of policy conclusions will not be discussed here but will be addressed in Chapter 6.

Not surprisingly, slow growth and unfavourable shifts in the sectoral composition of output aggravated South Africa's major economic problem, unemployment. South Africa now has an extremely high unemployment rate historically and also in comparison with other middle income countries. The numbers (see Figure 2.10) are taken from Altman (2005, 425) who based her calculation on data from Statistics South Africa. The strict definition includes only those actively looking for jobs, while the broad definition additionally accounts for discouraged workers. Since the Labour Force Survey, which provides the numbers, asks for any economic activity, the numbers should not be overstating the problem and cater for work in the informal sector as well (Altman, 2005, 427).

Unemployment is unevenly distributed among different groups of the population. Africans are at a much higher risk of being unemployed than Coloureds, Indians or whites. Using the strict definition, the unemployment rate for whites was 6% in 2002, compared to 37% for Africans (Altman, 2005, 426). This reflects the skills composition of the different population groups. Much in line with international figures, women have higher unemployment than men, while unemployment in rural areas atypically is higher than in urban areas (Lewis, 2001, 75). This is caused by the much smaller role of the agricultural sector in South Africa. Since there is no subsistence sector to fall back on and since the state provides no special support for the unemployed, it is closely correlated with poverty (Seekings and Nattrass, 2005, 317f.).

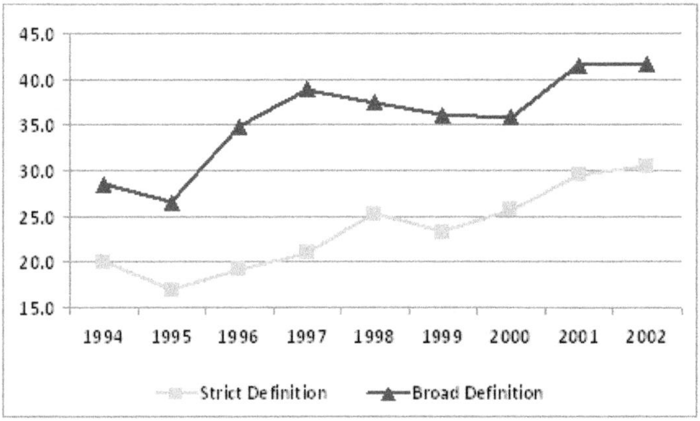

Figure 2.10: Unemployment Rates

Source: Altman (2005, 425)

Virtually all sectors contributed to the employment crisis, including agriculture and mining, the public sector, and manufacturing. The decrease in jobs in the public sector and mining can be attributed to specific factors (fiscal constraints and the decline in the gold price respectively), but overall, rising capital intensity in production certainly was the crucial factor. While this was partly due to a shift in activities, authors such as Lewis also note that unions managed to push up wages particularly for semi-skilled and unskilled workers (Lewis, 2001, 14) and thereby increased the relative price of (most notably unskilled) labour. Considering that these groups are by far the hardest hit by unemployment, he states that "the neoclassical conclusion that unskilled and semi-skilled labour has to a large extent been priced out of the market seems unavoidable" (ibid.). The opening of the economy to international competition in the 1990s has accelerated this trend through both higher import penetration in labour-intensive sectors and higher capital-intensity in exports. This analysis is shared by policy makers in South Africa. Back in 1996, minister of finance Trevor Manuel stated that "as South Africa proceeds with trade liberalisation and adapts to international competition, downward pressure will be placed on unskilled wages. If this is not accommodated by the labour market, then unemployment will rise." (cited in Marais, 2001, 182).

So would lower real wages for the unskilled ease the unemployment crisis? Apart from the fact that the trends observed by Lewis are not undisputed (see Marais, 2001, 183; Bhorat and Cassim, 2004, 25; Seidman Makgetla, 2004, 265) there are a number of concerns with such a strategy: firstly, in an environment of extreme poverty and inequality, a strategy of lowering wages of the unskilled risks a further deterioration of the situation of poor households. Considering South Africa's long history of exploitation of cheap African labour, it is indeed questionable whether such a strategy is politically viable for the ANC whose political raison d'être lies in overturning historical inequalities. Secondly, it is unreasonable to expect that structural trends such as the mechanisation of commercial agriculture and the switch to deep-ore mining which requires higher capital intensity for technological reasons will be reversed by a decrease in the relative price of labour (Bhorat et al., 2002, 25).

To conclude, given South Africa's factor endowment, job creation on a significant scale will most likely come from an improved performance of labour-intensive manufacturing sectors that predominantly employ unskilled labour. These sectors have performed poorly over the last decade, indeed over the last 30 years or so. At the same time, MEC sectors continued their dominance and thereby bear testimony to the path dependence of the economy's evolution over time. These trends have been reinforced by an industrial policy strategy that continued to openly support these sectors and did not do enough to actively encourage diversification.

After a theoretical interlude in Chapter 3, I will try to shed more light on this path dependence and the role of linkages between sectors—particularly between mining and MEC sectors—to corroborate these findings. In this vain I will conduct a simulation of a linkage-based New Economic Geography model based on South Africa's economic structure (Chapter 4) and an econometric analysis of linkage strength between sectors (Chapter 5). In Chapter 6, I will come back to the historical analysis and complement it with the most recent shift in policy priorities—the making of a South African developmental state. A core part of this developmental state consists of a more interventionist industrial policy, and I will use both the historical and the quantitative assessments of South Africa's manufacturing sector to evaluate the new policy and its chances for success.

Chapter 3

Linkages in Economic Theory

One prominent aspect of South African industrial development is the continuing strength of sectors close to its mineral endowment. There are numerous potential explanations for this fact, but one I want to shed more light on in this dissertation is the role of linkages between sectors. I interpret linkages narrowly, as the flow of intermediate goods between sectors as recorded in input-output tables (a more elaborate definition of forward and backward linkages follows below). They certainly played a crucial role in South Africa's early economic development, when mining activities created backward linkages to upstream industries such as chemicals and explosives, and forward linkages to industrial buyers of their output, so called downstream industries. In post-war economic development, the mining boom again galvanised the manufacturing sector. Linkages certainly played a role in industrial policy discussions as well, and the state's strategic involvement in sectors such as basic chemicals or iron and steel was partly motivated by facilitating linkages between primary extractive industries and downstream manufacturing. The extent of such effects of course has to be evaluated empirically, which I attempt in later chapters.

Before that, a theoretical foundation is necessary. In economic theory, the concept of linkages is an old one which came to prominence thanks to the rise of development economics after World War Two. I will briefly cover this literature (Section 3.1) before turning my attention to a more recent reformulation of the concept: linkages have been formalised in models of the New Economic Geography (NEG)(3.2). I will use such a model to describe

South Africa's industrial development in Chapter 4 and therefore introduce NEG in a second part of this chapter.

3.1 Linkages in Development Economics

Development Economics is here used as a catch-all to subsume those authors dealing with the long run development of economically backward countries.

German economist Friedrich List may be better known for his arguments on infant industry protection, yet the underlying idea presented by him is equally interesting: in his main work, first published in 1841, he stresses the importance of productive capabilities that are built up in the development process, and how the pursuit of certain industrial activities calls forth production and is productivity enhancing in other sectors of the economy (List, 1950). For him, there is an important difference between a nation using its resources in agricultural production, and one that focuses on manufacturing. The latter is preferable since manufacturing activities lead to productivity increases in all other sectors. Moreover, they trigger processes of institutional, infrastructural and political progress (ibid., 230). Diversification and the emergence of new industries is not a 'natural' phenomenon that can be relied on happening in a market economy however. He argues that protective tariffs are necessary to protect 'infant industries' from competition—the underlying argument being that productivity increases over time and with scale (ibid., 415ff.). So I find two ideas here that are still very relevant more than a century later: the emphasis on the structural composition of production and linkages between sectors, and the crucial role the state is playing in shaping and influencing this structure.

After 1945, the impending independence of colonies sparked an interest in questions of development that was answered by the nascent discipline of development economics. Often, the concept of linkages was at the very core of these works. In addressing challenges of industrialisation in the European periphery, Rosenstein-Rodan argues for a "large scale planned industrialization" (Rosenstein-Rodan, 1943, 205) in order to enable the exploitation of complementarity of industries. He explicitly refers to external economies as introduced by Marshall (1938) here: the social marginal product of an activity exceeds the private marginal product since it creates linkages—both directly by pushing suppliers of inputs over a certain profitability threshold, and indirectly by raising aggregate demand due to the employment of formerly idle manpower.

Another major contribution came from Myrdal (1957). Rather than perceiving the economy as a system that tends toward a stable equilibrium, he introduced the notion of a vicious (or virtuous) circle where exogenous shocks lead to a self-reinforcing process of cumulative causation. In terms of economic development these processes lead to regional inequalities where certain regions boom thanks to external economies and others decline. Again, policy implications are clear: the state has to provide leadership in identifying projects or industries that can spark positive cumulative processes.

Albert O. Hirschman then went on to explicitly define backward and forward linkages, the former inducing local production of inputs once demand for these inputs reaches a critical scale, the latter providing inputs locally for downstream producers (Hirschman, 1966). He also enriched the concept by stressing two necessary conditions for linkages to work: scale effects—without economies of scale the concept of linkages would be meaningless since every economic activity is linked to many others—and private entrepreneurial or public responsiveness to incentives. Linkages can also be understood as providing investment opportunities and therefore act as guidance for private and state investment (Hirschman, 1981). Here, Hirschman comes very close to ideas of 'unbalanced growth' (see for example Streeten, 1959). Hirschman also stresses the importance of transport costs. Linkage effects would not be relevant in their absence, since inputs in production could always be imported without a disadvantage. However, transport costs are significant, particularly for developing countries that often face long distances to large markets. In this formulation, the core elements of a linkage-driven model are already assembled: input-output links between industries, scale economies and significant positive transport costs. A bit later, these effects will be shown to form the core of the NEG model with linkage effects.

Before turning to the model, I want to complete this survey by discussing more recent contributions, even at the risk of over stretching the notion of development economics here. Authors that analyze the rapid rise and industrialisation of East Asia and other developing countries from an institutionalist perspective often stress the role of industrial development and diversification of the manufacturing sector. Moreover, in policy discussions, the East Asian effort is often evoked as a role model for South Africa.

In detailed and empirically rich accounts Wade (1990), Amsden (2001) and others described the interventionist and sector specific industrial policy of East Asian countries that deliberately discriminated between sectors and 'got the prices wrong' to steer industrial development. Policy makers used protective trade policies, subsidised credit and export support as carrots to promote investment in certain sectors while at the same time monitoring and evaluating performance with the credible threat of withdrawal of support as stick. Within a neoclassical theoretical framework, economies of scale and scope, learning effects, information and coordination externalities provide justification for targeted intervention and support for specific manufacturing sectors (Chang, 1994; Rodrik, 2004).

The sectors singled out for support were chosen according to dynamic factors. So countries were trying to create (rather than exploit existing) comparative advantage in industries with prospects of "long-term growth in output, profits, and wages" (Wade, 1990, 355). Amsden cites the case of Taiwan, where the government picked industries "based on six criteria: large linkage effects; high market potential; high technology intensity; high value-added; low energy intensity; and low pollution" (Amsden, 2001, 137).

The importance of structural dynamics within developing countries has also resurfaced in recent debates. Ocampo (2005) stresses the importance of a dynamic production structure capable of constantly generating new activities. The importance of sectoral diversification in the long-run development process has also recently been empirically shown in an important paper by Imbs and Wacziarg (2003). Rodrik (2007), in a related effort, then goes on to deduce the necessity of industrial policy to support entrepreneurs, since innovators usually do not reap the full benefits of their risky investments in developing countries.

Very recently, Hausmann and Klinger (2006) and Hausmann and Rodrik (2006) derived a concept they call the product space, where products are positioned to each other according to their closeness. The underlying theoretical assumption is that the production of each good requires specific inputs (skills, intermediate goods). Now some goods are closer to each other than others because the specific inputs required in one's production can relatively easily be transferred and used in the neighbourly good. The actual pattern of the product space is calculated by evaluating goods exported by more than 100 countries. Two goods are close when their joint exportation by one country occurs frequently. The emerging structure shows that there are products in the core, closely linked to many others, and peripheral goods that are only weakly connected to other goods. In terms of industrial policy, the implication the authors draw is that governments have to choose which sectors to support by providing those sector-specific inputs that are not made available by markets. Ideally, they choose sectors which are close to the existing production pattern and which move the economy closer to the core of the product space, facilitating further diversification.

To summarise a wide and rather dispersed range of authors, I would argue that both theoretical and empirical work has shown that linkages play a crucial part in the path industrialisation is taking in a country. They provide opportunities for further activities—in the case of a minerals economy such as South Africa these opportunities naturally appear around the resource endowments. This corresponds to the actual development experience of South Africa. Yet linkages alone cannot be relied on to generate investment. Following Hirschman, I understand them more as an opportunity still to be exploited by some agent. Usually this role is taken over by private business, but—and this is what can be learned from the East Asian experience—government should and can play a guiding role in the sectoral allocation of investment when the market cannot be relied upon. It should do so by forging a vision of which path the economy is supposed to take (see for example Chang, 1998)[1]; and by picking sectors for support that are on the one hand strongly linked to existing activities, and that on the other hand display dynamic potential as described above.

One last note regarding mineral endowments is necessary at this point. There is a significant body of literature dealing with the particular role natural resources play in the development process. Auty (1993) provides a comprehensive account of the so called resource curse thesis, according to which natural resources are at best a mixed blessing for developing countries. An overvalued exchange rate, high volatility in earnings, and a skewed production structure are all cited as possible and detrimental consequences of a large mining sector. Hirschman argued that the primary sector, including mining activities, is usually weakly linked to the rest of the economy and therefore was skeptical about its role in the industrialisation process as well (Hirschman, 1981, 86). Yet, in a cross-country study of 91 developing countries, Davis (1995) does not find evidence supporting the resource curse thesis—mineral economies did on average outperform the remainder

[1]Rodrik and Hausmann go even further in calling their paper on industrial policy *Doomed to Choose* (Hausmann and Rodrik, 2006)

of countries. Still only one country in his panel managed to lose its status as mineral economy over the observed time period by sufficiently diversifying its export base. "This indicates that [...] it is difficult if not impossible to force diversification of a resource-endowed economy contrary to comparative advantage." (Davis, 1995, 1772) The South African experience as described above does partially corroborate these findings: the Minerals Energy Complex is rather self-contained in terms of input-output linkages, yet at the same time its very existence gives evidence to the fact that linkage effects were at play in the rise of South Africa's capital intensive industries.

A linkage-based approach to industrial policy tailored to suit South Africa's needs would therefore have to take into account the critical role of the mining sector and the Minerals Energy Complex. In a similar vein, Ramos (1998) describes production clusters that develop around initial resource endowments in developing countries. While this is partly a market-based (or natural) process, the theoretical arguments mentioned above also justify government promotion and support for these clusters (see also Porter, 1990).

3.2 Linkages in the New Economic Geography

Natural resources and factor endowments of regions can only partly explain the spatial distribution of economic activities. It is easy to see why Johannesburg was founded virtually on top of the rich South African gold fields, yet this alone will hardly be enough to account for the enormous density of economic activity witnessed in Gauteng (the province Johannesburg is located in) today: taking up just 1,4% of the total surface of South Africa, Gauteng accounts for about one third of its GDP (and 8% of the continent's for that matter!). A large and long standing tradition of geographical economics tries to explain phenomena of 'second nature', defined as endogenous forces, brought about by human action, that influence and shape the economic landscape and lead to large regional imbalances and clustering of economic activities (Ottaviano and Thisse, 2004, 2565). Yet, this branch of research played no role in mainstream economic theory. As Krugman (1997, 33) notes, ideas of economic geography do not feature in standard economics textbooks at all. To him, this is due to technical diffulties with modeling economies of scale and the resulting imperfect competition. In brief reviews of this literature, Krugman (1997) and Fujita et al. (2001) argue that ideas of von Thünen, Christaller, Lösch and others did provide insight into issues of spatial economics, but all fell short in terms of the methodological and theoretical rigour expected in mainstream economic analysis (see for example Fujita et al., 2001, 33).

The *New Economic Geography* (henceforth NEG), a now more or less consolidated area of research work that was started and brought to prominence by authors such as Fujita, Venables and Krugman (the seminal reference being Krugman 1991a) provides for a treatment of spatial questions within the framework of neoclassical general equilibrium models. Whether it does justice to the rich tradition of geographical economics is a disputed question that I will not try to answer here (for a critical discussion see for example Martin, 1999). This omission is justifiable because I will concentrate on one particular family of NEG models—the vertical linkages (henceforth VL) models. While being very close to the core NEG work in terms of model structure, they owe a lot of intellectual debt to development economics as discussed in Section 3.1. Many papers in NEG cite the classics of development economics such as Hirschman and Myrdal almost as if they were a canon one has to refer to. Krugman himself dedicates one whole book (Krugman, 1997) to this cause. He explains how the ideas of development economists and economic geographers—interesting and relevant as they were—failed to influence the mainstream of economic theory. The argument is essentially identical to the explanation why geographical economics remained at the periphery of the discipline. Taking Hirschman's forward and backward linkages as an example, Krugman argues that they only matter if combined with increasing returns to scale in production. Hirschman was aware of this, yet then, economies of scale were difficult to model in a general equilibrium context because they are irreconcilable with perfect competition. Once mathematical modelling became a standard device of economics, the linkages and related arguments involving complementarities or circularity were pushed to the margins of economic theory (Krugman, 1997, 25ff.). Only the innovations introduced in Dixit and Stiglitz (1977) allowed economists to return to these questions within a general equilibrium model framework. NEG models—which are essentially based on the Dixit/Stiglitz framework—allow their reintroduction because they assume economies of scale in production and because they add a spatial dimension (transport costs) to the economy. The two factors combined lead to mathematically told stories that do have a close resemblance to arguments in development economics reviewed above.

I will start this exposition of NEG by briefly presenting the original contribution of Krugman (1991a) verbally. The so-called core-periphery (CP) model is outlined in more detail in Fujita et al. (2001, chap. 4 and 5) and Baldwin et al. (2003, chap. 2). I will then go on to depict the basic VL model in detail—the logic of the model being very close still to the CP model. In the next chapter the multi-industry VL with exogenous growth is presented, complete with parameter values for a minerals economy and simulation results. This model is an extension to the basic model that allows integrating a specific technological structure in the form of input-output tables. An exogenous growth process is then introduced to study the effect of growth on the development and location of industries.

3.2.1 The Logic of NEG: The Core-Periphery Model

The logic of NEG models is probably best explained by starting where it all started: with Krugman's first core-periphery (CP) model (Krugman, 1991a). It constitutes an attempt to understand how and why the manufacturing sector within a national economy might come to be locally concentrated in a core of the economy, a core which then provides the rest of the economy or the periphery with its manufactured goods. Krugman assumes that there are two sectors, the agricultural or traditional sector and the manufacturing or modern sector. The traditional sector is characterised by constant returns to scale and perfect competition. There are no transport costs and the sector produces a homogeneous good. The manufacturing or modern sector displays decreasing average costs and firms produce a variety of differentiated goods. Transport costs are positive in manufacturing, and decreasing average costs will lead to a limited number of manufacturing production sites. Agriculture on the other hand will be evenly spread. Demand comes from farmers, who are dispersed across the country, and from workers in manufacturing. Since the prevailing technology in manufacturing leads to a concentration in production, final demand from manufacturing wages will be equally concentrated—and a pattern of circular causality emerges. Workers (firms) will move to the core because demand is high, and their very move to the core further increases demand in the core.

The actual spatial distribution of manufacturing activity depends on the parameters of the model: if the manufacturing sector is small and transport costs are high, then manufacturers will locate close to where farmers live, leading to a structure of small towns serving local markets. If then, over time, manufacturing increases in importance, transport costs fall and economies of scale become stronger, it is easy to see how "the tie of production to the distribution of land will be broken. [...] Population will start to concentrate and regions to diverge; once started, this process will feed on itself" (Krugman, 1991a, 487).

Technically, increasing returns to scale are difficult to model, yet a monopolistic competition type market structure as introduced by Dixit and Stiglitz (1977) provides a tractable if very specific formulation. Utility of consumers is of a two-tier structure. They have Cobb-Douglass utility for the two types of goods (agricultural goods and manufactured goods) which of course implies that they spend a constant share of their income (μ and $1-\mu$ respectively) on agricultural goods and on the aggregate of manufactured goods. Krugman then goes on to define a sub-utility function for manufactured products. It is of the constant elasticity of substitution (CES) form, so that individuals' utility increases with the number of varieties offered. The critical parameter here is the elasticity of substitution σ, where $\sigma > 1$. If σ is close to 1, consumers have great love for variety, if σ increases, differentiated manufactured products become better substitutes and the desire for variety decreases.

Production in manufacturing on the other hand involves fixed costs, so together with the specific form of demand this market structure implies that each firm will produce only one good—a slightly differentiated product—in one location. The big advantage and simplification of the Dixit/Stiglitz framework is that there is no strategic behaviour of firms. One must assume an infinite (or very large) number of competitors in the market to achieve this result. Then, optimal pricing does not depend on one competitor's behaviour but is simply a constant mark-up over marginal costs. Since market entry is free, profits will be driven down to zero—the mark-up will just be high enough to cover fixed costs. The constant mark-up has another convenient yet unusual implication: there is one unique level of sales at which operating profit equals fixed costs. Therefore the equilibrium output of a single firm does not depend on market size. A bigger market will lead to an increased number of firms only (Baldwin et al., 2003, 41). One last addition to this technical cook book are iceberg transport costs. It is assumed that a constant fraction of goods 'melts away' in transport, in other words transport costs are proportional to marginal production costs. The desirable implications are that no separate transport sector needs to be modelled and firms will engage in mill pricing. They will charge the same producer price for both consumers in the local and in the remote market, transport costs incurred in the latter are paid for by consumers. With all these features in place, one can analyze the model with numerical simulations.

In the short run, labour is assumed to be immobile. Depending on its initial distribution, real wages will differ in the two regions due to the home market effect (a larger market implies higher sales and higher profits, these are passed on to workers through higher wages) and the market crowding or competition effect (firms in the smaller manufacturing sector face less competition and so pay higher wages). In the long run, workers are mobile, and the migration equation describes workers' movement to regions with higher real wages. When workers move, manufacturing production in the destined region increases—decreasing the cost of living (because more varieties are available locally without incurring transport costs) and thereby further enlarging the gap in real wages. The home market effect is at times referred to as a backward linkage, the cost of living effect as a forward linkage (see for example Ottaviano and Robert-Nicoud, 2006, 114).

The eventual outcome—that is the geographical distribution of manufacturing production, be it a core periphery pattern or a symmetric spread of activity—obviously depends on the initial distribution of the manufacturing sector and on the choice of parameters, particularly the magnitude of trade costs. When trade costs are high, dispersion forces are strong and manufacturing production will take place in both regions. With low trade costs, agglomeration will occur in the region that had some initial (historical) advantage.

3.2.2 Vertical Linkages Models: An Exposition

Since Krugman's initial contribution, a host of different models with similar features and applications have been presented (for an overview and extensive summaries see Fujita et al., 2001; Baldwin et al., 2003). In the context of industrial policy and industrial development, models with vertical linkages (VL) are particularly interesting. The original contributions in this sub-field are from Krugman and Venables (Krugman and Venables, 1995; Venables, 1996). Fujita et al. (2001, chap. 14-16) and Baldwin et al. (2003, chap. 8) present text book versions and, recently, Ottaviano and Robert-Nicoud provided a synthesis of VL models (Ottaviano and Robert-Nicoud, 2006).

What the VL models have in common is that the spatial dynamics result not from movement of labour between regions as in the CP model, but from "intersectoral reallocation of factors within the same location" (Ottaviano and Robert-Nicoud, 2006, 114). These models are set in an international context where labour is assumed to be immobile between regions, yet will move according to wage differentials between the traditional and the manufacturing sector within one location. Firstly, this implies that permanent real wage differentials between countries are possible. Secondly, the driving force of agglomeration now is the manufacturing sector itself which not only produces but also consumes manufacturing goods as inputs. The production function closely resembles the consumption function in the original CP model, which implies that firms spend constant shares of their total production costs on labour and on manufacturing products respectively, with the latter entering in a CES form so that a greater locally available input variety of manufacturing products reduces costs.

It is then possible to redefine the linkage effects. If more firms settle in a region, firms in the region profit from a greater local variety of inputs which are bought without transport costs—a forward linkage. At the same time, more firms in a region imply a higher demand for manufactures as inputs—a backward linkage. While these linkage effects act as agglomerative force, the rising manufacturing wage level in the core relative to the periphery acts as dispersion force which at some point might incite firms to establish themselves in the periphery.

The Formal Model

I will now present in more detail the basic version of the VL model as published in Krugman and Venables (1995) and Fujita et al. (2001, chap. 14). The main difference to these outlines is that I work in a discrete setting from the beginning. For a detailed representation of all derivations the reader is referred to Chapter 4 where a modified and extended version is applied to the research question of this dissertation.

The basic VL model presented here is very close to the original CP model sketched above. There are two regions which are identical—there are no 'first nature' or geographical differences between them. Following the literature I will call them North (region N) and South (region S). In each region, there is a manufacturing sector M which is characterised by increasing returns to scale and positive transport costs (of the iceberg form) between regions, and a traditional sector A with constant returns to scale in production and zero transport costs. Goods of both sectors are traded between the two regions.

Consumer Behaviour

The representative consumer's utility is described in a two-tier function. She has a Cobb-Douglass utility function dividing her income between the two types of goods, manufactured and agricultural goods (M and A respectively).

$$U = M^{\mu} A^{1-\mu} \tag{3.1}$$

A constant share of income μ is spent on M, the composite of manufactured goods, and a constant share $1 - \mu$ is spent on agricultural goods. As in the CP model, manufacturers produce slightly differentiated products. The composite of these goods is defined as the quantity index M—a sub-utility function that takes the following form:

$$M = \left[\sum_{i=1}^{n} m_i^{\rho} \right]^{1/\rho}, \quad 0 < \rho < 1 \tag{3.2}$$

where n (the number of varieties) is large. This is a constant elasticity of substitution (CES) utility function. ρ is indicative of the love for variety of consumers for the different available products m_i. If ρ is close to zero, consumers value variety greatly, if it is close to one, then the differentiated products become better substitutes and variety is less important. n represents the number of firms and equals the number of available varieties due to the fact that there are increasing returns in manufacturing—implying that a profit-maximizing firm will produce only one variety. To better understand the CES form, I calculate the elasticity of substitution σ of two varieties.

$$\sigma = \left[\frac{\partial(m_2/m_1)}{\partial MRS} \right] \left[\frac{MRS}{(m_2/m_1)} \right]$$

MRS stands for *marginal rate of substitution* and can be derived as the fraction of marginal utilities of goods m_1 and m_2. Utility maximisation implies that the resulting $\left(\frac{m_2}{m_1}\right)^{1-\rho}$ can be substituted by the price ratio $\left(\frac{p_1}{p_2}\right)$. Then

$$\sigma = \frac{\partial \left(\frac{p_1}{p_2}\right)^{\frac{1}{1-\rho}}}{\partial \left(\frac{p_1}{p_2}\right)} \left(\frac{m_2}{m_1} \right)^{1-\rho}$$

Simplifying yields

$$\sigma = \frac{1}{1-\rho}$$

As indicated above σ is big when ρ is close to one. In this case, the differentiated manufacturing products are near perfect substitutes and consumers do not value variety highly. When σ is small ρ is close to zero and consumers display a great love for variety.

Assuming that consumers' income is Y and p^A and p_i are the prices for agricultural and manufactured goods respectively, the budget constraint can be written as follows:

$$Y = p^A A + \sum_{i=1}^{n} p_i m_i \tag{3.3}$$

The utility maximization problem is solved in two steps. First I derive demand for manufactured goods (equations 3.4 to 3.9), in a second step I will divide income between manufacatured goods and agricultural goods (equations 3.10 to 3.11). For manufactured goods, the representative consumer wants to minimize expenditure for achieving a certain utility level M. So the optimisation problem becomes

$$min \sum_{i=1}^{n} p_i m_i \quad s.t. \quad \left[\sum_{i=1}^{n} m_i^{\rho} \right]^{1/\rho} = M \tag{3.4}$$

The marginal rate of substitution equals $\frac{p_i}{p_j} = \left(\frac{m_i}{m_j}\right)^{1-\rho}$. From this, an expression for m_i can be derived.

$$m_i = m_j \left(\frac{p_j}{p_i}\right)^{\frac{1}{1-\rho}} \tag{3.5}$$

I substitute 3.5 into the constraint to get compensated demand for m_j

$$M = \left[\sum_{i=1}^{n} \left(m_j \left(\frac{p_j}{p_i}\right)^{\frac{1}{1-\rho}} \right)^{\rho} \right]^{1/\rho}$$

Bringing m_j to the left I get

$$m_j = \frac{p_j^{\frac{1}{\rho-1}}}{\left[\sum_{i=1}^{n} p_i^{\frac{\rho}{\rho-1}} \right]^{1/\rho}} \quad M \tag{3.6}$$

This is the compensated demand function for m_j. It depends negatively on p_j and positively on the other varieties' prices. There is another, insightful way to describe m_j. Multiplying m_j by its price p_j and integrating over all varieties, we get total expenditure on the left and a price index on the right.

$$m_j p_j = p_j^{\frac{\rho}{\rho-1}} \left[\sum_{i=1}^{n} p_i^{\frac{\rho}{\rho-1}} \right]^{-1/\rho} \quad M$$

Summing up over all varieties j=1 to n:

$$\sum_{j=1}^{n} m_j p_j = \left[\sum_{j=1}^{n} p_j^{\frac{\rho}{1-\rho}} \right] \left[\sum_{i=1}^{n} p_i^{\frac{\rho}{\rho-1}} \right]^{-1/\rho} \quad M$$

Simplifying yields

$$\sum_{j=1}^{n} m_j p_j = \left[\sum_{i=1}^{n} p_i^{\frac{\rho}{1-\rho}} \right]^{\frac{\rho-1}{\rho}} \quad M \tag{3.7}$$

M being the quantity composite, the expression on the right can be thought of as a price index. Following Fujita et al. (2001, 47) I name it G.

$$G \equiv \left[\sum_{i=1}^{n} p_i^{\frac{\rho}{1-\rho}} \right]^{\frac{\rho-1}{\rho}} = \left[\sum_{i=1}^{n} p_i^{1-\sigma} \right]^{\frac{1}{1-\sigma}} \tag{3.8}$$

The price index relates income to utility. It represents the minimum expenditure required to buy one unit of M. It is therefore not an average price but derived from the utility function—and it displays its characteristics as well. To illustrate this, I assume for a moment that all prices are equal. Then, G becomes $(np_i^{1-\sigma})^{\frac{1}{1-\sigma}}$ or $n^{\frac{1}{1-\sigma}}p$. Once the number of varieties n increases, the price index G will fall—leading to an increase in consumers' utility.

Compensated demand can now be rewritten using G.

$$m_j = \left(\frac{p_j}{G} \right)^{-\sigma} M \tag{3.9}$$

The second step of utility maximization consists of dividing total income between expenditure on manufactured and on agricultural goods. Using equation 3.1 and rewriting the budget constraint with G results in the maximisation problem

$$max \quad U = M^{\mu} A^{1-\mu} \quad s.t. \quad GM + p^A A = Y \tag{3.10}$$

This standard Cobb-Douglass utility function leads to well known results of agricultural demand A being $(1-\mu)Y/p^A$ and demand for manufactured goods $M = \mu Y/G$. To get consumer demand for each variety of manufactures, this expression for M is substituted into 3.9 to get

$$m_j = \mu Y p_j^{-\sigma} \frac{1}{GG^{-\sigma}} = \mu Y \frac{p_j^{-\sigma}}{G^{-(\sigma-1)}} \tag{3.11}$$

In a last step, indirect utility can be written down by substituting demand for agricultural and manufacturing goods (terms A and M) into 3.1:

$$U = \mu^{\mu}(1-\mu)^{1-\mu} Y G^{-\mu} (p^A)^{-(1-\mu)} \tag{3.12}$$

As established further above, an increase in the number of varieties of manufactured goods on offer n reduces G, and 3.12 shows that this will increase utility. *Varietas delectat.*

Transportation Costs

As in the CP model, transportation costs in the manufacturing sector are modelled in the iceberg form. That is, a fraction of the good shipped to its destination melts away in the process. So there is no need for a separate transport sector in the model. Crucially, iceberg transport costs also ensure that a firm charges the same price for locally consumed goods and for exports—it engages in mill pricing (Baldwin et al., 2003, 18).

I will come back to the issue of mill pricing in the section on *producer behaviour*. For now, it suffices to illustrate the concept and its implications for delivery prices. Assume that a manufactured good is produced in N. When consumed in the region, there are no transport costs, so the price in the North will be p_N. Yet, when it is exported to S, only a fraction $1/T_{NS}$ of the good arrives. T_{NS} stands for the amount of the manufactured good that has to be shipped for one unit to arrive in S. In terms of prices, a mill price of p_N for one unit implies a delivery price of $p_N T_{NS} = p_{NS}$ in the South.

These costs will obviously affect the price index, which has to be rewritten for each region. The price index in S in a discrete setting with R regions would look as follows:

$$G_S = \left[\sum_{r=1}^{R} n_r (p_r T_{rS})^{1-\sigma} \right]^{1/(1-\sigma)} \tag{3.13}$$

It is assumed here that all varieties have the same price (this assumption will be shown to hold later). Then n_r equals the number of firms (i.e. varieties) in each region, and transport costs are taken into consideration for all goods that are shipped in from other regions. So demand in the South for a product from another region, e.g. N can be derived by adapting 3.11:

$$m_{jS} = \mu Y_S (p_N T_{NS})^{-\sigma} G_S^{(\sigma-1)} \tag{3.14}$$

Due to the nature of transport costs, this level of consumption is not equal to the amount that has to be produced in order for m_{jS} to arrive. The parameter T has to be considered. So total sales of a single variety produced in N, q_{jN} can be expressed as

$$q_{jN} = \mu \sum_{r=1}^{R} Y_r (p_N T_{Nr})^{-\sigma} G_r^{\sigma-1} T_{Nr} \tag{3.15}$$

3.15 is the sum of demand for the variety j in all regions $r = 1, .., S, N, ..R$ and includes the fraction of the good that melted in transport (T_{Nr}).

Producer Behaviour

As in the CP model, there are two sectors in each region. The agricultural sector is characterised by constant returns to scale in production, hence perfect competition, and no trade costs between regions. The single input in agriculture is labour l. To produce one unit of agricultural products A, a_A units of labour are needed. The cost function in agriculture therefore equals

$$C_A = w(a_A l) \tag{3.16}$$

where w stands for wages of workers, and it needs a_A units of labour l to produce the agricultural good. Perfect competition leads to marginal cost pricing, so the price of the agricultural good p^A equals wa_A. Since trade in agriculture is free, prices in the sector will equalise over regions, which under certain conditions (as long as there are both sectors in both regions) leads to an equalisation of wages as well.

The manufacturing sector produces a variety of manufacturing products q_i and uses both labour l and intermediate goods as inputs. In the CP model, the manufacturing sector used skilled labour only. Note that there is no differentiation between agricultural labour and manufacturing (or skilled) labour in the VL model—in marked contrast to the CP model. Labour therefore can move freely between these two sectors. Additionally, firms in the manufacturing sector face increasing returns to scale. Add to this the preference for variety of consumers and it becomes clear why no firm will produce a variety that is already supplied by one of its competitors. Each firm will produce one distinct variety at one distinct location.

Decreasing average costs are expressed in a fixed cost component F in the cost function. Both inputs, labour and a CES aggregate of intermediates (identical to the utility formulation of consumers), are used in this fixed input requirement F—in equal proportion to their use in the variable input requirement a_M. Technology is identical for all varieties and in both regions. One crucial simplification of this version of the VL model is that intermediates stem from the manufacturing sector itself, so basically "manufacturing uses itself (in addition to labour) as an input, that is, that the same aggregate of manufacturing varieties demanded by consumers is also an input into the production of each variety" (Fujita et al., 2001, 241). Linkages effects exist despite there being only one industrial sector! Specifically, inputs are divided in a fixed share $1-\alpha$ of labour and α of intermediates (the manufacturing composite M). The latter is the same as the aggregate of manufacturing varieties demanded by consumers.

Assuming for now that fixed costs are covered, then the production function in the manufacturing sector in North equals

$$q_N = \big[\alpha^{-\alpha}(1-\alpha)^{\alpha-1} l_N^{1-\alpha} \left[\sum_{r=1}^{R} n_r q_{rN}^{\rho}\right]^{\alpha/\rho}\big] / a_M \tag{3.17}$$

$\alpha^{-\alpha}(1-\alpha)^{\alpha-1}$ are constants necessary to derive a cost function as simple as the one below, l_N represents labour input, on which $1-\alpha$ of total costs is spent, and $\left[\sum_r n_r x_{rN}^{\rho}\right]^{1/\rho}$ represents inputs stemming from intermediates, which takes up a constant share α of all expenditure. Firms have to spend an equally partitioned amount on the fixed cost component F. n is the number of varieties of manufacturing goods produced in each region, x_{rN} the input of each variety produced in region r and ρ again indicates the extent of preference for variety, this time of firms.

The cost function of the manufacturing sector takes the form

$$C_M = (F + a_M q_N)\left[w^{1-\alpha} G_N^{\alpha}\right] \tag{3.18}$$

where G_N is the price index in N:

$$G_N = \left[\sum_{r=1}^{R} n_r (p_r T_{rN})^{1-\sigma}\right]^{1/1-\sigma} \tag{3.19}$$

Due to the specification, the price index for intermediates corresponds to 3.13, the price index for consumers. This is due to the fact that input demand from firms can be derived in two steps—in line with consumer demand. The demand for a single variety of manufactured goods equals 3.9, and a constant share of costs of firms α is devoted to manufacturing goods. So intermediate demand for a single variety (INT) becomes

$$m_{iINT} = \alpha T C p_i^{-\sigma} G^{\sigma-1} \tag{3.20}$$

To arrive at total sales of a variety produced in North, consumer demand 3.15 plus the fraction T lost in transport have to be added. I get

$$q_{iN} = \left[\mu \sum_{r=1}^{R} Y_r + \alpha \sum_{r=1}^{R} TC_r\right] (p_N T_{NS})^{-\sigma} G_r^{\sigma-1} T_{Nr} \tag{3.21}$$

Firms maximise profits by equating marginal revenue with marginal costs. Marginal revenue can be expressed as $p(1+\frac{1}{\epsilon})$. So the elasticity of demand $\epsilon_{q,p}$ has to be calculated.

$$\epsilon_{q,p} = \frac{\partial q}{\partial p}\frac{p}{q}$$

Firms take the price index G as given. This is an important feature of Dixit/ Stiglitz: there is no strategic interaction between competitors. Then it is a matter of simple derivation to get $-\sigma$ as the elasticity of demand. To arrive at optimal price setting, marginal revenue and marginal costs can now be equated.

$$MR = MC \quad \Rightarrow \quad p(1+\frac{1}{-\sigma}) = (w^{1-\alpha} G^{\alpha}) a_M \tag{3.22}$$

I replace σ with $\frac{1}{1-\rho}$ to get the profit maximizing price

$$p = \frac{\left(w^{1-\alpha}G^{\alpha}\right)a_M}{\rho} \tag{3.23}$$

Firms set prices by charging a constant mark up over marginal costs.

Analysing 3.21 also helps to understand the concept of mill pricing. The elasticity of demand will be $-\sigma$ for domestic demand as well as for demand in other locations since transport costs enter proportional to the value of goods. For this reason, firms will charge the same mill price p for local and foreign consumption. The end price in the remote region corresponds to the respective marginal costs and therefore has to include transport costs and can be written as pT.

The technology of firms stated in the production function 3.17 already constitutes the first source of linkage effects. Since intermediates enter in a CES form, firms profit from a greater variety of intermediates available to them locally—it will lead to a decrease in their price index. One can think of this linkage as a *forward linkage.* A greater number of suppliers of intermediate goods in a region reduces costs for firms using these intermediates in their production.

In Dixit/Stiglitz, there is free entry into markets, so profits are driven down to zero. I use this condition to define the equilibrium size of a manufacturing firm.

$$\Pi = pq - \left(w^{1-\alpha}G^{\alpha}\right)\left[F + a_M q\right] \tag{3.24}$$

where

$$p = \frac{(w^{1-\alpha}G^{\alpha})a_M}{\rho}$$

Replacing ρ with $\frac{\sigma-1}{\sigma}$ and setting $\Pi = 0$ yields equilibrium firm size q^*

$$q^* = \frac{F(\sigma-1)}{a_M} \tag{3.25}$$

Note that 3.25 implies that equilibrium firm size does not depend on the size of the market, but only on cost parameters and consumers' love for variety. So an increase in market size leads to an increase in the number of firms in the market only (and thereby further diversifies manufacturing supply) but leaves firm size unaffected.

It is now possible to re-write expenditures on manufactures E in a particular location. It consists of demand from consumers and of intermediate demand by firms.

$$E_r = \mu Y + \alpha n_r p_r q^* \tag{3.26}$$

The zero profit condition ensures that the total value of a firm's production (pq^*) equals its total costs. So with α the part of costs devoted to inputs, the second term on the right is simply all firms' expenditure on intermediates. This expenditure represents the second source of linkages, so called *backward linkages*. The more firms operate in one location, the higher their intermediate demand, and this demand raises total demand for manufacturing products.

To find the number of firms in the market, one has to define the size of the market—in other words, labour supply. For simplicity, let labour supply equal 1 in both countries. As described above, labour is intersectorally mobile, so farm workers can move into manufacturing and vice versa, but labour is internationally immobile. Take λ to be the share of labour that is engaged in manufacturing. Above, I defined the value of total manufacturing in a country, and since a constant share $(1-\alpha)$ of costs is spent on workers, the total wage bill in manufacturing can be derived.

$$w\lambda = (1-\alpha)npq^* \tag{3.27}$$

From 3.25 we know equilibrium firm size, so n^*, the equilibrium number of firms, becomes

$$n^* = \lambda \frac{w\rho}{(w^{1-\alpha}G^{\alpha})F(\sigma-1)(1-\alpha)} \tag{3.28}$$

Using n^* and the profit maximizing price 3.23, the price index for region North 3.19 in a 2-region setting can be rewritten as

$$\begin{aligned} G_N^{1-\sigma} = & \left[\lambda_N w_N^{1-\sigma(1-\alpha)} G_N^{-\sigma\alpha} \frac{p^{\sigma} a_M^{1-\sigma}}{F(\sigma-1)(1-\alpha)}\right] + \\ & \left[\lambda_S w_S^{1-\sigma(1-\alpha)} G_S^{-\sigma\alpha} \frac{p^{\sigma} a_M^{1-\sigma}}{F(\sigma-1)(1-\alpha)}\right] T^{1-\sigma} \end{aligned} \tag{3.29}$$

This equation is not very handy, so following Fujita et al. (2001, 242f.) I introduce some normalizations. I choose units so that the marginal input requirement a_M equals ρ and equilibrium output of a firm q^* equals $1/(1-\alpha)$.

Then the profit maximizing price and the price index can be reformulated to get

$$p = w^{1-\alpha} G^{\alpha} \tag{3.30}$$

for a much simplified price and

$$G_N^{1-\sigma} = \lambda_N w_N^{1-\sigma(1-\alpha)} G_N^{-\sigma\alpha} + \lambda_S w_S^{1-\sigma(1-\alpha)} G_S^{-\sigma\alpha} T^{1-\sigma} \tag{3.31}$$

as the simplified price index for the region N in a two-regions setting.

Short Run Equilibrium

I can now define the short run equilibrium. It is important to understand that entry is free even in the short run, so profits will still be zero. Yet in the short run, labour is immobile, so wages can differ between the two regions.

Using the normalisations introduced above, the price indices for regions N and S become

$$G_N^{1-\sigma} = \lambda_N w_N^{1-\sigma(1-\alpha)} G_N^{-\sigma\alpha} + \lambda_S w_S^{1-\sigma(1-\alpha)} G_S^{-\sigma\alpha} T^{1-\sigma} \tag{3.32}$$

and

$$G_S^{1-\sigma} = \lambda_S w_S^{1-\sigma(1-\alpha)} G_S^{-\sigma\alpha} + \lambda_N w_N^{1-\sigma(1-\alpha)} G_N^{-\sigma\alpha} T^{1-\sigma} \tag{3.33}$$

respectively. 3.32 and 3.33 are crucial expressions and embody central aspects and features of the model. If for example λ, the share of manufacturing in a region, increases in N, then the price index G_N will fall—and firms profit from cheaper intermediate inputs. This is what I defined above as a *forward linkage*. Also, these equations show how the price indices depend on both wages and, via intermediates, on the price indices themselves.

Now that both consumer and producer behaviour are known, it is time to look at market clearing conditions. Market clearance is ensured in an indirect way by defining the so-called *wage equations*. They determine the level of wages manufacturing firms are allowed to pay for them just to break even—in other words, the wage level at which the zero profit condition is fulfilled. To arrive at the wage equations, I first equate q^*, equilibrium output by firms, with demand for a particular manufacturing variety as described in 3.21.

$$q^* = \left[\mu \sum_{r=1}^{R} Y_r + \alpha \sum_{r=1}^{R} TC_r\right] (p_N T_{NS})^{-\sigma} G_r^{\sigma-1} T_{Nr}$$

Using the normalisations introduced above, E for total expenditure on manufactured goods, and bringing wages (which are directly linked to prices via mark-up pricing) to the left I get the wage equations for regions N and S:

$$\frac{(w_N^{1-\alpha} G_N^{\alpha})^{\sigma}}{1-\alpha} = E_N G_N^{\sigma-1} + E_S G_S^{\sigma-1} T^{1-\sigma} \tag{3.34}$$

$$\frac{(w_S^{1-\alpha} G_S^{\alpha})^{\sigma}}{1-\alpha} = E_S G_S^{\sigma-1} + E_N G_N^{\sigma-1} T^{1-\sigma} \tag{3.35}$$

For firms to break even, they have to charge a certain price. This price depends on both the wage level and the price index, the latter coming into the picture due to the existence of intermediate inputs. Together with the normalisation for q^* this accounts for the left side of the wage equation. On the right, it is obvious that spending on manufactures comes from consumers and firms (both included in E), from the home market and, additionally, from exports to the other region.

The wage equation implies that increased spending in a region will push up wages since demand for a single variety will increase—a backward linkage. The expansion of a sector also leads to a greater variety of industrial goods on offer, which decreases the costs of industrial inputs. This effect shows up in G on the left side of the wage equation and leads to higher wages as well—it can be interpreted as a forward linkage. A countering effect is the increased competition that follows a larger variety on offer. This effect is represented in G on the right hand side of the equation and tends to reduce the manufacturing wage. Changes in the manufacturing wage in relation to changes in the regional distribution of manufacturing activity as described here will be the driving force of the adjustment process from the short-run to the long-run equilibrium.

Total expenditure E is defined as

$$E_N = \mu Y_N + \frac{\alpha w_N \lambda_N}{1-\alpha}, \quad E_S = \mu Y_S + \frac{\alpha w_S \lambda_S}{1-\alpha} \tag{3.36}$$

where expenditure comes from consumers (first term) and from the industrial sector itself via intermediate demand. Consumers spend a share μ of their income on manufactured goods, while firms' respective expenditure is of the share α, derived from the cost function. From 3.27 we know that the value of manufacturing output is npq^* and that it can be expressed as $\frac{w\lambda}{1-\alpha}$, leading to the second term of the expression.

Income Y comes from both sectors. The total labour force equals 1, so income generated in manufacturing is simply $w\lambda$. Turning to income generated in agriculture, we know that labour is the sole factor of production. For reasons of simplicity we assume an extremely simple and linear production function: $q_A = (1 - \lambda)$, where $(1 - \lambda)$ is the amount of labour used in agriculture. a_A from equation 3.16 is set to unity. Since the agricultural good acts as the numéraire, the marginal product of labour in the sector and hence the agricultural wage are also unity.

$$Y_N = w_N \lambda_N + (1 - \lambda_N), \quad Y_S = w_S \lambda_S + (1 - \lambda_S) \tag{3.37}$$

The wage gap v between sectors is

$$v_N = w_N - 1, \quad v_S = w_S - 1 \tag{3.38}$$

Together, equations 3.32 to 3.38 characterise the short run equilibrium.

Long Run Equilibria

In the short run, wages will differ between sectors, so there is an incentive for workers to move to the sector with higher wages. The assumption is simply that workers move out of agriculture and work in the manufacturing sector when wages in manufacturing are higher or $v > 0$. The law of motion is defined as follows:

$$\dot{\lambda} = v(\lambda(1 - \lambda)) \tag{3.39}$$

So there are three possible long run equilibria in a region, in which there is no incentive for workers to leave their sector: wages are equalised across sectors—both sectors will operate; all production is concentrated in manufacturing and manufacturing wages are higher or equal to (a virtual) agricultural wage; or lastly all production is concentrated in agriculture and wages are higher or at least equal to (a virtual) manufacturing wage.

$$\begin{aligned} w &= 1, \quad \lambda \in (0, 1), \\ w &\geq 1, \quad \lambda = 1, \\ w &\leq 1, \quad \lambda = 0 \end{aligned} \tag{3.40}$$

These equilibria depend on the initial distribution of manufacturing activities and on parameter values. The most common representation of the model is to look at equilibria depending on the significance of transport costs. High transport costs usually lead to a symmetric long-run equilibrium, meaning that manufacturing production takes place in both regions. This also means that both countries are active in the traditional and in the modern sector, meaning that wages all over are unity. The reason for this spatial distribution is that in the case of high transport costs, it pays to be close to consumers, and farmers—equally spread over the regions—are a significant part of final demand.

When transport costs fall, the importance of being close to these 'remote' consumers erodes and the symmetric equilibrium becomes unstable. So if manufacturing production increases only slightly in one region, this will increase the manufacturing wage in the region, leading to a further movement of workers into manufacturing in the region. Put more technically, forward and backward linkages (outweighing the competition effect) trigger an agglomeration process and lead to industrial concentration in one region, while the other specializes in agriculture—the core-periphery outcome.

3.2.3 A Simulation Exercise

To illustrate the characteristics of the model, I will present some results from a numerical simulation done with Mathematica. First, equations 3.32 to 3.38 are numerically solved in a two-regions setting to arrive at the short run equilibrium. Then, workers' movement (triggered by wage differentials) is simulated as a discrete adjustment process.

The short run equilibrium depends critically on parameter values which are set as follows:

$$\begin{array}{|l|}\hline \sigma = 5 \\ \alpha = 0.5 \\ \mu = 0.4 \\ \gamma = 0.5 \\ \hline \end{array}$$

Setting $T = 3$ means that the simulation starts in a situation where transport costs are high. If λ_N and λ_S are set to 0.7 and 0.1[2] respectively (representing an initial spatial distribution of manufacturing of the core-

[2] Were the initial values 0 and 1, there would be no movement of workers. However, this turns out not to be a stable equilibrium. To test for stability, I use starting values slightly different from the extreme values.

periphery type) then the wage gap v_N is negative and v_S positive. There is an incentive in the North for workers to leave the manufacturing sector and move into agriculture and vice versa in the South.

The law of motion is formulated as follows in the simulation[3]:

$$\dot{\lambda} = \gamma v(\lambda(1 - \lambda))$$

Movement of workers leads to a symmetric long run equilibrium—λ_N and λ_S are both 0.4, so manufacturing production is equally split between the two regions. This result is not sensitive to the initial values of λ_r but driven by high transport costs. This becomes obvious when one lets transport costs fall. Using the symmetric outcome as starting values for λ_r, the symmetric equilibrium remains the long run outcome up until $T = 1.95$. Once T falls below this threshold (the so-called *break point*), the symmetric equilibrium becomes unstable. The region that gains a slight advantage in manufacturing will experience specialisation in the modern sector, the other region will deindustrialise. The outcome is the core-periphery equilibrium. As laid out above, the strength of linkages causes the concentration of manufacturing activity in one region.

With very low transport costs ($T = 1.5$) any initial distribution will lead to a core-periphery outcome in the long run. Which region ends up as the industrialised core, and which one as the periphery depends on the initial conditions. A slight advantage for the North in the beginning suffices to lead to total agglomeration of manufacturing in the core in the long run. Interestingly, the core-periphery outcome remains the long run equilibrium up until a level of transport costs of $T = 2.2$. Only at $T = 2.25$ will an initial core-periphery patttern become unsustainable and the two regions move to a symmetric outcome. This latter level of transport costs is called the *sustain point* in the literature (Baldwin et al., 2003, 30f.). Break and sustain points can also be derived algebraically. A detailed derivation can be found in Fujita et al. (2001, 248f.).

To describe the model, we can therefore identify three different outcomes, depending on the level of transport costs. Given the parameter values assumed in this simulation, the core-periphery outcome will always be the long run equilibrium for low transport costs ($1 < T < 1.9$). At an intermediate

[3]The slight difference to Equation 3.39 is the inclusion of parameter γ which—set at 0.5—slows the movement of workers. It is necessary in a discrete simulation exercise such as this one to prevent overshooting.

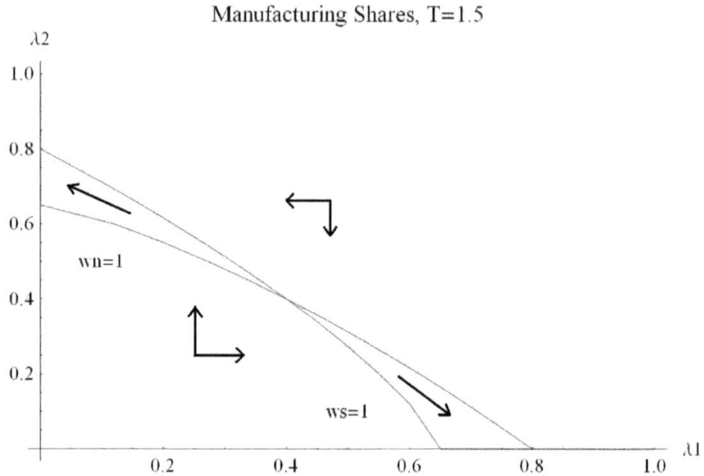

Figure 3.1: Manufacturing employment at $T = 1.5$

level ($1.95 < T < 2.2$), the long run equilibrium depends on the initial conditions. A core-periphery structure will give rise to a core-periphery long run equilibrium, a symmetric distribution of activities will lead to a symmetric long run equilibrium. With high transport costs ($T > 2.25$), the equilibrium will always be symmetric, no matter the initial conditions.

There are various ways to graphically present the results of such a simulation exercise. The best known is the Tomahawk diagram which displays stable equilibria in relation to transport costs. I choose a different way here, depicting the share of each region's labour force active in manufacturing were the manufacturing wage to be unity in one of the regions, hence equal to the agricultural wage. In a situation of low transport costs—from above we know that this implies a core-periphery outcome—the stable long run equilibria are the corner solutions, when either $w_N = 1$ or $w_S = 1$ intersect with the axes.

To interpret Figure 3.1, consider $w_N = 1$ first. This curve depicts all combinations of λ_N and λ_S at which manufacturing wages in the North are unity, or at which there is no incentive for workers in the North to leave the sector they are active in at the moment. This is the case when all manufacturing is concentrated in the North, but also in the symmetric equilibrium ($\lambda_N = \lambda_S = 0.4$) and all other combinations on the curve. At any point to the right of $w_N = 1$, the manufacturing wage is less than unity and λ_N would decrease because of wage incentives, at any point to the left λ_N is higher than unity and workers would move into the modern sector. The same is true for the South (where any point above $w_S = 1$ implies manufacturing wages below unity and leads to a fall in λ_S), and it becomes clear why only the corner solutions are stable equilibria: any point to the left (to the right) of both lines would lead to an increase (to a decrease) of manufacturing activity in both regions. If the two regions are on a hypothetical point $\lambda_N = 0.7, \lambda_S = 0.1$ (on $w_N = 1$), then wages of manufacturing workers in the South are below unity and they would move into agriculture. λ_S would decrease, λ_N would increase further until the two regions arrive in the core-periphery solution. The same would hold for a comparable situation close to the other corner solution. Finally, the symmetric equilibrium is not stable since a slight movement of λ in any region would trigger a specialisation process and lead to one of the two corner solutions.

In the case of high transport costs ($T = 3$) we already know to expect the symmetric equilibrium. The graphic representation of wage developments confirms this (see Figure 3.2). Only the symmetric equilibrium is stable, an inspection of any other point in the graph will confirm the tendency of workers to move in a way that leads to an equal distribution of manufacturing activity.

The latter case is certainly the most interesting. At intermediate transport costs ($T = 2.15$ in this simulation) we saw above that the outcome depends on the initial distribution of manufacturing activity—it might be symmetric or a core-periphery pattern. Figure 3.3 shows the results in terms of wages. There are five equilibria overall now, the two corner solutions, the symmetric equilibrium and two intermediate solutions. Only the first three turn out to be stable. To see why, take the curve $w_S = 1$. If the regions are situated on the left-most part of the curve (λ_S between 0 and 0.2), then Northern workers have an incentive to leave manufacturing since manufacturing wages are below unity. In this case (and at very low levels of λ_S) the corner solution—the core-periphery pattern—will prevail.

In contrast, if we presume that the two regions are on the second from left part of $w_S = 1$, then workers in the North earn wages in manufacturing that exceed agricultural wages. This will lead them to move into the modern sector, increasing λ_N and decreasing λ_S. The economies move towards

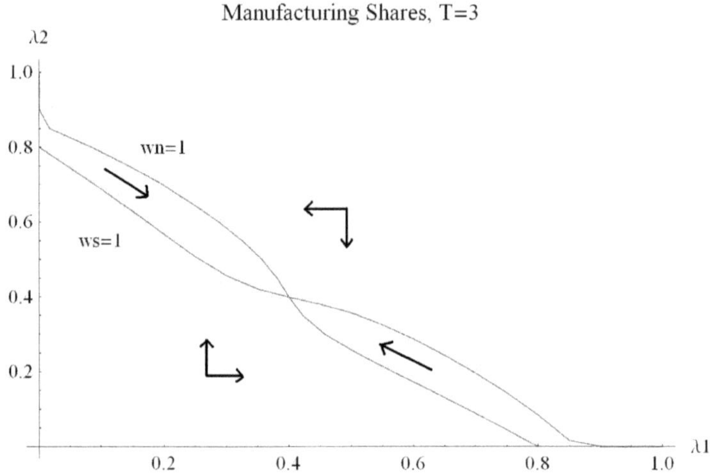

Figure 3.2: Manufacturing employment at $T = 3$

the symmetric equilibrium. This exercise can easily be continued, but the outcome should be clear by now: depending on the starting position, the two regions will either end up in a core-periphery pattern (with the core in the North if it has a strong initial advantage or vice versa) or in a symmetric equilibrium (if the initial position is sufficiently close to the symmetric position).

3.2.4 Conclusion

This *simple* vertical linkages model reestablishes the results of the Core-Periphery model: depending on initial conditions, the geographical distribution of economic activity changes endogenously, potentially leading to processes of industrialisation and de-industrialisation respectively. The ultimate cause for such specialisation processes[4] are the backward and forward linkages that manufacturing firms create locally once they set up shop in a region. This is the crucial difference to the Core-Periphery model, where ag-

[4]The term specialisation seems more appropriate then the term agglomeration in this case, since both regions concentrate on one particular activity in the core-periphery outcome, rather than one region taking up all economic activity.

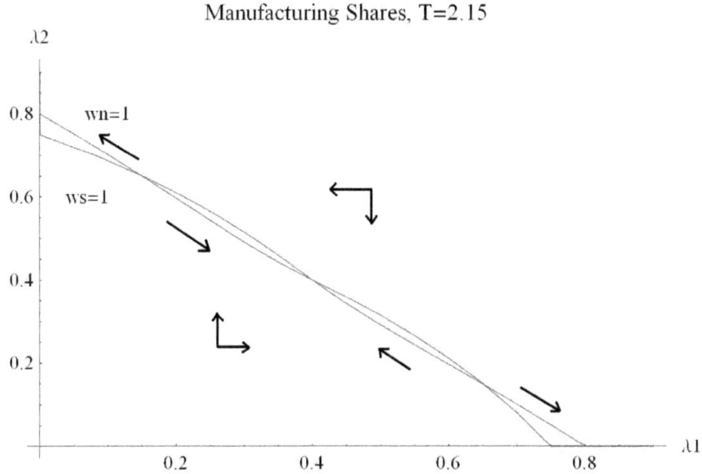

Figure 3.3: Manufacturing employment at $T = 2.15$

glomeration processes are driven by the geographical movement of workers and their purchasing power.

Since linkages play an important role in South African industrial development, the vertical linkages model provides an entry point into a discussion of its industrial development. However the limitation of the model to one homogeneous industrial sector would not permit to take the specific structure of South African industry into consideration. Therefore, the next chapter introduces a vertical linkages model with multiple sectors and also provides simulation analysis that takes into account some of the peculiar features of the South African economy that were described in Chapter 2.

Chapter 4

A Simulation of Linkage Effects

South African industrial development has led to an economic structure that is rather peculiar given its factor endowments: production is capital-intensive and concentrated to a large extent in capital-intensive sectors. This pattern is even stronger when one looks at international competitiveness and the country's exports. This is surprising and requires explanation when considering that South Africa has an abundance of unskilled labour at its disposal.

In Chapter 2 I argued that its mineral endowment, and the industrial development that was triggered by it, are responsible for this structure. Linkages between the mining sector and closely related industrial sectors shaped the economy while labour-intensive manufacturing sectors remained weakly developed throughout history. Almost from the beginning of the mining operations, input sectors such as explosives and chemicals, electricity generation and even mining machinery were started in the country. Equally important, the foreign exchange earned through the export of minerals allowed policy makers to support the emergence of an inward-oriented manufacturing sector that produced consumer goods for the growing domestic market. While this pattern was established in the period between the First and the Second World War, it continued (and became more accentuated) after 1945 and can serve to describe even today's economy to a large extent.

The tight links between mining and a range of other sectors—electricity, which is overwhelmingly based on coal mining, chemical industries, and basic metals such as steel—has led Fine and Rustomjee (1996) to the coining of the term *Minerals Energy Complex.* It is a notion that is picked up in this work and is useful when thinking of the South African industrial development process as driven by linkages between these sectors.

A second notion that is often evoked is South Africa's intermediate position in international trade relations. It struggles to compete with developed countries in the export of high-tech and skills-intensive goods, and it faces equally stiff competition in labour-intensive goods, where low-wage regions particularly from Asia undercut its competitiveness. The former is caused by a shortage of skills, the latter by relatively high wage costs. South Africa is a middle income country with a corresponding cost structure, its history of oppression and exploitation of African labour make wage cuts a politically extremely sensitive issue, and its minerals exports also put an upward bias on the exchange rate of the Rand.

I take these two core features of the economy—linkages between mining and certain industrial activities shaping industrial development, and South Africa's intermediate position in the global economy, where it faces competition from both ends of the skills spectrum—and try to reproduce them in a vertical linkages model with multiple sectors (that allow to model linkages between them) and three regions (that can cater not only for a core and a periphery, but also an intermediate region).

4.1 The Multi-Industry Model

The logic of vertical linkages models was explained above. For the model presented here, I will mostly draw on work done by Puga and Venables (1996, 1999). They provide a particularly interesting framework that lends itself to applications on development economies and industrial development. They set up a multi-country and multi-industry framework where each industry is imperfectly competitive and industries are linked by an input-output structure. Starting with an initial core periphery distribution of manufacturing, they then add an exogenous growth process that expresses itself in increased demand for manufactured goods. At first, strong linkage effects let new firms in the core satisfy additional demand, driving up wages and increasing inequality between regions. At a certain wage level, it becomes profitable for firms to forego benefits from linkages in the centre, and take advantage of low wages in the periphery by moving there. They thereby create linkages and trigger a self-sustaining industrialisation process in the periphery—a story reminiscent of old ideas like circular causality and cumulative causation.

In the 1996 paper, Puga and Venables simulate this process for a set of hypothetical scenarios where industries differ in terms of labour intensity, upstream and downstream position or linkage strength and then look into which industries leave an existing agglomeration first. In the 1999 application, they aggregate their input-output structure from the actual South Korean input-output matrix. Forslid et al. (2002) provide an application in a European context, albeit with a focus on changing trade costs rather than growth, and Fujita et al. (2001, Chapter 15) have an exposition of the Puga/Venables model in their overview as well.

4.1.1 Logic of the Model

One striking feature of world economic development in the last few decades is the rapid growth of Asian economies such as South Korea and Taiwan. Much of their success is attributed to the formidable performance of their manufacturing firms which managed to penetrate world markets and export increasingly sophisticated goods to the rest of the world. Often, their growth is analysed in terms of national policies, and their experience has influenced discussions on industrial and more broadly economic policy in developing countries. In chapter 6, which tackles very recent industrial policy changes in South Africa, this influence will become very visible. However, the vertical linkages model as presented here aims to provide a different explanation. Rather than looking at country differences, it is assumed that countries are similar in their technology and their factor endowments. The differences in industrial activity are explained by agglomeration effects that result from some initial advantage and forward and backward linkages.

There are multiple regions, and each of the regions possesses a traditional and a multitude of manufacturing sectors. These sectors are linked to each other via an input-output matrix. A by now well known combination of factors allows for agglomeration processes: the existence of positive transport costs, increasing returns to scale in production and linkages between sectors. Because of positive transport costs, it is important for firms to be located close to consumers (which in this setting can be both final consumers or households, and other firms that use their product as an input) and to the producers of input that they themselves use in production. In combination with increasing returns to scale, this ensures that firms will choose a singular location close to the main market, rather than spreading production geographically as they could with constant returns to scale. Lastly, input-output linkages represent the sectoral connections that reinforce agglomeration. Once an upstream industry is located in a certain region, it becomes very attractive for downstream sectors to set up shop close by.

One region has—for some historical region that is not necessarily explained in the model—an initial advantage and therefore becomes the core of manufacturing activity. All manufacturing production is concentrated in the region because of the backward and forward linkages at play. The other regions represent the periphery and are specialised in agriculture. The existing agglomeration and the linkages are a strong incentive for any new manufacturing firms to settle in the core. However, there is an opposing force: wages in the core will be higher than in the periphery. As in the model laid out above, wages rise with manufacturing activity in a region.

These two opposing tendencies provide for interesting developments once a growth process is introduced. It is modeled very simply as an increase in demand for manufacturing goods that results from exogenous technical progress and a related increase in labour productivity. With higher demand for manufacturing goods, additional firms will come into operation. At first, they will locate in the core because of linkages. However, more activity widens the wage gap, and at one point it will pay for a firm to start its business in the periphery, where it forgoes proximity to suppliers and customers, but employs labour at lower wages. Unsurprisingly, firms in labour-intensive sectors and firms with weak linkages to other firms will move first. With growth continuing, the region that attracted these first movers will develop a manufacturing sector over time, creating its own linkages, but also experiencing rising wages—it will turn into a second core. This process repeats itself with the other regions, describing a development process where one region after the other experiences development spurts which lead to industrialisation and higher wage levels.

In order to represent South Africa's situation as closely as is possible in this model framework, I will introduce a number of variations below. There will be three regions, one representing the core with a concentration of manufacturing activity, and two peripheral ones. Out of five different manufacturing sectors, one will use an additional input in production—it can be thought of as minerals. This sector therefore represents the mining and mineral beneficiation sectors. The minerals good will be exogenously priced, and is only available in one of the two peripheral states. Apart from this differing minerals endowment, the regions will be identical as was the case above. Starting from this position, I will try to show how a growth process that causes additional manufacturing production will lead to a particular pattern in the emergence of manufacturing activity in the periphery: firms in sectors that are closely linked to mining through input-output linkages will set up shop in the region which disposes of minerals—a trivial result. However, firms in labour intensive sectors that have little connections to the mining industry will evade the mineral-rich region because of higher wages, and they will rather settle in the third region, which thus starts a process of labour-intensive industrialisation.

As a result, the resource-rich country remains caught in a development path that is not labour-intensive. Linkage effects and wage differentials prevent the attraction of more labour-absorbing industries. This seems to be a reasonable, albeit by necessity extremely simplified, representation of South African industrial development.

4.1.2 The Formal Model

The model resembles the one presented in Chapter 3, but there are a number of important differences. I will therefore present it in detail and step by step, following the overall structure of the earlier presentation, but with a focus on those aspects that have changed.

Consumer Behaviour

The representative consumer draws utility from the consumption of a homogeneous agricultural good, and from industrial goods of five different sectors s. A minimum amount of the agricultural good has to be consumed—this amount $\overline{Y}$ can be thought of as a subsistence level of food consumption. All income Y up to $\overline{Y}$ is spent on the agricultural good by the representative consumer. For income above $\overline{Y}$, she allocates constant shares of her income to each of the six sectors. The utility function is thus a linear expenditure system as developed by Stone (1954).

Moreover, within each of the five manufacturing sectors $s = 1...5$, consumers display a preference for variety: they draw utility from consuming different varieties of the manufactured good produced in the sector. m_i is the quantity of a variety consumed, and there is a range of n varieties on offer in a sector, which is determined in the model.

M_s	*Composite index of the quantity of consumption of manufactured goods produced in sector s*
m_{is}	*Consumption of a variety i of the manufactured good produced in sector s*
A	*Consumption of the agricultural good*
p_A, p_{is}	*Price of the agricultural and the manufactured good respectively*
Y	*Income of the representative consumer*
$\overline{Y}$	*Subsistence level of consumption of the agricultural good*
μ_s	*Share of income above* $\overline{Y}$ *spent on sector s*
$0 < \rho < 1$	*Indicator for the love for variety; the smaller it is, the greater is the preference for variety*
σ	*Elasticity of substitution between varieties, the bigger it is, the greater is the preference for variety*
G_s	*Price index in sector s*
T_{NS}	*Transport costs for shipping a good from region N to region S*
δ_s	*Share of workforce in a region employed in sector s*
K	*Land used in agricultural production*
l	*Labour*
α_s	*Share of intermediates stemming from sector s used in production*
w_{rs}	*Wages in region r and sector s*
v_{rs}	*Wage differential in region r between agricultural sector and manufacturing sector s*
E_{rs}	*Total expenditure in region r on goods of manufacturing sector s*
g	*Mineral input into mining sector*
α_g	*Share of mineral input used in the mining sector*

Table 4.1: Variables and Parameters in the Model

As a result, the utility function consists of two tiers. The upper tier defines expenditure allocation to the six sectors and is a variation of the

Cobb-Douglass form.

$$U = (A - \overline{Y})^{1-\sum \mu_s} \prod M_s^{\mu_s} \tag{4.1}$$

This utility formulation implies that a share $1 - \sum \mu_s$ of income above the subsistence level will be spent on the agricultural good, and μ_s on the manufacturing sector s. The lower tier expresses the consumer's preference for variety within the subsectors. It defines M_s as a constant elasticity of substitution function and is equivalent to the subutility function in the simple VL model above, 3.2.

$$M = \left[\sum_{i=1}^{n} m_{is}^{\rho} \right]^{1/\rho}, \quad 0 < \rho < 1 \tag{4.2}$$

ρ is the indicator for the strength of a consumer's love for variety for the different available products m_{is}. n represents the number of firms and varieties available. As before, the elasticity of substitution can be calculated and equals

$$\sigma = \frac{1}{1-\rho}$$

A large σ (ρ is close to one) indicates that the differentiated manufacturing products are near perfect substitutes and consumers do not value variety highly. When σ is small ρ is close to zero and consumers display a great love for variety.

The budget constraint looks as follows:

$$Y = p_a A + \sum_{s=1}^{5} G_s M_s \tag{4.3}$$

where G is a yet to be defined price index. In order to derive demand functions, it is necessary to maximize utility in two steps. The lower tier is addressed first to determine demand for a variety of a manufacturing good within any sector s. Total expenditure on varieties within the sector is minimised subject to the constraint that overall utility equals M_s.

$$min \sum_{i=1}^{n} m_i p_i \quad s.t. \quad \left[\sum_{i=1}^{n} m_i^{\rho} \right]^{\frac{1}{\rho}} = M_s \tag{4.4}$$

Setting up the Lagrangian function and differentiating for m_i and m_j respectively yields a price ratio of varieties m_i and m_j

$$L = \sum p_i m_i + \lambda \left[M_s - \left[\sum m_i^{\rho} \right]^{\frac{1}{\rho}} \right]$$

$$\frac{p_i}{p_j} = \frac{m_i^{\rho-1}}{m_j^{\rho-1}}$$

From here, it is easy to find an expression for m_i

$$m_i = \left(\frac{p_j}{p_i} \right)^{\frac{1}{1-\rho}} m_j$$

Plugging this result back into the constraint yields

$$M_s = \left[\sum_{i=1}^{n} \left((\frac{p_j}{p_i})^{\frac{1}{1-\rho}} m_j \right)^{\rho} \right]^{\frac{1}{\rho}}$$

Simplifying yields

$$M_s = \left[\sum_{i=1}^{n} p_i^{\frac{\rho}{\rho-1}} \right]^{\frac{1}{\rho}} m_j p_j^{\frac{1}{1-\rho}}$$

Demand for an individual variety m_j therefore turns out to be

$$m_j = M \frac{p_j^{\frac{1}{\rho-1}}}{\left[\sum_{i=1}^{n} p_i^{\frac{\rho}{\rho-1}} \right]^{\frac{1}{\rho}}} \tag{4.5}$$

This is the compensated demand function. By rearranging terms, it can be rewritten to include a so-called price index G as is shown in equations 3.7 and 3.8. G thus equals

$$G = \left[\int p_j^{\frac{\rho}{\rho-1}} d_j \right]^{\frac{\rho-1}{\rho}} \tag{4.6}$$

G represents the minimum cost of obtaining one unit of the quantity index M. Not surprisingly, G also reflects consumers' desire for variety. If a larger number of varieties is available at a correspondingly lower price, G

will fall. The compensated demand function for m_j can thus be rewritten by substituting the price index G into 4.5.

$$m_j = M\left(\frac{p_j}{G}\right)^{\frac{1}{\rho-1}} \tag{4.7}$$

Or equivalent, if ρ is replaced by the elasticity of substitution σ:

$$m_j = M\left(\frac{p_j}{G}\right)^{-\sigma}$$

Once the demand for a variety within a sector s is known, the attention is turned to the upper tier of the utility maximisation problem. We maximise 4.1 subject to the budget constraint 4.3. Again, we set up the Lagrangian function:

$$LA = (A - \overline{Y})^{1-\sum \mu_s} \prod M_s^{\mu_s} + \lambda(Y - p_A A - \sum G_s M_s)$$

Differentiating the Lagrangian function for M_s, A and λ and setting them to zero yields local maxima:

$$\frac{\partial LA}{\partial M_s} : \mu_s \frac{U}{M_s} = \lambda G_s$$
$$\frac{\partial LA}{\partial A} : (1 - \sum \mu_s)\frac{U}{A - \overline{Y}} = \lambda p_A$$
$$\frac{\partial LA}{\partial \lambda} : Y = p_A A + \sum G_s M_s$$

Take the sum of $G_s M_s$ over all industrial sectors plus the traditional sector to get

$$\sum_{s=1} G_s M_s + (A - \overline{Y})p_A = \sum_{s=1} \mu_s + (1 - \sum_{s=1} \mu_s)(\frac{U}{\lambda}) = \frac{U}{\lambda}$$

In a next step, rewrite this expression and substitute Y as derived above

$$Y - \overline{Y}p_A = \frac{U}{\lambda}$$

It is now possible to derive demand functions for the agricultural good and for manufacturing goods in each of the five sectors. Starting with the traditional sector and replacing $(\frac{U}{\lambda})$ in the local maximum above, I get

$$(A - \overline{Y})p_A = (1 - \sum_{s=1} \mu_s)(Y - \overline{Y}p_A)$$

The demand for agricultural goods A then is

$$A = \frac{(1 - \sum_{s=1} \mu_s)(Y - \overline{Y} p_A)}{p_A} + \overline{Y} \tag{4.8}$$

The representative consumer spends a fraction of income above the minimal consumption requirement on the traditional good. Additionally, this minimal consumption requirement is spent on the traditional good as well.

The demand for industrial goods is derived in a similar manner. First, I derive demand for the composite of one industrial sector M_s. Substitution equivalent to the procedure in the traditional sector yields

$$M_s = \frac{\mu_s(Y - \overline{Y} p_A)}{G_s} \tag{4.9}$$

The consumer spends a fraction μ_s of income over and above $\overline{Y}$ on sector s. However, we are interested in demand for a single variety produced by a firm within the sector. To achieve this, I replace M_s in Equation 4.7 by 4.9. Then, demand for a single variety becomes

$$m_{sj} = \frac{\mu_s(Y - \overline{Y} p_A)}{G_s} \left(\frac{p_{sj}}{G} \right)^{\frac{1}{\rho - 1}}$$

Simplification yields the demand function for a single variety j in sector s:

$$m_{sj} = \mu_s(Y - \overline{Y} p_A) p_j^{\frac{1}{\rho - 1}} G_s^{\frac{\rho}{1 - \rho}} \tag{4.10}$$

Expressed in σ, the elasticity of substitution, rather than in ρ, demand can be rewritten as

$$m_{sj} = \mu_s(Y - \overline{Y} p_A) p_j^{-\sigma} G_s^{\sigma - 1} \tag{4.11}$$

Demand for a variety obviously depends on expenditure by consumers on the sector as established above. Within the sector, demand depends negatively on the price of the variety, and positively on the price index G_s—an increase in the price index indicates fewer varieties, hence less competition and therefore a larger share for one variety. It is also easily checked that the price elasticity of demand equals σ and is therefore constant.

As a last step in describing consumer behaviour, we can derive indirect utility $V(Y, p_A, G_s)$ by substituting demand for A and M_s in the utility function 4.1.

$$V = (1 - \sum_s \mu_s)^{1 - \sum \mu_s} \prod_s \mu_s^{\mu_s} (Y - \overline{Y} p_A) p_A^{-(1 - \sum \mu)} \prod_s G_s^{-\mu} \tag{4.12}$$

The indirect utility function is useful when stressing once more the core feature of the particular formulation of utility and demand: consumers' love for variety in the industrial sector. To formally re-establish this result, assume for now that prices p_{sj} for all varieties $j = 1, ..n$ in a sector s are equal. Then the price index G as expressed in 4.6 becomes $p_s n^{(\rho-1)/\rho}$. If n increases, the price index G falls and utility increases. The extent of this preference for variety clearly depends on the parameter ρ—if it is close to one, a change in n has little effect, if it is close to zero, then more varieties strongly affect G and preference for variety is relatively larger.

Many Regions

So far, there has been little geography in this NEG-model. However, the purpose of this exercise is to analyse a country's industrial development in a three-region setting. I will assume that consumers have identical preferences in the three regions, however one important adaption is necessary nonetheless: both agricultural and industrial goods will be tradable, allowing countries to import or export them corresponding to their specialisation in production.

For the sake of simplicity, it is generally assumed that trade in the agricultural good is costless to keep this sector as simple as possible. In the industrial sectors on the other hand trade is not free but generates transport costs of the iceberg-form. The NEG owes this formulation to von Thünen who introduced the concept already in the 19th century. What it assumes is that a fraction $1 - 1/T$ of the transported good melts on the way to its destination, so that only $1/T$ of the good arrives. This formulation has two major advantages: firstly, it is not necessary to formulate a separate transport sector. Secondly, firms will charge the same mill price to domestic and to foreign consumers.

To see why it is necessary to look at firm behaviour and their profit-maximising price setting. For now, it suffices to understand the basic concept of iceberg transport costs. Assume that a manufactured good is produced in the North–region N. When consumed in the region, there are no transport costs, so the price of the good in the North will be p_N. Yet, when it is exported to the South–region S, only a fraction $1/T_{NS}$ of the good arrives. T_{NS} stands for the amount of the manufactured good that has to be shipped for one unit to arrive in S. In terms of prices, a mill price of p_N for one unit implies a delivery price of $p_N T_{NS} = p_{NS}$ in the South. Note also that T_{NN} equals one.

Transport costs will impact on the price indices in various regions and sectors, so they have to be reformulated. There are three regions $R = 1, 2, 3$ in this formulation. Moreover, it is necessary to assume that prices for individual varieties within a sector are equal, which is indeed the case here and will be shown later. Then, the price index in sector s of region 1 becomes

$$G_{1s} = \Big[\sum_{r=1}^{3} n_{rs}(p_{rs}T_{1r})^{\frac{\rho}{\rho-1}}\Big]^{\frac{\rho-1}{\rho}} \tag{4.13}$$

and might vary over locations. If a large proportion of goods are produced locally, the price index will be relatively low, in the opposite case (one might think of such a region as periphery) it will be relatively higher. Due to the nature of transport costs, demand has to be reformulated, and total sales of a variety have to include T, the amount of the good lost in transport. So total sales of a single variety q in location 1 are

$$q_1 = \mu_s \sum_{r=1}^{3} (Y_r - \overline{Y_r} p_A)(p_j T_{1r})^{-\sigma} G_s^{\sigma-1} T_{1r} \tag{4.14}$$

They depend on total income in all regions available for the consumption of manufacturing goods, consumers' preferences with regard to the different manufacturing sectors, the variety's price and transport costs. With regards to the demand elasticity, as above it is constant and equal to σ. Note that it does not depend on transport costs either. As indicated above, this will be convenient at a later stage when we look at the price setting of firms.

Producer Behaviour

With consumer behaviour and demand established, we can look at the behaviour of firms. In the traditional sector, there is perfect competition, trade between regions is costless and its output will be used as numéraire. In the manufacturing sectors, the market form is monopolistic competition, as introduced by Dixit and Stiglitz (1977).

Turning our attention to the agricultural sector first, we assume a production function that is increasing in the input labour, yet with diminishing returns. Following Fujita et al. (2001, 257) it takes the following form:

$$q_A = \frac{K}{\gamma}\Big(\frac{(1 - \sum_s \delta_s)}{K}\Big)^{\gamma} \tag{4.15}$$

K can be thought of as an agriculture-specific input into production such as land. The other input factor of course is labour. A share of $(1 - \sum_s \delta_s)$ of the total labour force in a region (which is set to one for simplicity) work in the agricultural sector. The rest of workers are distributed over the five manufacturing sectors, with sector s employing δ_s workers.

The marginal product of labour in agriculture is positive yet diminishing. If a region industrialises—in other words if workers are drawn out of agriculture and move into manufacturing—then the marginal product increases and so does the agricultural wage. Since workers move freely between sectors within a region, the industrialisation process also increases the equilibrium manufacturing wage. This is a core feature of the model which is primely responsible for the setting up of new industries in the periphery.

Since the agricultural good acts as numéraire, the agricultural wage will equal the marginal product of labour in the sector. Formally,

$$w_A = \left(\frac{(1 - \sum_s \delta_s)}{K}\right)^{\gamma-1} \tag{4.16}$$

In each manufacturing sector, firms will produce with increasing returns to scale since there is a fixed-cost component involved in the production process. Because of this, each firm will produce one variety only. Because of consumers' love for variety, we also know that each variety will be produced by only one firm. The number of firms in a sector will thus equal the number of varieties on offer. The inputs used are labour and intermediate goods that come from the five manufacturing sectors. The formulation is thus equivalent to the simple VL model—equation 3.17. The production function for a typical firm in sector s then equals

$$F + cq_s = (1 - \sum \alpha_s)^{\sum \alpha_s - 1} \prod_s \alpha_s{}^{-\alpha_s} l^{\alpha_l} \prod_s M_s^{\alpha_s} \tag{4.17}$$

To put the production function in this manner immediately points to one of its crucial attributes: the inputs, labour and intermediate goods, are used in both the fixed and the variable component of production. In other words, to set up the factory, the firm incurs fixed costs F, of which a proportion $1 - \sum \alpha_s$ is spent on workers, and the rest (shares α_s) on inputs from the different manufacturing sectors. The same proportionality applies to variable costs. On the right hand side, the first two terms are constants that ensure a simple cost function (see below). l represents the labour input in production, M_s the intermediate input from a particular sector s.

M_s again represents a manufacturing goods composite for a specific sector and consists of a number of differentiated varieties. Firms display a love for variety in their input demand equivalent to consumer preferences. For the sake of simplicity, the formulation will be exactly equivalent. Reformulating, we get

$$F + cq_s = (1 - \sum_s \alpha_s)^{\sum \alpha_s - 1} \prod_s \alpha_s{}^{-\alpha_s} l^{1-\sum \alpha_s} \prod_s \Big[\sum_r n_{rs} x_{rs}^{\rho}\Big]^{\frac{\alpha_s}{\rho}} \quad (4.18)$$

The CES aggregator $\left[\sum_r n_{rs} x_{rs}^{\rho}\right]^{1/\rho}$ shows how a firm uses differentiated inputs x stemming from sectors $s = 1,..5$ and from all three regions. It has a preference for variety, and the strength of this preference depends on ρ.

To arrive at profit maximization and price setting of an individual manufacturing firm, we need to know the cost function first. This involves some tedious algebra, but the result is a rather intuitive cost function. Starting with the production function 4.17 the Lagrangian function can be set up:

$$LA = wl + \sum_s G_s M_s + \lambda\Big[q - (1 - \sum_s \alpha_s)^{\sum \alpha_s - 1} \prod_s \alpha_s{}^{-\alpha_s} l^{1-\sum \alpha_s} \prod_s M_s^{\alpha_s} \frac{1}{c} + \frac{F}{c}\Big]$$

Then

$$\frac{\partial LA}{\partial l} : w = \lambda(1 - \sum \alpha_s) l^{-\sum \alpha_s} (1 - \sum_s \alpha_s)^{\sum \alpha_s - 1} \prod_s \alpha_s{}^{-\alpha_s} \prod_s M_s^{\alpha_s} \frac{1}{c}$$

$$\frac{\partial LA}{\partial M_{s1}} : G_{s1} = \lambda \alpha_{s1} M_{s1}^{\alpha_{s1}-1} \prod^{2-5} M_s^{\alpha_s} (1 - \sum_s \alpha_s)^{\sum \alpha_s - 1} \prod_s \alpha_s{}^{-\alpha_s} l^{1-\sum \alpha_s} \frac{1}{c}$$

$$\frac{\partial LA}{\partial M_{s2}} : G_{s2} = \lambda \alpha_{s2} M_{s2}^{\alpha_{s2}-1} \prod^{2-5} M_s^{\alpha_s} (1 - \sum_s \alpha_s)^{\sum \alpha_s - 1} \prod_s \alpha_s{}^{-\alpha_s} l^{1-\sum \alpha_s} \frac{1}{c}$$

$$\frac{\partial LA}{\partial \lambda} : q = (1 - \sum_s \alpha_s)^{\sum \alpha_s - 1} \prod_s \alpha_s{}^{-\alpha_s} l^{1-\sum \alpha_s} \prod_s M_s^{\alpha_s} \frac{1}{c} - \frac{F}{c}$$

From this, by division we arrive at much simplified price ratios:

$$wl\alpha_{s1} = G_{s1} M_{s1} (1 - \sum \alpha_s)$$
$$G_{s2} M_{s2} \alpha_{s1} = G_{s1} M_{s1} \alpha_{s2}$$

If we want to express input demand for l and M_s in terms of output and prices, these ratios have to be plugged back into the production function.

Input demand for labour l can be derived by inserting $M_s = \frac{wl\alpha_s}{G_s(1-\sum\alpha)}$ in the production function. The relevant term $\prod_s M_s^{\alpha_s}$ becomes

$$\prod_s M_s^{\alpha_s} = (wl)^{\sum\alpha_s}(1-\sum\alpha_s)^{-\sum\alpha_s}\prod(\frac{\alpha_s}{G_s})^{\alpha_s}$$

and l turns out to be

$$l = \frac{(F+cq)(1-\sum\alpha_s)\prod G_s^{\alpha_s}}{w^{\sum\alpha_s}}$$

The equivalent procedure produces input demand for the composite M_s of one industrial sector. I insert $l = G_{s1}M_{s1}(1-\sum\alpha_s)/(w\alpha_{s1})$ into the production function which turns out to be

$$F + cq = \prod\alpha_s^{-\alpha_s}\alpha_{s1}^{\sum\alpha_s - 1}w^{\sum\alpha_s - 1}\prod M_s^{\alpha_s}M_{s1}^{1-\sum\alpha_s}G_{s1}^{1-\sum\alpha_s}$$

With a further substitution, this expression can be greatly simplified. The product of manufacturing composites $\prod M_s^{\alpha_s}$ can be split up, extracting $M_{s1}^{\alpha_{s1}}$ and replacing the remaining sectoral composites $s2$ to $s5$ by $M_{s2} = G_{s1}M_{s1}\alpha_{s2}/(G_{s2}\alpha_{s1})$ and so forth. Then

$$F+cq = \prod\alpha_s^{-\alpha_s}\prod^{2-5}\alpha_s^{\alpha_s}\alpha_{s1}^{\sum\alpha_s-1}\alpha_{s1}^{-\sum^{2-5}\alpha_s}w^{\sum\alpha_s-1}G_{s1}^{1-\sum\alpha_s}G_{s1}^{\sum^{2-5}\alpha_s}\prod^{2-5}G_s^{-\alpha_s}M_{s1}^{1-\sum\alpha_s}$$

Simplication yields

$$F + cq = \alpha_{s1}^{-1}M_{s1}w^{\sum\alpha_s-1}G_{s1}^{1-\alpha_{s1}}\prod^{2-5}G_s^{-\alpha_s}$$

From this, I derive an expression for M_{s1}

$$M_{s1} = \frac{(F+cq)\alpha_{s1}}{w^{\sum\alpha_s-1}G_{s1}^{1-\alpha_{s1}}\prod^{2-5}G_s^{-\alpha_s}}$$

Lastly, factor demand is inserted into the total cost function $TC = wl + \sum G_s M_s$. Then, TC can be expanded to

$$TC = w\left(\frac{(F+cq)(1-\sum\alpha_s)\prod G_s^{\alpha_s}}{w^{\sum\alpha_s}}\right) + \sum G_s\frac{(F+cq)\alpha_s}{w^{\sum\alpha_s-1}G_s^{1-\alpha_s}\prod^{2-5}G_s^{-\alpha_s}}$$

Simplify to get

$$TC = (F+cq)w^{1-\sum\alpha_s}\left[(1-\sum\alpha_s)\prod G_s^{\alpha_s} + \sum G_s\frac{\alpha_s}{G_s^{1-\alpha_s}\prod^{2-5}G_s^{\alpha_s}}\right]$$

and finally

$$TC = (F + cq)\left[w^{1-\sum\alpha_s}\prod G_s^{\alpha_s}\right] \tag{4.19}$$

This simple and intuitive cost function shows how production costs (both the fixed cost component and variable costs) depend on wages and price indices of intermediate inputs, impacting according to the share of expenditure that goes towards their use.

We can now formulate the profit maximization problem of a manufacturing firm.

$$\Pi = pq - (F + cq)\left[w^{1-\sum\alpha_s}\prod G_s^{\alpha_s}\right] \tag{4.20}$$

where total demand q is taken from equation 4.14. The firm will set production so that marginal revenue equals marginal costs or $p(1+\frac{1}{\epsilon}) = MC$. The monopolistic competition formulation implies that the firm—producing a distinct variety—acts as a local monopolist and does not consider its competitor's reaction. It thus takes the price index G as given, which in turn implies that the elasticity of demand is σ.

Algebraically,

$$p(1 + (\frac{1}{-\sigma})) = c\left[w^{1-\sum\alpha_s}\prod G_s^{\alpha_s}\right]$$

Replace σ by ρ and reformulate to arrive at the price set by the producer of a variety:

$$p = \left[w^{1-\sum\alpha_s}\prod G_s^{\alpha_s}\right]\frac{c}{\rho} \tag{4.21}$$

Prices are set at a constant mark-up $\frac{c}{\rho}$ over marginal costs. On the other hand, entry into the market is free, and profits will be driven down to zero accordingly. We use the zero-profit condition to determine the size of an individual firm.

Setting $\Pi = 0$ and using 4.21 we get

$$\left[w^{1-\sum\alpha_s}\prod G_s^{\alpha_s}\right]\frac{c}{\rho}q = (F + cq)\left[w^{1-\sum\alpha_s}\prod G_s^{\alpha_s}\right]$$

Simplifying yields equilibrium output of a firm

$$q^* = \frac{F\rho}{(1-\rho)c} \quad or \quad q^* = F\frac{(\sigma-1)}{c} \tag{4.22}$$

Firm size thus depends on the cost parameters (positively on fixed costs, negatively on variable costs) and on the prefence for variety of consumers. The higher the representative consumer's love for variety as expressed in σ or in ρ, the smaller the output of an individual firm—more firms will offer more varieties in smaller quantities. Note also what does not affect firm size: the overall size of the market. If total demand increases, it will not change supply behaviour of a single firm. What it does cause however is the entry of new firms—a larger market then leads to a larger choice of varieties and thereby reduces the price index G in the market. More formally, to express the number of firms as a function of market size, equate the total wage bill in a sector s with the share of total revenue in that sector that goes to wages:

$$\delta_s w = (1 - \sum \alpha_s) npq$$

Thus, the equilibrium number of firms becomes

$$n^* = \frac{\delta_s w}{(1 - \sum \alpha_s) pq} \tag{4.23}$$

Before writing down the short run equilibrium, we have to reformulate total demand for goods because we now know that firms also demand industrial products as part of their input demand. Total demand from consumers including the amount of goods lost in transport was recorded in 4.14. Now demand from firms has to be added. Due to the formulation of their production function 4.17 they spend a fixed proportion α_s of their total costs on products stemming from sector s. Within sectoral demand, they have a preference for variety equivalent to consumer behaviour, depending on the parameter ρ.

So total demand for a variety i in sector s can be written as

$$q_{si} = \sum_r E_{rs} \left[p_i^{-\sigma} \left(\frac{G}{T}\right)^{\sigma - 1} \right] \tag{4.24}$$

where expenditure on sector s, E_s in one particular region is defined as

$$E_s = \mu_s (Y - \overline{Y} p_A) + \sum_z \alpha_{zs} npq \tag{4.25}$$

Consumers spend a share μ_s of income above the minimum agricultural good requirement $\overline{Y}$ on the sector, and firms from sectors $z = 1...5$ spend an according share α_{zs} of their total sales—reflecting the input-output linkages between sectors.

Short Run Equilibrium

We are now in a position to write down the short run equilibrium of the model. It is expressed in the price indices, the so-called wage equations, expenditure and income. In order to simplify notation, a number of normalizations are introduced.

$$p_A = 1$$
$$c = \rho$$
$$q^* = \frac{1}{1 - \sum \alpha_s}$$

We start by defining expenditure E_{rs} in a region r on products of the manufacturing sector s. Use the normalisations above and transform 4.25 accordingly to get

$$E_{rs} = \mu_s(Y_r - \overline{Y_r}) + \sum_z \alpha_{zs} \frac{\delta_s w}{(1 - \sum \alpha_s)} \tag{4.26}$$

The first term on the right hand side is consumption expenditure on a sector (dependent on μ_s), the second term intermediate demand from firms (dependent on α_{zs}).

Income Y_r in a region r comes from workers' wages in manufacturing and from income in the agricultural sector. Thus

$$Y_r = \sum_s w_s \delta_s + \frac{K}{\gamma}\Big(\frac{(1 - \sum_s \delta_s)}{K}\Big)^\gamma \tag{4.27}$$

Turning to the price indices, we reformulate 4.13 to get the price index in region r_1 and sector s

$$G_{r_1 s}^{1-\sigma} = \sum_r n_{rs}(p_{rs} T_{r_1 r})^{1-\sigma}$$

After the normalisations introduced above, the price p as in 4.21 and the number of firms n (see equation 4.23) can be simplified and rewritten as

$$p = w^{1-\sum \alpha_s} \prod G_s^{\alpha_s}$$
$$n = \frac{\delta_s w}{(1 - \sum \alpha_s) p q^*}$$
$$n = \frac{\delta_s w}{w^{1-\sum \alpha_s} \prod G_s^{\alpha_s}}$$

Plug these into the price index to get

$$G_{r_1 s}^{1-\sigma} = \sum_r \frac{\delta_s w}{w^{1-\sum \alpha_s} \prod G^{\alpha_s}} \left(w^{1-\sum \alpha_s} \prod G^{\alpha_s}\right)^{1-\sigma} T^{1-\sigma}$$

Simplification yields the final version of the price index for region r_1 and its sector s:

$$G_{r_1 s}^{1-\sigma} = \sum_r \delta_s w^{1-\sigma(1-\sum \alpha_s)} \prod_s G_{rs}^{-\alpha\sigma} T_{r_1 r}^{1-\sigma} \tag{4.28}$$

Equation 4.28 shows that the price index in a region first of all depends on transport costs to the region—the higher they are, the higher the price index will be. Also, this implies that a remote region that imports a larger share of its manufactured goods will face higher price indices. The term $\delta_s Lw$ is an indicator of the market size of respective regions. Lastly, the price index depends on prices of individual varieties, and since prices are set as a mark-up over marginal costs, wages and input prices enter the equation as well.

Lastly, we define the so-called manufacturing wage equations. Manufacturing wages are crucial since they will determine the dynamics of the model. Yet they are intuitively hard to grasp since there is no closed form expression for them. We arrive at them by using what Baldwin et al. (2003, 19) call the "market clearing conditions". From 4.22 we know the output a firm produces at which it can exactly recover its fixed costs and so has zero profits. From demand by consumers and firms, we thus know that this output level q^* must equal

$$q^* = \sum_r E_{rs} \left[p_i^{-\sigma} \left(\frac{G}{T}\right)^{\sigma-1} \right]$$

Rearrange to bring the price on the left hand side. This price p_i is the break even price that a firm must charge in order to achieve zero profits. If it sets its price at a lower level, it will go out of business because it operates at a loss, if it sets its price at a higher level, competitors will enter the market and drive the price down.

$$p_i^{\sigma} = \frac{1}{q^*} \sum_r E_{rs} \left[\left(\frac{G}{T}\right)^{\sigma-1} \right]$$

Lastly, price setting is linked to manufacturing wages due to mark-up pricing. Thus, we can indirectly define the manufacturing wage at which firms achieve zero profits, given income, price indices and transport costs in all locations.

$$\left[w^{1-\sum\alpha_s}\prod G_s^{\alpha_s}\right]^\sigma = \frac{1}{1-\sum\alpha_s}\sum_r E_{rs}\left[\left(\frac{G}{T}\right)^{\sigma-1}\right] \tag{4.29}$$

This is the so-called wage equation. We can use it plus the price indices to illustrate the main forces at work in the model: backward and forward linkages and the market-crowding or competition effect. The question to be asked is whether any given short run equilibrium with resulting income, expenditure, price indices and wages in all regions represents a stable equilibrium. In order to find out, assume that a small number of workers move into manufacturing in one region and δ_s changes accordingly—will that trigger further specialisation in manufacturing (in other words: will manufacturing wages increase further) because of linkage effects? Or will the competition effect prevail and thus prevent further specialisation?

- *Backward Linkages:* Backward linkages stem from the increasing size of the local market that results from more manufacturing production in the region. This increase works through both input demand by manufacturing firms and through additional final demand by workers and is relevant because of the existence of positive transport costs. In equations 4.26 to 4.29 the backward linkage shows up in expenditure on manufacturing goods E. If δ_s increases, so does expenditure in the region. This shifts up demand curves for local producers and leads to an increase in wages.

- *Forward Linkages:* Forward linkages represent the cost reduction for downstream producers that is associated with the local availability of intermediate inputs. In the model, this effect relies on the preference for variety of firms: if more varieties of an input good are available locally, the price index of that input will decrease. When δ_s increases in 4.28, the regional price index in the respective sector falls. In terms of wages, this reduction in input costs tends to increase the equilibrium wage further, as can be seen in G_s on the left hand side of the wage equation.

- *Competition Effect:* The competition effect provides an opposing tendency. The increase in δ_s that reduces the price index also implies that the demand for each firm's variety shifts down. This will tend to reduce the equilibrium wage and is represented in the model in G_s on the right hand side of the wage equation. Lastly, an increase in δ_s simultaneously leads to a decrease in agricultural employment $(1 - \sum_s \delta_s)$. This raises the marginal product of agricultural labour and thus agricultural wages. Competition for workers thus puts another break on industrialisation.

Wages are the reward for the mobile factor, labour. The short run equilibrium as defined above in equations 4.26 to 4.29 yields a wage rate in each of the manufacturing sectors. They might and will in all likelihood differ, depending on the respective forward and backward linkages and the competition effect. These differing wages in the manufacturing sectors, or, more precisely, the wage differential between the agricultural sector and manufacturing sectors, then determine the sectoral movement of workers in the long run and thus the dynamics of the model. If wages are higher in manufacturing, workers will move there and the region amasses industrial production. In the opposite case, they will leave the modern sector and the region deindustrialises. Note that firms always operate at zero profits, which means that they immediately move into or out of a sector according to the profit signal. Workers on the other hand do not move in the short run but only switch occupation in the long run equilibrium.

On Dynamics

The wage differentials in the short run trigger movements of workers to those industries that offer higher wages. In the long run equilibrium, wages will equalise across sectors. Note that they do not equalise across regions since labour is not interregionally mobile. This is one of the core differences between the core-periphery and the vertical linkages driven NEG models.

Therefore it is important to define the mobility equations that describe the movement of workers. The incentive to move is provided by the wage differential between the traditional sector and a particular manufacturing sector. We define the wage differential in region r and sector s v_{rs} as

$$v_{rs} = w_{rs} - \left(\frac{(1 - \sum_s \delta_s)}{K_r} \right)^{\gamma - 1} \tag{4.30}$$

If v_{rs} is positive, agricultural workers will leave their sector and move into manufacturing sector s thereby increasing its size and triggering above mentioned adjustments. The mobility equation is then defined as

$$\dot{\delta_{rs}} = v_{rs}\gamma(\delta_{rs}(1 - \delta_{rs})) \tag{4.31}$$

The change over time in a sector's workforce depends on its wage differential to the agricultural sector. The formulation in 4.31 ensures that the movement stops in the corner solutions—if all workers are working in sector s, $(1 - \delta_{rs})$ is zero and movement stops, if the sector does not exist ($\delta_{rs} = 0$), the same applies.

Long run interior equilibria can be established with simulation analysis—results will depend on parameter values chosen. Both will be described in detail in the sections below. Before that, one last building block of the model has to be introduced however—the exogenous growth process. We are not so much interested in the causes of growth in this model, but in its effects on the sectoral composition of output. Therefore, the formulation will be very simple: technological progress steadily increases the productivity of labour. Following Fujita et al. (2001, 264), labour is denoted in efficiency units L. Thus $L\delta_{rs}$ is the number of efficiency units operating in country r and sector s, and w_{rs} is the wage per efficiency unit. So if the economy grows thanks to an increase in L, workers' income through wages increase.

The short run equilibrium has to be reformulated to accommodate for these changes.

$$E_{rs} = \mu_s(Y_r - \overline{Y_r}) + \sum_z \alpha_{zs} \frac{L\delta_s w}{(1 - \sum \alpha_s)} \tag{4.32}$$

$$Y_r = \sum_s w_s L\delta_s + L\frac{K}{\gamma}\Big(\frac{(1 - \sum_s \delta_s)}{K}\Big)^{\gamma} \tag{4.33}$$

$$G_{r_1 s}^{1-\sigma} = \sum_r L\delta_s w^{1-\sigma(1-\sum \alpha_s)} \prod_s G_{rs}^{-\alpha\sigma} T_{r_1 r}^{1-\sigma} \tag{4.34}$$

$$\Big[w^{1-\sum \alpha_s} \prod G_s^{\alpha_s}\Big]^{\sigma} = \frac{1}{1 - \sum \alpha_s} \sum_r E_{rs}\Big[\big(\frac{G}{T}\big)^{\sigma-1}\Big] \tag{4.35}$$

The growth process is relevant because of the particular form of utility and demand: once income exceeds $\overline{Y}$, a fixed proportion is spent on manufacturing goods. In total, this implies that the demand for manufacturing goods grows faster than the demand for agricultural goods. These shifts are responsible for sectoral changes: additional manufacturing production will happen in regions where it is most profitable, either due to linkage effects or due to lower wage costs. The development of this growth-induced process over time and the various forces that drive these results will be analysed below.

4.1.3 The Mining Sector

The first of the non-traditional sectors will represent the mining sector. In addition to inputs from all other sectors, it also uses a mineral input in production. I call it g. A constant share α_g of total costs is spent on the mineral input in the mining sector. In all other sectors, α_g equals zero. From this follows the production function[1] for the mining sector:

$$F + cq_g = l^{1-\sum \alpha_s - \alpha_g} g^{\alpha_g} \prod_s M_s^{\alpha_s} \tag{4.36}$$

I further assume that the price of the mineral input is exogenously given. This simplifies my analysis considerably and is not an unreasonable assumption—given the size of South Africa's economy and the global market for natural resources. It is denoted p_g. Total costs in the minerals sector in the region profiting from being endowed with it thus are

$$TC = (F + cq)\left[w^{1-\sum \alpha_s - \alpha_g} p_g^{\alpha_g} \prod G_s^{\alpha_s}\right] \tag{4.37}$$

In the other regions, the mineral input has to be imported. Its import bears iceberg transport costs of the magnitude T, so the input cost accordingly is $p_g T$.

Just as in the rest of the sectors, firms in the mining sector set prices as a mark-up over marginal costs, which—thanks to the normalisations introduced above—disappears. The price set in the mining sector p_{min} therefore is

$$p_{min} = w^{1-\sum \alpha_s - \alpha_g} p_g^{\alpha_g} \prod G_s^{\alpha_s} \tag{4.38}$$

Returning to the short run equilibrium, the price indices and the wage equations have to be adapted to cater for the special role of the mining sector. The price index of the sector as described in 4.34 changes to

$$G_{r_1 s}^{1-\sigma} = \sum_r L\delta_s p_g^{-\alpha_g \sigma} w^{1-\sigma(1-\sum \alpha_s - \alpha_g)} \prod_s G_{rs}^{-\alpha\sigma} T_{r_1 r}^{1-\sigma} \tag{4.39}$$

[1] This is a simplified version, omitting the constants

in the region with the mineral endowment. In the other regions, the price of the mining input enters as $(Tp_g)^{-\alpha_g \sigma}$. The wage equation is adapted accordingly. Again, in the mineral-rich region, I replace the price set by firms in the mining sector in the wage equation to get

$$\left[p_g^{\alpha_g} w^{1-\sum \alpha_s - \alpha_g} \prod G_s^{\alpha_s}\right]^{\sigma} = \frac{1}{1-\sum \alpha_s} \sum_r E_{rs} \left[\left(\frac{G}{T}\right)^{\sigma-1}\right] \tag{4.40}$$

In the other regions, transport costs for the mineral input will be considered on the left hand side again. Now that the special features of the minerals sector are established, numerical simulation will shed more light on the model and its characteristics. The focus of attention will lie on the role of the mineral endowment and its consequences on sectoral growth in the three regions.

4.2 Simulation Results

In this section, I present results for two simulations. The first uses a very simplified input-output matrix to illustrate the features of the model, particularly the effect of the mineral endowment on sectoral industrial development and wages in the respective regions. In the second simulation, I attempt to use a more realistic input-output matrix that more accurately describes the South African case.

4.2.1 Three Regions, Five Industries: a Simple Case

The simulation presented here uses parameter values that are standard in the literature and describe a situation of low transport costs where a core-periphery outcome is expected. They are described in more detail in the appendix.

The crucial aspect that needs to be highlighted and that differs from work done before is the input-output matrix that links the five manufacturing sectors. Table 4.2 displays all values of α_s for industry 1 in column 1, for industry 2 in column 2 and so forth. So each column presents the total of intermediate inputs from other modern sectors for the respective sector. Sector 1, the mining sector, additionally uses the mineral good as input. α_g, the share of the mineral resource in the production of the mining sector is set to $\alpha_g = 0,5$ to represent its dominance in this sector.

	MEC		*Non-MEC*		
	α_{1s}	α_{2s}	α_{3s}	α_{4s}	α_{5s}
α_{s1}	0,11	0,12	0,02	0,02	0,02
α_{s2}	0,1	0,1	0,02	0,02	0,02
α_{s3}	0,02	0,02	0,08	0,09	0,1
α_{s4}	0,02	0,02	0,07	0,09	0,09
α_{s5}	0,01	0,01	0,07	0,08	0,09

Table 4.2: Input-Output Matrix

The matrix is constructed so that industries 1 and 2 are heavily linked. So the second industry represents those activities that use the mining industry's output heavily and also provide significant inputs to the mining industry. In terms of the South African economy that provides the underlying reference for this simulation, the second sector can be identified as those manufacturing sectors that together with mining itself make up the Minerals-Energy Complex; that is base chemicals, petroleum products, and plastics, non-metallic mineral products, base metals, and electricity. Sectors 3 to 5 on the other hand are weakly linked to the resource-intensive core of the economy—both in terms of forward and backward linkages. However, they display strong linkages among themselves. They represent non-MEC manufacturing sectors in the simulation.

The simulation is done with Mathematica. For an initial value of $L = 1$, the short run equilibrium price indices, wages, expenditure and income are calculated. From this, the wage differentials v_s are gathered in all three regions and their respective sectors. Workers then move according to the law of motion as defined in 4.31. A long-run equilibrium is reached once they have no more incentive to leave their sector. In the graphic representations below, I display subsequent long run equilibria for increasing values of L—thus a simulation of the growth process.

Region 1 represents the core region, region 2 profits from the minerals endowment, and region 3 is the periphery. In the starting position, the core region specializes in activities 3 to 5, the second region in those activities close to the mineral endowment, and the third region is the periphery, accounting for no modern production at all. When the economy starts to grow, the first two regions start to amass sectoral activity according to the initial sectoral distribution. Country 3 remains peripheral. At a critical

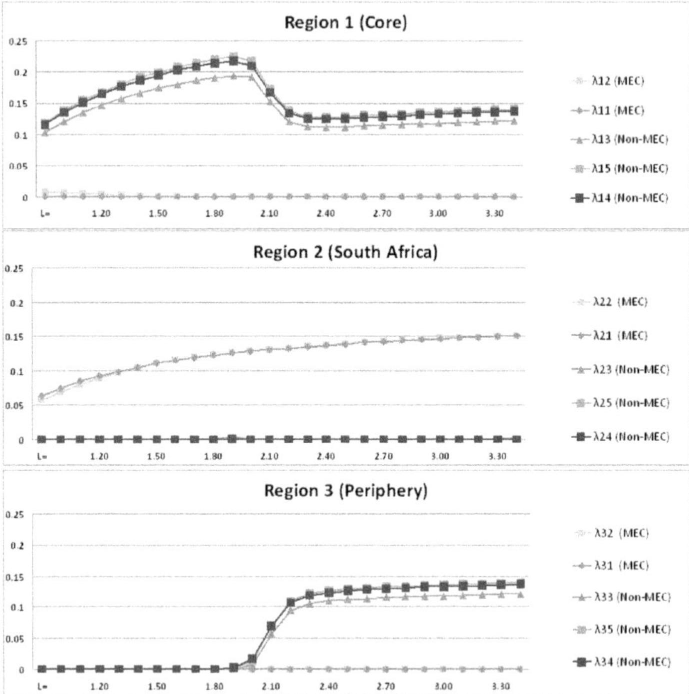

Figure 4.1: Sectoral Development

level however, incentives change and it becomes attractive for some manufacturing firms to leave the core region and set up shop in the periphery. The simulation results show that—despite a small hike in region 2—region 3 establishes itself as a manufacturing region (see Graph 4.1). The mineral-rich region keeps its competitive advantage in the first two sectors, but the other industries are now more equally divided between region 1 and region 3. Firms in these sectors do not set up shop in region 2.

What are the driving forces of these results? The linkage structure imposed on the model clearly plays a decisive role. Strong linkages between industries 1 and 2 explain why they are tied in the second region. These linkages also explain the closely correlated development of industries 3 to 5.

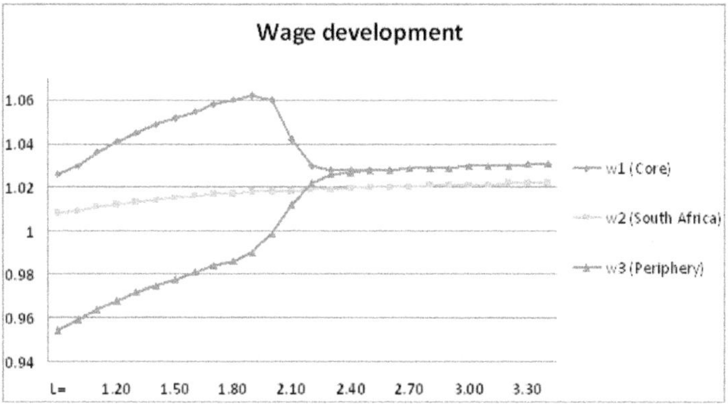

Figure 4.2: Regional wages

However, the input-output matrix cannot explain why the growth process triggers industrialisation in region 3—without any manufacturing activity and thus without any benefits accruing from linkage effects—and not in region 2. The reason for this are wage costs (see Graph 4.2). Not surprisingly, the core is the high wage region initially. Higher economic activity drives up manufacturing wages through the channels discussed above. The growth process further increases manufacturing wages in the core, until, at the break point, the wage costs are so high that it pays for some firms to establish themselves in the periphery.

Between the two peripheral regions, the mineral-rich region has some manufacturing activity—thus there will be linkage-related advantages for firms that emerge there. However, as can be seen in Graph 4.2, the presence of firms in sectors 1 and 2 implies that wages in the region are higher than in region 3 that is fully specialized in the traditional sector. The wage differential between them is large enough to overshadow linkage advantages and therefore manufacturing activity in sectors 3 to 5 emerges in region 3, the low-wage region.

Once some firms have made that step, the region profits from local linkage effects as well and quickly industrialises. Wages will rise accordingly and the country soon reaches the level of the industrialised core in terms of wages. Region 2 grows continuously in terms of wages, but fails to attract a broader set of industries: its development is clearly tied to the mineral endowment. Albeit an advantage initially, it puts an upper limit on sectoral growth and eventually also on wages and thus welfare in the region, because it prevents a diversification process.

4.2.2 Three Regions, Ten Industries: South Africa

The results obtained above stem—to a good extent—from the peculiar form of the input-output matrix chosen above. In order to reestablish the results with an industry structure closer to what we observe, I run a simulation with 3 regions and 10 industries that uses an input-output matrix modelled on South Africa's industrial structure.

The derivation of the matrix is explained in the Appendix. The outcome is a 10x10 matrix as presented in Table 4.3. Sector 1, mining and quarrying, represents the mining sector from above and uses the mineral as additional input again. Apart from this, parameter values are very similar to those chosen above (see Appendix), that is we are in a setting of low transport costs. The three countries are identical in all respects except the minerals endowment. Region 2 has access to the mineral without transport costs, the other regions have to import it and thus have to bear additional transport costs.

With regards to the input-output matrix, it is clear the sector 'petroleum products, chemicals, rubber and plastic' is the one that is most closely linked to the mining sector. A share of $0,145$ of its total production costs is spent on inputs stemming from the minerals sector. This corresponds to the empirical literature that identifies this sector as crucial component of the MEC. The other manufacturing sectors that are usually subsumed under the label MEC are basic metals, a sub-group of the sector-grouping 'metals, metal products, machinery and equipment' in the table. However, its backward linkage to the mining sector $(0,086)$, albeit larger than that of the rest of sectors, is less important than the linkage of the chemicals sector.

A major difference to the hypothetical 5 industries-case presented above is that 'the rest of the economy', that is the sectors that are not considered part of the MEC, are not in a systematic way closely linked with each other. This was an artefact above and will be visible in the results below. One does observe stronger linkages between certain sectors however, notably the importance of metal products in the transport equipment sector and, to a lesser extent, in the electrical machinery sector.

	Min	*Food*	*Tex*	*Wood*	*Chem*	*NMM*	*Metals*	*ElecM*	*Trans*	*Furn*
Min	0,002	0,001	0,000	0,001	0,145	0,018	0,086	0,000	0,002	0,033
Food	0,000	0,079	0,005	0,001	0,003	0,000	0,000	0,000	0,000	0,000
Tex	0,001	0,001	0,039	0,001	0,003	0,000	0,001	0,001	0,010	0,004
Wood	0,005	0,022	0,001	0,105	0,006	0,002	0,003	0,002	0,002	0,016
Chem	0,035	0,029	0,018	0,032	0,276	0,007	0,024	0,017	0,026	0,014
NMM	0,003	0,006	0,000	0,000	0,003	0,010	0,001	0,002	0,004	0,000
Metals	0,039	0,018	0,005	0,010	0,024	0,007	0,253	0,028	0,065	0,024
ElecM	0,005	0,000	0,000	0,000	0,000	0,000	0,006	0,031	0,011	0,001
Trans	0,014	0,004	0,001	0,001	0,003	0,000	0,002	0,000	0,321	0,000
Furn	0,000	0,000	0,001	0,002	0,001	0,000	0,001	0,002	0,000	0,007

Min	*Mining and Quarrying*
Food	*Food, beverages and tobacco*
Tex	*Textiles, clothing and leather*
Wood	*Wood and paper; publishing and printing*
Chem	*Petroleum products, chemicals, rubber and plastic*
NMM	*Other non-metallic mineral products*
Metals	*Metals, metal products, machinery and equipment*
ElecM	*Electrical machinery, radio, TV, instruments*
Trans	*Transport equipment*
Furn	*Furniture and other manufacturing*

Table 4.3: Input-Output Matrix

Results of the simulation show a similar pattern of sectoral industrial development. However it differs from the simulation above in important aspects. Turning the attention to the development of the 10 sectors in the three regions first (see Figure 4.3), it is obvious that the growth process is more continuous for the majority of sectors in the three regions than before. The one major exception is the 'Chem' sector, that is initially located in the core region and relocates to the minerals-rich region once a certain growth level is attained. This relocation is triggered by the wage differential becoming big enough for some firms to relocate, and happens in this particular sector because of the strong linkages to the minerals sector that is overwhelmingly located in region 2. These changes lead to a familiar pattern of sectoral development in the region: mining and the closely related sectors dominate the economy. Given the input output structure of South Africa, this applies for the petroleum products, chemicals and plastics sector. The rest of the economy virtually stagnates, there is no significant growth in any of the other sectors despite a continuous increase in world wide demand for manufacturing products.

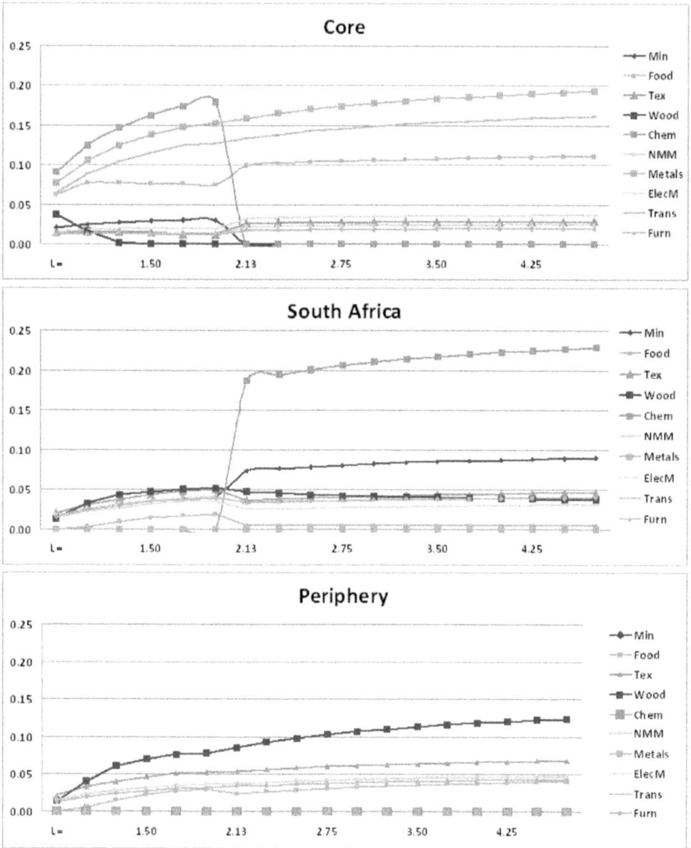

Figure 4.3: Sectoral Development

This additional demand is satisfied by firms that emerge either in the core region, where they build on existing advantages of agglomeration—expressed in the form of linkages that render intermediate inputs cheaper in this model, or in region 3, the periphery. The core, while loosing activity in the 'Chem' sector, grows strongly in the metal products sector, and this growth pulls along transport equipment and electrical machinery, that are both strongly

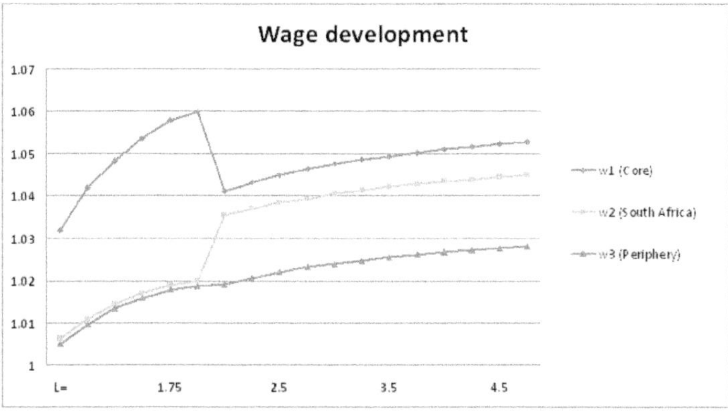

Figure 4.4: Regional wages

linked to metal products. Less intuitive is the strong performance of the food sector in the core.

With regards to the periphery, its growth is concentrated predominantly in the wood and paper and in the textiles industry. Those two sectors exceed their counterparts in the mineral-rich region in size. The periphery unsurprisingly does not engage in mining or closely linked industries at all. Intuitively plausible as well, there is no metal products and transport equipment production in it either.

The major difference to the first simulation is that region 3 does not fully industrialise and thus overtake the minerals-rich region. The reason for this difference lies in the more realistic input-output matrix. Inter-industry linkages in the 'non-mineral' sectors (sectors 3-5 above) are nowhere near as strong and therefore do not trigger a rapid industrialisation process in all of them once activity emerges in one of them.

This difference is also visible in the development of wages. In the early stages of the growth process, the wage gap widens between the core region and the two peripheral regions. The relocation of the 'Chem' sector then strongly increases economic activity and wages in the minerals-rich region, bringing it to a wage level much closer to the core region. Region 3 remains a low-wage region. As a result of the wage difference between regions 2 and

3 however, most sectors outside mining and chemicals are more important in the periphery than region 2.

So while the second simulation does not replicate the strong welfare results of the first exercise (an overtaking of the minerals-rich region by the peripheral region in terms of wages), it does retain the sectoral implications of input-output linkages and the mineral endowment: it is the sector closely linked to mining that will relocate to the mineral-rich region, and this increased economic activity in one sector, by driving up wages in the economy as a whole, dampens economic activity in a host of other sectors. Given the parameter values chosen here, these results are strongest for the sectors 'wood and paper; publishing and printing', 'textiles, clothing and leather' and 'electrical machinery, radio, TV, and instruments', that all develop more dynamically in the peripheral region.

The core region retains its high wages mostly through dominance in 'metals, metal products, machinery and equipment', 'transport equipment' and, certainly less intuitive, 'food, beverages and tobacco'.

At this point, it is important and necessary to stress the limits of this analysis. Many, if not most, important factors influencing sectoral development have been abstracted from, not least additional production inputs in other sectors (for example in the wood and paper sector). Regarding the simulation, it is therefore apparent that one cannot speak of an empirical application proper of an economic geography model. I therefore second Forslid et al. (2002) who called simulations of a similar kind "theory with numbers" (Forslid et al., 2002, 281). What the simulation does provide though is a theoretical argument that justifies further investigation into the importance of linkages and thus 'real' empirical work.

In the next chapter, I will attempt to do just this and provide some empirical evidence for the importance of linkages in the context of South African industrial development and the growth performance of its various sectors.

Chapter 5

Linkages at Work? Empirical Results

The history of South African industrial development and the results of the simulation both provided evidence that linkages between different sectors might influence industrial development in the country. However, neither provide 'hard' empirical evidence about their actual strength and impact. In order to rectify this omission, I propose to use a structural vector autoregression model (SVAR) to assess sectoral development in South Africa from 1970 to 2006. The model explicitly tests for the impact of input-output linkages on the growth performance of sectors.

The chapter starts with an overview of existing empirical work in the New Economic Geography field and on linkage effects, particularly those studies with direct relevance for South Africa. In the second part, the SVAR methodology is introduced in detail. The third part presents the model and estimation results. I conclude with an interpretation of the results.

5.1 Empirics of Linkage Effects

Existing empirical applications of NEG models are reviewed briefly below. Since there are a number of problems in these applications and since this study has a broader focus on linkage effects that does not limit itself to the model results, I also add a brief description of studies that attempt to assess linkage effects in South Africa.

5.1.1 Empirics of the New Economic Geography

Turning to empirical applications of NEG first, it is noteworthy that they still lag their theoretical counterparts in terms of quantity and coherence, despite a recent surge in publications (Head and Mayer, 2004, 2611 and Brakman and Garretsen, 2006, 569). In his critical assessment of NEG, Martin finds this to be embedded in the very nature of the models that to him "[...] do not lend themselves easily to empirical estimation or application, since they are typically too abstract, over simplified and too idealised." (Martin, 1999, 70) Empirical work therefore mostly limits itself to the testing of certain properties of the models.

Krugman offered first insights into agglomeration effects by calculating locational Gini coefficients as an index of industry concentration (Krugman, 1991b, 54ff.). These coefficients compare the incidence of particular industries in regions to total manufacturing production. Krugman finds high concentration for most US industries. Ellison and Glaeser substantially enrich this concept in two contributions (Ellison and Glaeser, 1997, 1999). They measure industry concentration against an accidental distribution and still find concentration in most sectors. Yet they caution that often, agglomeration will result from natural advantages (Ellison and Glaeser, 1997). In their second paper they try to empirically isolate the effect of natural advantages (or first nature) on concentration and find that "about 20% of observed geographic concentration can be explained by a small set of advantages." (Ellison and Glaeser, 1999, 315). Apart from indices of concentration, Head and Mayer (2004) provide an exhaustive overview of empirical tests on various propositions of the New Economic Geography.

Regarding linkage effects in particular, Ellison and Glaeser (1997) measure coagglomeration of industries with strong upstream-downstream relationships. For the constructed pairs of industries 77 out of 100 downstream industries that are heavily using one input are locally coagglomerated with the upstream producer (Ellison and Glaeser, 1997, 917) which is a strong indication that vertical linkage effects are indeed at play in spatial agglomeration processes. Building on the multi-sector VL model presented in Puga and Venables (1996) and in Fujita et al. (2001), Forslid et al. (2002) calibrate a 14 sector model with a complete input-output structure derived from IO-matrices to study the effects of economic integration, which they simulate by a fall in trade costs over time, on industry concentration for four European regions.

However, these results have to be interpreted with care. Hypotheses derived from NEG models are often equivalent to hypotheses derived from other theories—thus their empirical testing and corroboration is "not necessarily evidence of the relevance of NEG, but could support competing theories and hypotheses." (Brakman and Garretsen, 2007, 99) Ottaviano (2007) points to a second identification problem: the 'within-equivalence' of vertical linkages models and those NEG models based on factor mobility (e.g. the core-periphery model). He shows that the 'footloose entrepreneur' (FE) model, a variation of the core-periphery model, has the same structural features and equivalent equilibrium properties to the vertical linkages footloose entrepreneur (VLFE) model, a variation of the vertical linkages models. Thus, observed agglomeration could stem from either labour mobility as predicted in the core-periphery setting or from linkages, but it is not possible to uniquely attribute it to one of the two effects (Ottaviano, 2007, 64).

To my knowledge, there is no empirical work investigating agglomeration due to linkage effects in South Africa. However, a number of contributions try to estimate concentration tendencies with respect to manufacturing industries in South Africa and the Southern African region, in particular the Southern African Development Community (SADC). McCarthy provides a qualitative assessment of the potential effects of a free trade area established in SADC and suggests that some polarisation in favour of South Africa due to agglomeration effects as described in the new economic geopgraphy is to be expected (McCarthy, 1999). For a similar purpose, Petersson (2002) calculates centrality and concentration indices for SADC countries and South African provinces. He finds strong evidence for a core periphery structure (with South Africa as the regional core and the Gauteng region as core region of South Africa) and concentration of production in industry, particularly in labour and scale intensive sectors. In more recent work, Hess (2005) uses the locational Gini coefficient to establish that while some industries tend to concentrate in the core of SADC, there is also some concentration in peripheral countries (e.g. textiles and wearing apparel). Heavy industries such as industrial chemicals, iron and steel and non-ferrous metals are increasingly located in South Africa however (Hess, 2005, 52). Fedderke and Szalontai (2005) re-establish these results for manufacturing sectors within South Africa and also find that the high levels of concentration are harmful for output and productivity growth.

5.1.2 Linkage Effects in South Africa

While there is a shortage of empirical work on South Africa with explicit reference to the NEG framework, that cannot be said about linkage effects in general.

Fine and Rustomjee (1996) base their seminal work on industrial development on detailed examinations of input-output linkages, particularly with reference to the MEC. They show that mining and closely related manufacturing industries are a cohesive unit, with almost 60% of MEC-inputs stemming from the MEC itself and close to 30% of its output returned to the MEC (Fine and Rustomjee, 1996, 81). Non-MEC manufacturing on the other hand displays only weak linkages to the MEC.

The importance of linkages has also been stressed in a number of sectoral case studies recently. Roberts (2006, 166) analyses the metal products sector and finds that the most important input—basic iron and steel from within the confines of the MEC—is largely supplied by Iscor, the South African steel monopolist. Thus, the competitiveness of firms in the sector depends to a large extent on the pricing of this key input. Studies of the chemicals and plastics sector (see Roberts, 2001; Dobreva, 2006) reach similar conclusions: the downstream sector, in this case plastic firms, are strongly using chemicals as an input, and again suffer from the market power of large upstream producers.

The most recent and also most exhaustive work in this vain, which is not limited to sector case studies but aims to provide an overview over the whole economy is Tregenna (2007). Her study shows total backward linkages are strongest in the manufacturing sector (using a standard-type classification), thus the provision of an additional unit of output of manufacturing goods would require the production of 2,14 additional units of total output. Backward linkage effects for agriculture, mining and services are significantly lower (1,89, 1,76, and 1,81 respectively) (Tregenna, 2007, 105). Tregenna also calculates employment multipliers (how many jobs would be created if final demand for a sector's output increases by one million Rand) and finds them to be higher in services than in manufacturing. These results have to be interpreted carefully however due to the well-known problems in the measurement of employment in South Africa. Unfortunately she does not report results for more deeply disaggregated data, which would be interesting from the perspective of this study. She also uses the standard distinction between manufacturing and mining activities, and thus does not distinguish between MEC and non-MEC manufacturing.

5.2 Testing for Linkage Effects—A SVAR Approach

Rather then testing for agglomeration effects, and thus inviting the identification problems referred to above, I choose a different, indirect strategy to analyse the significance of linkage effects. Following a paper by Abeysinghe and Forbes (2005), who engage in a similar exercise with regards to international trade relations, a structural VAR is developed that tests the effects of a shock in one sector on the other sectors in the economy. In the transmission of shocks, the role of linkages is explicitly catered for.

I will first introduce the vector auto-regression (VAR) and the structural VAR method, and then describe the specific model, data and results in detail.

5.2.1 Structural VARs

Originally, econometricians treated time series data not any different from other data and formulated traditional regression models. However, non-stationarity of many economic variables led to 'spurious' results and triggered the development of a different approach based on time series analysis—the Box-Jenkins approach (Kennedy, 2003, 319f.). Instead of relying on explanatory variables deducted from economic theory, the past values of the variable in question were used to predict its future development. "Thus in essence it is a sophisticated method of extrapolation." (ibid.).

The dependent variable is first differentiated sufficiently to render it stationary. Then it is expressed in its own past values and current and past error terms—leading to the acronym ARIMA (autoregressive integrated moving average). Once the appropriate model (lag length, number of differentiations) is selected, it can be used to forecast the dependent variable. Because ARIMA-models outperformed traditional economists' formulations, they were adapted and extended to a multivariate setting, producing the so-called VAR models.

Vector Autoregression

The vector autoregression approach was introduced by Sims (1980). He stated that existing large simultaneous equation models "contain too many incredible restrictions" (ibid., 14) and therefore introduced the VAR approach, where all variables in the system are endogenous and depend on their own and all the other variables' lagged values. There are thus no restrictions introduced a priori, which also implies that the approach is atheoretical.

The variables can then be written down as a vector which is explained by its own lagged values plus an error vector. The characteristics and limitations of the VAR approach are now explained in more detail by using the example of a bivariate system with one lag. This presentation follows the outline in Enders (1995, 294ff.).

Assume that the time paths of the two variables y_t and z_t mutually affect each other. Then

$$y_t = b_{10} - b_{12}z_t + \gamma_{11}y_{t-1} + \gamma_{12}z_{t-1} + \epsilon_{yt} \tag{5.1}$$

$$z_t = b_{20} - b_{21}y_t + \gamma_{21}y_{t-1} + \gamma_{22}z_{t-1} + \epsilon_{zt} \tag{5.2}$$

Assume further that y_t and z_t are both stationary, and that the error terms ϵ_{yt} and ϵ_{zt} are uncorrelated white noise disturbances with standard deviations σ_y and σ_z. In the above equations, there is a contemporaneous effect of y_t on z_t and vice versa—their size being expressed in b_{12} and b_{21}, respectively. The epsilons are pure shocks in the two variables. However, these equations are not reduced-form equations. The endogenous variables of the system (y_t and z_t) appear on the right hand side as well, thus violating a core assumption of linear regressions. The reason for this violation is that these regressors are correlated with the error terms due to the interdepence of the various endogenous variables that are determined simultaneously (Kennedy, 2003, 180). To lend themselves to estimations, they have to be rewritten in their reduced form, so that every endogenous variable is expressed as a function of exogenous (including lagged endogenous) variables.

Using matrix algebra, 5.1 and 5.2 become

$$\begin{bmatrix} 1 & b_{12} \\ b_{21} & 1 \end{bmatrix} \begin{bmatrix} y_t \\ z_t \end{bmatrix} = \begin{bmatrix} b_{10} \\ b_{20} \end{bmatrix} + \begin{bmatrix} \gamma_{11} & \gamma_{12} \\ \gamma_{21} & \gamma_{22} \end{bmatrix} \begin{bmatrix} y_{t-1} \\ z_{t-1} \end{bmatrix} + \begin{bmatrix} \epsilon_{yt} \\ \epsilon_{zt} \end{bmatrix} \tag{5.3}$$

or in short form: $Bx_t = \Gamma_0 + \Gamma_1 x_{t-1} + \epsilon_t$. This can be premultiplied by B^{-1} to get $x_t = B^{-1}\Gamma_0 + B^{-1}\Gamma_1 x_{t-1} + B^{-1}\epsilon_t$. Simplifying notation allows us to rewrite this equation as $x_t = A_0 + A_1 x_{t-1} + e_t$ or, expressed in explicit form,

$$y_t = a_{10} + a_{11}y_{t-1} + a_{12}z_{t-1} + e_{1t} \tag{5.4}$$

$$z_t = a_{20} + a_{21}y_{t-1} + a_{22}z_{t-1} + e_{2t} \tag{5.5}$$

where a_{i0} are the elements of A_0, a_{ij} of matrix A_1, and e_{it} of vector e_t. This is the so-called standard or reduced form of the VAR, and equations 5.4 and 5.5 can be estimated. Note however that the error terms e_{it} are now composed of the two original shocks ϵ_{yt} and ϵ_{zt}. Thus, without further restrictions, the impact of one of these pure shocks on the dependent variables cannot be identified. Formally,

$$B^{-1} = \frac{1}{1 - b_{12}b_{21}} \begin{bmatrix} 1 & -b_{12} \\ -b_{21} & 1 \end{bmatrix}$$

Thus, $B^{-1}\epsilon_t$ reveals the error terms

$$e_{1t} = \frac{\epsilon_{yt} - \epsilon_{zt}b_{12}}{1 - b_{12}b_{21}} \tag{5.6}$$

$$e_{2t} = \frac{\epsilon_{zt} - \epsilon_{yt}b_{21}}{1 - b_{12}b_{21}} \tag{5.7}$$

As before, b_{12} and b_{21} are the parameters that indicate the contemporaneous effect of one variable on the other. If they are non-zero, then the structural shocks cannot be identified from the estimated (standard form) VAR. The errors e_{it} do have the desirable properties of being stationary, i.e. having zero means, a constant variance and zero autocovariances (Enders, 1995, 296) and thus do fulfill the preconditions for an OLS estimation. On the other hand, their covariance will typically be non-zero, so the two error terms will be correlated.

Identification

5.1 and 5.2 cannot be estimated directly, but 5.4 and 5.5 can be. OLS will yield estimates for the parameters a_{i0} and a_{ij} and we can calculate variances and the covariance of the residuals, $var(e_{it})$ and $cov(e_{1t}, e_{2t})$. But the nine estimates are not enough to identify the original equations that have ten unknowns, b_{i0}, γ_{ij}, and the standard deviations σ_y and σ_z. Identification requires additional restrictions of the original system.

One possible restriction is to set one of the coefficients of 5.1 and 5.2 equal to zero. If, for example, $b_{21} = 0$, then y_t has no contemporaneous effect on z_t, and the system is exactly identified. The original time series can be rewritten as

$$y_t = b_{10} - b_{12}z_t + \gamma_{11}y_{t-1} + \gamma_{12}z_{t-1} + \epsilon_{yt} \tag{5.8}$$

$$z_t = b_{20} + \gamma_{21}y_{t-1} + \gamma_{22}z_{t-1} + \epsilon_{zt} \tag{5.9}$$

The error terms of the reduced form become

$$e_{1t} = \epsilon_{yt} - \epsilon_{zt}b_{12} \tag{5.10}$$

$$e_{2t} = \epsilon_{zt} \tag{5.11}$$

This form of identification is called a Choleski decomposition (Enders, 1995, 303). The error terms show that the contemporaneous effect of y_t on z_t being zero can be restated as the original shocks ϵ_{yt} and ϵ_{zt} both influencing y_t, but z_t being only affected by ϵ_{zt}.

Impulse Responses

In order to trace the effects of shocks on the variables over time, the vector autoregressive system needs to be rewritten in its moving average form. This is accomplished in analogy to the representation of a single variable autoregression in moving average form. Take a simple AR(1)-process

$$Y_t = \varphi Y_{t-1} + \epsilon_t$$

If $\varphi = 1$, this process represents a random walk and thus is non-stationary. However, the first difference of the random walk is stationary since ϵ_t is stationary. We thus call the random walk integrated of order one (I(1)). In order to test for stationarity, so-called 'unit roots tests' test for this very characteristic. If $\varphi \prec 1$, the series is stationary, in case it is above one, it would explode. We assume that Y_t is stationary and can then express it as a moving average process.

$$Y_{t-1} = \varphi Y_{t-2} + \epsilon_{t-1} \Rightarrow Y_t = \varphi^2 Y_{t-2} + \varphi\epsilon_{t-1} + \epsilon_t$$

$$Y_{t-2} = \varphi Y_{t-3} + \epsilon_{t-2} \Rightarrow Y_t = \varphi^3 Y_{t-3} + \varphi^2 \epsilon_{t-2} + \varphi \epsilon_{t-1} + \epsilon_t$$

Since $\varphi \prec 1$,

$$Y_t = \epsilon_t + \varphi \epsilon_{t-1} + \varphi^2 \epsilon_{t-2} + \varphi^3 \epsilon_{t-3} + ... + \varphi^q \epsilon_{t-q}$$

The moving average representation of the VAR also requires stationarity. We use matrix notation as above and have

$$x_t = A_0 + A_1 x_{t-1} + e_t$$

Recursive replacement yields

$$x_t = A_0 + A_1(A_0 + A_1 x_{t-2} + e_{t-1}) + e_t = (I + A_1)A_0 + A_1^2 x_{t-2} + A_1 e_{t-1} + e_t$$

and, after replacing n times

$$x_t = (I + A_1 + A_1^2 + ... + A_1^n)A_0 + A_1^{n+1} x_{t-(n+1)} + \sum_{i=0}^{n} A_1^i e_{t-n}$$

In case of stability (A_1^n disappears as n grows towards infinity) the above equation can be rewritten as

$$x_t = \mu + \sum A_1^i e_{t-i} \tag{5.12}$$

where $\mu = \begin{bmatrix} \overline{y} & \overline{z} \end{bmatrix}^t$. Equivalently

$$\begin{bmatrix} y_t \\ z_t \end{bmatrix} = \begin{bmatrix} \overline{y} \\ \overline{z} \end{bmatrix} + \sum \begin{bmatrix} a_{11} & a_{12} \\ a_{21} & a_{22} \end{bmatrix}^i \begin{bmatrix} e_{1t-i} \\ e_{2t-i} \end{bmatrix}$$

where

$$\overline{y} = \frac{[a_{10}(1 - a_{22}) + a_{12}a_{20}]}{(1 - a_{11})(1 - a_{22}) - a_{12}a_{21}}, \quad \overline{z} = \frac{[a_{20}(1 - a_{11}) + a_{21}a_{10}]}{(1 - a_{11})(1 - a_{22}) - a_{12}a_{21}}$$

The current value of vector x_t is expressed as a sequence of error terms e_{it}, whose effect on x_t can now be traced through time. Note however that these again are the composed errors and not the structural shocks ϵ_{it}. To identify the effect of a structural shock, first rewrite 5.6 and 5.7 in matrix form

$$\begin{bmatrix} e_{1t} \\ e_{2t} \end{bmatrix} = \frac{1}{1 - b_{12}b_{21}} \begin{bmatrix} 1 & -b_{12} \\ -b_{21} & 1 \end{bmatrix} \begin{bmatrix} \epsilon_{yt} \\ \epsilon_{zt} \end{bmatrix}$$

Replace the vector e_{it} in 5.12 by the above expression to get

$$\begin{bmatrix} y_t \\ z_t \end{bmatrix} = \begin{bmatrix} \overline{y} \\ \overline{z} \end{bmatrix} + \frac{1}{1 - b_{12}b_{21}} \sum \begin{bmatrix} a_{11} & a_{12} \\ a_{21} & a_{22} \end{bmatrix}^i \begin{bmatrix} 1 & -b_{12} \\ -b_{21} & 1 \end{bmatrix} \begin{bmatrix} \epsilon_{yt-i} \\ \epsilon_{zt-i} \end{bmatrix}$$

In order to simplify notation, define matrix ϕ_i as

$$\phi_i = \frac{A^i}{1 - b_{12}b_{21}} \begin{bmatrix} 1 & -b_{12} \\ -b_{21} & 1 \end{bmatrix}$$

with elements $\phi_{jk}(i)$. Thus, the VAR can be rewritten in a moving average form of the original shocks

$$\begin{bmatrix} y_t \\ z_t \end{bmatrix} = \begin{bmatrix} \overline{y} \\ \overline{z} \end{bmatrix} + \sum_{i=0}^{\infty} \begin{bmatrix} \phi_{11}(i) & \phi_{12}(i) \\ \phi_{21}(i) & \phi_{22}(i) \end{bmatrix} \begin{bmatrix} \epsilon_{yt-i} \\ \epsilon_{zt-i} \end{bmatrix} \tag{5.13}$$

The coefficients $\phi_{jk}(i)$ can now be interpreted as impulse responses. For example, $\phi_{12}(0)$ is the immediate impact of a shock in ϵ_{zt} on y_t—the so called impact multiplier. Similarly, $\phi_{22}(1)$ represents the impact of a shock in ϵ_{zt-1} on z_t. They can be plotted against i to yield the impulse response functions, or added up to yield the cumulated impulse responses. For illustration, take a single variable AR(1) process of the form $Y_t = 0,6Y_{t-1} + \epsilon_t$. A change of ϵ_t of one unit changes Y_t by one unit. In the subsequent period, the change in Y_{t+1} is 0.6, in period two 0.6^2 and so forth. The impulse response function in this simple case thus would be $\phi(i) = (0.6)^i$.

Yet, the crucial problem of identification remains to be solved. One possible solution that was explained above is to set one of the parameters expressing the contemporaneous effect of one variable on the other equal to zero. Sticking with the assumption taken above, $b_{21} = 0$ (y_t has no contemporaneous effect on z_t), the error terms reduce to 5.10 and 5.11. This method is also called "ordering of the variables" (Enders, 1995, 307) because a shock in z_t affects both series, while a shock in y_t does not instantly impact on z_t. z_t is thus called 'prior' to y_t. The observed errors e_{2t} can be attributed fully to the structural shock ϵ_{zt}, and the sequence ϵ_{yt} can be calculated with the help of 5.10.

Clearly, the ordering of variables is very important in this procedure and runs counter to the original advantage of VARs—that they do not require prior restrictions of the system. Ideally, the decision of how to order variables is motivated by economic theory, yet that is not always possible. Not surprisingly, this aspect is one of the major points of criticism of VARs voiced by a large number of authors (Kennedy, 2003, 347). Structural VARs as presented in the next section attempt to address this issue.

Structural VAR analysis

With little or no theoretical input, one has to be careful in interpreting the results of VARs identified in the way described above. It is useful in describing relationships between selected variables and in forecasting, but little can be said about causalities.

As a remedy, some authors have proposed identification procedures that are motivated explicitly by economic theory. Sims, in estimating a six-variable VAR, proposes coefficient restrictions in the matrix B that are consistent with economic theory (Enders, 1995, 330). Blanchard and Quah (1989) on the other hand restrict the cumulative effect of a demand shock, setting the respective $\sum \phi = 0$. The underlying assumption is that only a supply shock has a permanent effect on output. In the following section, linkages and sectoral development will be analyzed using another form of structural VAR analysis as proposed by Abeysinghe and Forbes (2005).

5.2.2 Linkages and Sectoral Development

As motivated above, I seek to investigate whether linkages between economic sectors are present and how large their contribution to individual sectoral development is. Methodologically I try to solve this puzzle by using an SVAR approach which not only allows to consider the direct input-output linkages between individual sectors, but also indirect effects that are not captured in IO-tables.[1]

The Econometric Model

The model is based on a structural VAR model developed by Abeysinghe and Forbes (2005), which they used for the analysis of trade linkages and

[1]This section is based upon joint work with Michael Wild (Schwank and Wild 2008)

output multiplier effects between countries. In our model the trade linkages are replaced by the linkages between sectors—stemming from intermediate inputs used in a sector that come from the rest of the economy. The reduced form representation of the output linkages is derived as follows.

Let Y be an individual sector's production, which is a composite of

$$Y = IM + A \tag{5.14}$$

where IM is the sector's output used as input in other sectors (intermediate output) and A is the part of output that is going to final consumption, exports and that is used in its own production. Rewriting equation (5.14) in a way where IM represents the sum of all the intermediate output going to the other (n-1) sectors gives

$$Y = \sum_{j=1}^{n-1} IM_j + A \tag{5.15}$$

We rewrite equation (5.15) in terms of growth rates to get

$$dY/Y = 1/Y \left[\sum_{j=1}^{n-1} dIM_j + dA \right] \tag{5.16}$$

In a next step, we assume that the intermediate output to sector j can be formulated as a function of total output in sector j.

$$IM_j = IM_j(Y_j) \tag{5.17}$$

Differentiating (5.17) with respect to Y_j gives

$$dIM_j = (\partial IM_j / \partial Y_j) dY_j \tag{5.18}$$

By inserting (5.18) into (5.16) we finally get

$$dY/Y = IM/Y \sum_{j=1}^{n-1} [\eta_j (IM_j/IM)(dY_j/Y_j)] + dA/Y \tag{5.19}$$

where $\eta_j = (\partial IM_j / \partial Y_j)(Y_j / IM_j)$ represents the elasticity of intermediate inputs flowing from the sector under scrutiny to sector j with respect to sector j's production. It is thus a measure of how strongly the intermediate output flowing to a specific sector will react to this sector's growth. By assuming now that this elasticity is the same across sectors and adding time and industry subscripts we can then rewrite and simplify equation 5.19 as

$$y_{it} = \alpha_i y_{it}^{im} + u_{it} \tag{5.20}$$

where $\alpha = (IM/Y)\eta$ and $y^{im} = \sum(IM_j/IM)y_j$. The elasticity η, assumed to be the same across sectors, can be taken out of the sum, which leaves other sectors's growth rates weighted by their contribution to the total intermediate output of the sector under scrutiny. The error term u_{it} captures omitted variables.

The core proposition of this formulation is that sectoral growth depends on the growth performance of other sectors in the economy. The extent of direct influence is determined by the intermediate output linkage IM_j. Yet, the model also captures indirect effects. For example, if output growth in the furniture manufacturing sector slows down, this obviously has a direct effect on the demand for machinery. There is also an indirect effect as the demand for transportation also diminishes, and thus transportation's demand of machinery. All the other determinants of sectoral growth will show up in the error term.

In a next step, and to amend our equations to econometric estimation, we transform the model and rewrite it as a structural vector autoregression. We thus assume that sectoral output performance can be explained by its own past output performance and the past output performance of all the other sectors in the economy. The latter enter weighted according to the linkage strength. This representation closely matches equation 5.20 where sectoral growth is explained by growth in the rest of the economy, weighted by the respective linkage strength. The transformation to an autoregressive process requires the assumption that the error terms u_{it} are correlated over time and across equations and that they follow a vector ARMA process as described in Abeysinghe and Forbes (2005, 359). Formally,

$$y_{it} = \lambda_i + \sum_{j=1}^{p} \phi_{ji} y_{it-j} + \sum_{j=0}^{p} \beta_{ji} y_{it-j}^{f} + \epsilon_i t \tag{5.21}$$

where λ_i is a vector of constants, the first sum captures all sectors' own lagged values and the second present and past values of the other sectors weighted by linkages. More precisely,

$$y_{it}^{f} = \sum_{j=1}^{n} w_{ij} y_{jt}$$

w_{ij}, the elements of the weighting matrix, are the shares of total intermediate output of sector i that go to the other sectors j (IM_j/IM). $i \neq j$. The sum of all shares of sector i's output to the other sectors must equal one. Equation (5.21) can be estimated separately for each sector of the economy. However, they can also be written as an SVAR system of equations. To illustrate, assume that there are three sectors in the economy, and the estimation takes only one lag into consideration. Then, the SVAR system of equations equals

$$\begin{bmatrix} 1 & -\beta_{01}w_{12} & -\beta_{01}w_{13} \\ -\beta_{02}w_{21} & 1 & -\beta_{02}w_{23} \\ -\beta_{03}w_{31} & -\beta_{03}w_{32} & 1 \end{bmatrix} \begin{bmatrix} y_{1t} \\ y_{2t} \\ y_{3t} \end{bmatrix} = \begin{bmatrix} \lambda_1 \\ \lambda_2 \\ \lambda_3 \end{bmatrix} + \\ + \begin{bmatrix} \phi_{11} & \beta_{11}w_{12} & \beta_{11}w_{13} \\ \beta_{12}w_{21} & \phi_{22} & \beta_{12}w_{23} \\ \beta_{13}w_{31} & \beta_{13}w_{32} & \phi_{33} \end{bmatrix} \begin{bmatrix} y_{1t-1} \\ y_{2t-1} \\ y_{3t-1} \end{bmatrix} + \begin{bmatrix} \epsilon_{1t} \\ \epsilon_{2t} \\ \epsilon_{3t} \end{bmatrix}$$

or, in a compact form,

$$(B_0 \cdot W)y_t = \lambda + (B_1 \cdot W)y_{t-1} + \epsilon_t \qquad (5.22)$$

where $(\cdot)$ stands for the element-products of the matrices. The matrix on the left hand side captures contemporaneous effects of the time series on each other, the 3x3 matrix on the right hand side captures the effect of own lagged values (ϕ_{ii}) and lagged values of the time series on each other (β_{1i}). The major difference of this approach to other SVAR works as stressed by Abeysinghe and Forbes (2005, 360) is that the model is overidentified as the elements of the weighting matrix w_{ij} are known, and that we do not have to assume that the error terms ϵ_{it} are uncorrelated as is usually the case, but can explicitly test for it.

Data Description

The model is applied to a number of settings at different levels of aggregation. A list of these sectors and the abbreviations used henceforth can be found in Table 5.1.

Our data set stems from the Quantec database, a commercial database which collects economic data for South Africa from different sources. The time period covered is 1970 to 2007, so we have 37 observations per time series. A highly aggregated sector composition—we look at the development of output in agriculture, mining, the secondary and the tertiary sector—constitutes our first layer of analysis. Unit roots tests confirm their presence, thus output enters in log first differences in the estimation. In order to assess the relevance of the MEC concept for sectoral development, we use two specifications, where the second divides the secondary sector in MEC activities (excluding mining) and non-MEC manufacturing. Figure 1 in the appendix shows the development of total output in these 5 sectors.

The corresponding weighting matrices that we need in the VAR are calculated by using data on the intermediate input used in each sector stemming from the rest of the economy. Crucially, we only consider domestic intermediate inputs, because only they will induce a backward linkage locally. This differentiation between domestic and total linkage effects is not always made in related analysis, perhaps due to a lack of data. Again, the Quantec database provides this information. Although we could have used only one weighting matrix for the whole period, we decided taking the accurate weighting matrix for each year, as this captures the change in input linkages over time. An exemplary matrix that indicates linkages between sectors is presented in Section 5.2.2—note that, in line with the model specification, the intermediate input stemming from the sector itself has been set to zero. Upon inspection, we see that the secondary sector is a large consumer of intermediate goods from other sectors, thus potentially and not surprisingly the sector with the most pulling power in the economy.

The second data set consists of a sample of output development and input linkages from 1970 to 2007 for the nine 2-digit sectors of the economy and is also taken from the Quantec database. Figure 2 in the appendix shows the individual sector's development over the whole period in absolute values. Again, we performed a unit root test in the level values and unsurprisingly detected it in almost every sector. Due to this and also to reflect the model's formulation in growth rates, the data is transformed into log first differences as well.

Lastly, we look at 10 manufacturing subsectors, applying the same procedure. Figure 3 in the appendix displays their output performance over the period under scrutiny. The outlier in sectoral development is the Petroleum, Chemicals and Plastics sector. It performed strongly throughout the last 37

Sectoral Abbreviations

1-digit Sectors

Agri	Agriculture, forestry and fishing
Min	Mining and quarrying
MEC	Pet, NMM, Basic Metals, Electricity
Sec	Secondary Sector (Man, Elec, Cons)*
Tert	All Services

2-digit Sectors

Agri	Agriculture, forestry and fishing
Min	Mining and quarrying
Man	Manufacturing*
Elec	Electricity, gas and water
Cons	Construction
Trad	Trade, catering and accommodation services
TrSC	Transport, storage and communication
FinI	Financial intermediation, insurance, real estate
Comm	Community, social and personal services

3-digit sectors

Food	Food, beverages and tobacco
Tex	Textiles, clothing and leather
Wood	Wood and paper; publishing and printing
Pet	Petroleum products, chemicals, rubber and plastic
NMM	Other non-metallic mineral products
Met	Metals, metal products, machinery and equipment
ElM	Electrical machinery and apparatus
Rad	Radio, TV, instruments, watches and clocks
Trans	Transport equipment
Furn	Furniture and other manufacturing

Table 5.1: Sectoral abbreviations, *when MEC is included, Sec and Man represent non-MEC manufacturing

years and did particularly well in the second half of the 1990s. Another important sector that grew strongly since the democratic opening is the Transport Equipment sector, reflecting the success of the industrial policy intervention in this specific area, the Motor Industry Development Programme.

In terms of linkages, there is no one sector within manufacturing that possesses a dominance equivalent to the manufacturing sector as a whole on a higher level. Overall, Transport Equipment draws the largest amount of inputs from other sectors—in accordance with the common understanding that automotive production is desirable because of its widespread linkages and thus justifying the support the sector receives.

Estimation Results

The estimation follows the approach by Zellner and Palm (1974) which estimates the model in the tradition of a seemingly unrelated regressions (SUR) model instead of using the standard SVAR approach. Thus, equation 5.21 is estimated for each sector separately. It can then be rewritten and expressed as a SVAR system so that impulse responses can be calculated.

Due to the fact that we only have yearly observations, we can include only one lag of each sector. We estimated the model in OLS, 2SLS and 3SLS. For the latter two approaches the residual correlations have been calculated and the Breusch-Pagan test on the diagonality of the residual-correlation matrix has been applied. Even though this test rejects the null of diagonality for some of the specifications (those involving 9 and 10 sectors), we decided to use the 3SLS estimates for our further analysis, as the number of significant correlation coefficients is lowest when compared to the 2SLS or OLS estimates. Tables 5.2, 5.3 and 5.4 display these coefficients for the three data sets, in the specification separating MEC activities from the rest of manufacturing. The other matrices are available on request, the number of significant non-zero correlations does not change, however. Those error term correlations that are significant at the 5% are printed in bold letters. For the highest level of aggregation there are no correlations significantly different from zero, indicating that the model is correctly specified. In the case of 9 (10 when one considers MEC manufacturing separately) sectors there are only 2. However, the 10 manufacturing subsectors include 9 statistically significant correlations, two of which are negative which is certainly surprising. This might be due to poor data quality or improper specification, it definitely implies that results must be interpreted very carefully for this level of aggregation because there are unresolved problems in the estimation.

Impulse Response Analysis

To answer the question about the direct and indirect impact of a change in one sector on the other sectors we use impulse response analysis (Hamilton, 1994). To this end we use the model estimated above and calculate the recursive relationships according to the VAR-results. This allows us to

	agri	min	mec	man	tert
agri	1.000				
min	-0.019	1.000			
mec	-0.184	0.204	1.000		
man	-0.209	0.047	0.256	1.000	
tert	0.170	0.291	0.216	-0.018	1.000

Table 5.2: Correlation for 3SLS

	Agri	Min	MEC	Man	Elec	Cons	Trade	TrSC	FinI	Comm
Agri	1.00									
Min	-0.19	1.00								
MEC	-0.09	0.03	1.00							
Man	-0.18	-0.22	0.23	1.00						
Elec	**0.39**	-0.15	0.07	-0.07	1.00					
Cons	-0.03	-0.05	-0.04	0.14	0.28	1.00				
Trade	0.19	0.06	0.14	0.07	0.16	-0.03	1.00			
TrSC	0.28	-0.15	**0.48**	-0.07	0.27	-0.09	0.01	1.00		
FinI	0.13	0.19	0.05	-0.25	-0.23	0.01	0.07	-0.03	1.00	
Comm	0.03	0.28	0.09	-0.23	0.22	-0.16	0.05	0.11	0.26	1.00

Table 5.3: Correlation for 3SLS, bold indicates significance at the 5 % level

isolate the effect of a unit shock in one sector on all the other sectors in the model. Technically, and as explained above in the theoretical section, the autoregressive system has to be transformed into a moving average form. The procedure is equivalent to the exposition in the theoretical section on impulse responses; starting with (5.22), by recursive replacement, we arrive at

$$y_t = \sum_{i=0}^{\infty} C_1^i u_{t-i} \tag{5.23}$$

where $u_{t-i} = (B_0 \cdot W)^{-1}\epsilon_{t-i}$ and $C_1 = (B_0 \cdot W)^{-1}(B_1 \cdot W)$. The impulse response matrix thus is $C_1^i(B_0 \cdot W)^{-1}$.

Looking at the overall economy at the highest level of aggregation first, the change of sectoral shares between 1970 and 2007 reveals that the tertiary sector has gained in importance, mostly at the expense of the primary sector, while the secondary sector remained roughly stable. A closer look, distinguishing between MEC and non-MEC manufacturing, reveals however that the latter declined in importance quite substantially, while MEC activities became more dominant (see Figure 5.1). Any statement about the

	Food	Tex	Wood	Pet	NMM	Met	ElecM	Rad	Trans	Furn
Food	1.00									
Tex	-0.07	1.00								
Wood	-0.21	0.31	1.00							
Pet	**-0.37**	0.18	0.05	1.00						
NMM	-0.25	0.17	**0.41**	-0.18	1.00					
Met	0.03	**0.49**	0.08	-0.04	0.16	1.00				
ElecM	**0.42**	**0.34**	0.04	0.15	-0.29	0.12	1.00			
Rad	**0.42**	0.25	-0.01	0.02	-0.06	-0.04	**0.62**	1.00		
Trans	-0.09	**-0.38**	0.31	-0.02	0.32	-0.22	-0.19	-0.23	1.00	
Furn	0.20	-0.03	-0.09	0.12	0.14	-0.21	0.08	0.12	**0.34**	1.00

Table 5.4: Correlation for 3SLS, bold indicates significance at the 5 % level

declining dependence of South Africa on its mining sector must therefore be qualified.

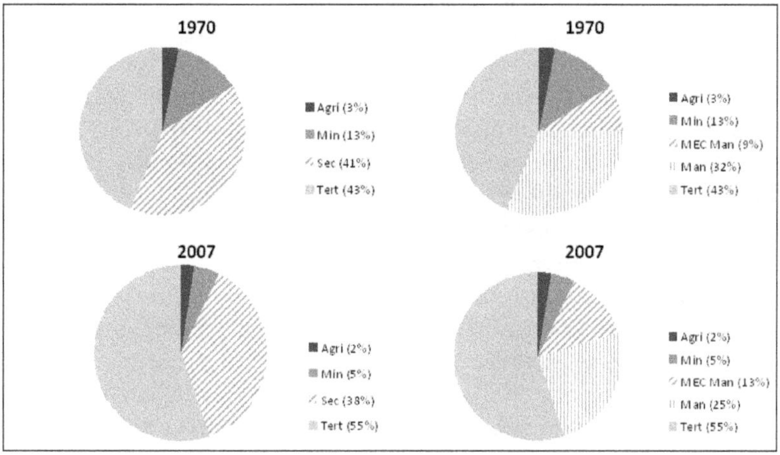

Figure 5.1: Share of Sectoral Output in Total Output in 1970 and 2007, Source: Quantec

On the other hand, a look at the weighting matrices used in the estimation (Table 5.5 shows an exemplary matrix for the year 2007) highlights the nonetheless central role of the secondary sector in the economy. The presentation of linkages is slightly unusual, so it requires explanation. Usually, the intermediate inputs used in a certain industry are displayed in rows,

used in	Agri	Min	Sec	Tert
	Intermediates from			
Agri	0.00	0.00	0.09	0.06
Min	0.00	0.00	0.09	0.15
Sec	0.97	0.96	0.00	0.79
Tert	0.03	0.04	0.82	0.00

used in	Agri	Min	MEC	Sec	Tert
	Intermediates stemming from				
Agri	0.00	0.00	0.07	0.07	0.06
Min	0.00	0.00	0.05	0.06	0.17
MEC	0.02	0.79	0.00	0.13	0.29
Sec	0.96	0.16	0.49	0.00	0.48
Tert	0.03	0.05	0.39	0.73	0.00

Table 5.5: Share of intermediate inputs stemming from sectors (column) used in sector (row), 2007. Source: Quantec

with each industry represented in a column. Here, the matrix has been transposed (for reasons that will hopefully become clear immediately), so each sector and the input it uses are to be found in the respective rows. The columns thus stand for the intermediate inputs domestically produced in the agricultural sector, and flowing to the rest of the economy—the intermediate input that remains within the sector has been set to zero in accordance with the theoretical model. These input flows to other sectors are reported as shares of total intermediate input goods produced in the respective sector. Therefore, they represent backward linkages—an expansion in a sector will increase its demand for intermediates, and thus induce expansion of production in upstream sectors.

In terms of the sectors analysed here, the secondary sector is by far the largest consumer of intermediate inputs. For example, more than 97% of agricultural goods that are used as intermediate inputs in the rest of the economy go to the secondary sector. Albeit agriculture being the strongest case, the centrality of manufacturing is also evident for the other sectors. The introduction of the MEC as a separate sector slightly changes this picture. Overall, the secondary sector, now encompassing only non-MEC manufacturing, still is the single largest demander of intermediates. Yet, as expected, and justifying this specific aggregation, intermediate mining goods are overwhelmingly used in the MEC.

Impulse responses to unit shocks in all sectors reveal a strong convergence to zero after 4 years. Table 5.6 thus displays the cumulated effects of a one-unit shock in each of the sectors on the other sectors over a period of four years. The table must be interpreted as follows: the shock in a certain industry has an accumulated effect on all the other industries as displayed in the respective row. For example, in the 4-sector setting a one-unit shock in the secondary sector leads to a 0.338 unit increase of output in agriculture

	Agri	Min	Sec	Tert
Shock in	*Cumulated impulse response*			
Agri	0.742	0.033	0.056	0.070
Min	-0.040	1.198	-0.121	-0.258
Sec	0.338	0.592	1.049	0.505
Tert	0.085	0.153	0.247	1.627

	Agri	Min	MEC	Sec	Tert
Shock in	*Cumulated impulse response*				
Agri	0.721	0.026	0.040	0.041	0.047
Min	-0.029	1.327	-0.070	-0.084	-0.156
MEC	0.044	0.563	1.101	0.113	0.194
Sec	0.437	0.355	0.408	1.330	0.503
Tert	0.151	0.232	0.307	0.433	1.592

Table 5.6: Cumulated impulse response after 4 periods

and relatively strong movements in other sectors of the economy as well—a result in line with the strong linkages detected in the manufacturing sector. The impacts of unit shocks in agriculture and mining are negligible, in the case of mining they are even negative. Lastly, spillovers from the services sector are smaller than those from manufacturing, but they are significant nonetheless, particularly when compared to agriculture and mining. Again, this is in line with linkage strength.

Once the MEC is considered separately, it becomes clear that the expansionary spillovers we observe from unit shocks in the secondary sector are mostly due to non-MEC manufacturing. An expansion of the MEC has a positive spillover on mining, but the effects on other sectors are comparatively small. A unit shock in MEC industries only leads to a 0.113 increase in manufacturing output in this specification, and growth spillovers to agricultural and services production are also much smaller than those observed with non-MEC manufacturing.

For a more detailed analysis, we looked at the nine (ten when MEC is stated separately) 2-digit sectors (disaggregating the secondary and the tertiary sectors). Graph 5.2 reestablishes the falling role of mining itself but the surge in MEC manufacturing activities. The growth in services was particularly strong in the transport, storage and communication, and in the financial intermediation, insurance and real estate sectors.

The corresponding weighting matrices are reported in the appendix (see Tables 3 and 4). With regards to the impulse responses, we can confirm

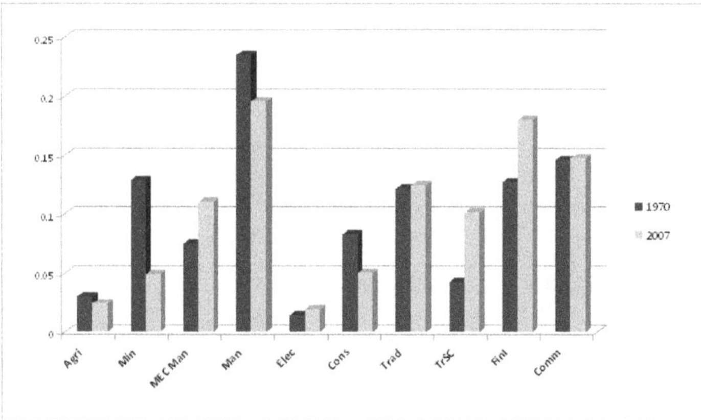

Figure 5.2: Share of Sectoral Output in Total Output in 1970 and 2007, Source: Quantec

	Agri	Min	Man	Elec	Cons	Trad	TrSC	FinI	Comm
Shock in				*Cumulated impulse response*					
Agri	0.736	0.022	0.034	0.036	0.023	0.034	0.026	0.041	0.053
Min	0.009	1.240	0.019	0.039	0.020	0.020	0.037	0.025	0.021
Man	0.558	0.711	1.196	0.725	0.318	0.650	0.409	0.858	0.587
Elec	0.005	0.045	0.011	1.711	0.044	0.010	0.007	0.019	0.007
Cons	0.160	0.227	0.343	0.233	2.250	0.259	0.162	0.403	0.195
Trad	0.133	0.170	0.266	0.395	0.541	1.664	0.364	0.862	0.237
TrSC	0.132	0.175	0.278	0.408	0.289	0.391	1.420	0.544	0.229
FinI	0.072	0.106	0.154	0.190	0.405	0.196	0.172	2.656	0.293
Comm	0.007	0.010	0.014	0.018	0.025	0.018	0.013	0.041	1.408

Table 5.7: Cumulated impulse response after 4 periods

the findings of the above specification at a higher level (see Tables 5.7 and 5.8). Agriculture and mining provide virtually no spillovers to the rest of the economy, while manufacturing appears to have significant pulling power. Interestingly, the construction sector has comparatively strong effects, given its size. Of the services sectors, community, social and personal services have by far the weakest effect, which is to be expected in the short run.

Once the MEC is reported separately (Table 5.8), we again find its pulling power small in comparison to the rest of the manufacturing sector (with the obvious exception of the mining industry). This is notable also

	Agri	Min	MEC	Man	Elec	Cons	Trad	TrSC	FinI	Comm
Shock in				*Cumulated impulse response*						
Agri	0.737	0.031	0.037	0.040	0.049	0.039	0.043	0.032	0.062	0.056
Min	0.007	1.223	0.011	0.012	0.024	0.014	0.013	0.020	0.017	0.013
MEC	0.163	0.728	1.111	0.279	0.637	0.315	0.362	0.308	0.611	0.343
Man	0.822	0.629	0.651	1.522	0.834	0.612	0.882	0.487	1.224	0.709
Elec	0.028	0.190	0.043	0.052	1.799	0.188	0.050	0.034	0.091	0.036
Cons	0.211	0.319	0.364	0.386	0.346	2.366	0.342	0.221	0.550	0.257
Trad	0.312	0.385	0.410	0.550	0.751	0.972	1.916	0.584	1.452	0.456
TrSC	0.265	0.369	0.412	0.482	0.717	0.596	0.649	1.492	0.976	0.403
FinI	0.150	0.205	0.211	0.273	0.337	0.600	0.326	0.258	2.793	0.397
Comm	0.047	0.064	0.069	0.085	0.108	0.138	0.103	0.070	0.206	1.372

Table 5.8: Cumulated impulse response after 4 periods

because the MEC is a significant consumer of intermediates from a number of sectors—yet this conventional backward linkage is not reflected to the same extent in the impulse response results.

Lastly, we have also attempted to model spillovers within the subsectors of manufacturing. As reported above, a substantial part of the error correlations in this specification are non-zero, which points to a misspecification of the model. Omitted variables are a likely cause, since we limit ourselves to a subsection of the economy here. Sectoral growth in the rest of the economy should be controlled for and we intend to do so in a follow up version of the paper. Therefore the following results have to be interpreted carefully and should be regarded as a first and tentative evaluation of the manufacturing subsectors.

Sectoral output shares in 1970 and 2007 (Figure 5.3) reveals the petroleum products, chemicals and plastics sector as the star performer within manufacturing over the last 37 years. Only transport equipment has gained in importance in a comparable manner—probably reflecting to an extent the efforts of the Motor Industry Development Programme. On the downside, labour-intensive sectors such as food and beverages and textiles now represent a much smaller part of total manufacturing, and the same is true for the metal, metal products and machinery sector.

The weighting matrix, printed for 2007 in the appendix (Table 5), further corroborates the positive role the transport equipment sector is playing in the economy: it is the sector with potentially the greatest pulling power, being the most important user of intermediate inputs from a variety of sectors. Other than transport equipment, food and beverages, the petroleum

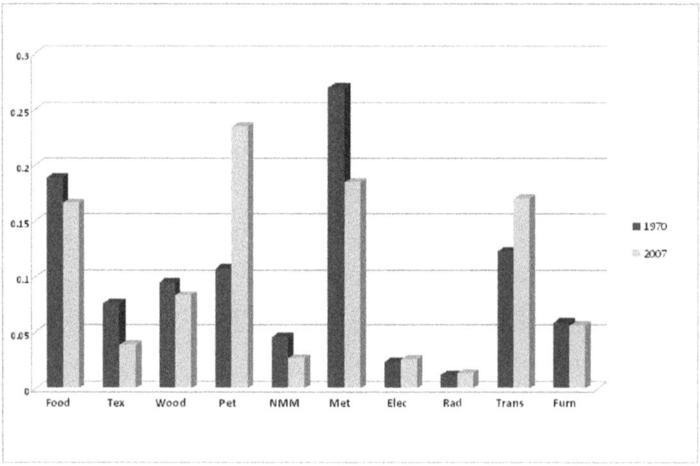

Figure 5.3: Share of Sectoral Output in Total Manufacturing Output in 1970 and 2007, Source: Quantec

products and chemicals sector significantly use intermediates from the rest of manufacturing sectors.

Results of the estimation and the corresponding impulse responses (Table 5.9) largely confirm these results. A unit shock in the transport equipment sector induces a 0.896 unit output increase in electrical machinery production, a 0.781 increase in textiles and clothing and a 0.760 increase in the metal products and machinery sector. Other sectors are pulled along as well. In contrast to the pure input linkages, the metal products and machinery sector creates stronger spillovers, particularly when compared to the petroleum products and chemicals sector. Given that the latter belongs to the MEC, these results provide a further hint (caution is due because of the specification problems) that MEC activities provide less of a spillover to the rest of the economy (in this case manufacturing) than non-MEC activities.

Conclusion

This chapter set out with a hypothesis derived from economic theory and the actual development experience of South Africa: that linkages are important

Shock in	Food	Tex	Wood	Pet	NMM	Met	ElecM	Rad	Trans	Furn
				Cumulated impulse response						
Food	1.332	0.067	0.083	0.090	0.092	0.074	0.066	0.056	0.096	0.053
Tex	0.519	1.071	0.077	0.159	0.085	0.094	0.079	0.070	0.110	0.156
Wood	0.115	0.079	0.987	0.149	0.049	0.067	0.057	0.076	0.073	0.176
Pet	0.372	0.215	0.130	1.346	0.201	0.193	0.170	0.153	0.236	0.200
NMM	0.068	0.064	0.061	0.099	1.003	0.085	0.065	0.053	0.087	0.057
Met	0.198	0.231	0.136	0.331	0.194	1.223	0.437	0.312	0.312	0.251
ElecM	0.079	0.080	0.064	0.164	0.117	0.190	1.113	0.338	0.099	0.128
Rad	0.031	0.037	0.027	0.040	0.023	0.040	0.111	0.979	0.028	0.128
Trans	0.508	0.781	0.227	0.583	0.475	0.760	0.896	0.723	1.442	0.380
Furn	0.101	0.140	0.144	0.121	0.055	0.120	0.075	0.117	0.074	1.226

Table 5.9: Cumulated impulse response after 4 periods

in the sectoral growth process of an economy. They provide opportunities for local upstream and downstream producers and thus shape the development path of an economy. In the case of South Africa, economic development was and continues to be strongly influenced by its minerals endowment. The manufacturing industry evolved around the mining sector, initially serving its needs, and even today, within manufacturing subsectors, those activities close to the natural resources of the country still play an important role.

We tried to empirically assess the strength of these linkages by estimating an SVAR model of sectoral output growth that explicitly incorporated the linkages between the various sectors in South Africa. With regards to the overall aggregations that we looked at first, the results strongly suggest that manufacturing as a whole is the sector with the greatest 'pulling power'in the economy, thereby justifying the continued attention it receives from policy makers. This is particularly true for those manufacturing activities that are not counted among the MEC. Positive shocks in the agricultural and mining sectors (and, to a lesser extent, the MEC) lead to much smaller growth spurts in the rest of the economy, and the same is also true for tertiary sectors that are comparable in size to manufacturing.

On a higher level of disaggregation, the growth performances of the ten subsectors within manufacturing in general are less dependent on each other, reflecting the fact that linkages to sectors outside manufacturing—neglected in this setting—play an important role. Linkage effects therefore have less explanatory power. The sector that stands out is the transport equipment sector that has by far the strongest growth effects on the rest of manufacturing. Compared to simple linkage via intermediate inputs, we also observe a relatively prominent role of the metals, metal products and machinery sector, which displays stronger growth impacts on the rest of manufacturing than the petroleum products and chemicals sector.

The policy conclusions that can be drawn from this support a widely accepted stance in the literature and in policy circles: that South Africa will need to support its manufacturing sector to achieve higher overall growth rates, and that within manufacturing, more diversification and less reliance on capital-intensive sectors close to the mineral endowment such as chemicals is needed. It also vindicates support for the auto industry, given its central role within the manufacturing subsectors.

Chapter 6

Industrial Policy Revisited

When reviewing South Africa's industrial development in Chapter Two, the goals, instruments chosen and outcomes of industrial policy have been highlighted consistently. After the theoretical and empirical work in Chapters Three to Five, I want to return to this theme now and take a closer look at very recent developments: the shifts of the South African government towards a more interventionist economic policy regime, noticeable since at least 2004, and explicitly linked also to a reformulation of industrial policy.[1]

Sectoral development and the linkages between these sectors have been the overarching focus of this thesis, and this chapter will attempt to remain within this framework. It will analyse the "National Industrial Policy Framework" (Department of Trade and Industry, 2007a), the main reference document for industrial policy makers, from this point of view. Particularly, I will try to assess whether this policy change is likely to facilitate more sectoral diversification—away from the dependence on resource-based sectors and towards more dynamically developing and possibly labour-intensive sectors, also contributing to a healthier and more stable balance of payments. However, I will not limit myself to sectoral analysis but also try to locate this policy shift within a broader observable change in policy towards a developmental state. An analysis of proposed measures, the actors and institutions involved in the process and a tentative evaluation of hitherto implementation in the realm of industrial policy provide a case study that allows to draw broader conclusions on South Africa's rocky path towards a developmental regime.

[1]This section is based on Schwank (2008).

The concrete and applied policy steps that together make up the policy shift are taken from official policy documents. Additional insight is gained from interviews with key stakeholders and policy makers involved in the process and academic experts in the field that have closely followed the evolution of industrial policy since the advent of democracy.

6.1 Developmental States

The notion of the 'developmental state' was first introduced by Chalmers Johnson in his landmark study on trade and industrial policy in Japan (Johnson, 1982). In it he defines the Japanese state as a plan-rational or developmental state, differentiating it from the market-rationality of the United States (ibid., 18ff.). According to Johnson, a developmental state leads the industrialisation drive of the economy by pursuing strategic social and economic goals, usually with an emphasis on industrial policy. "In the plan-rational state, the government will give greatest precedence to industrial policy, that is, to a concern with the structure of domestic industry and with promoting the structure that enhances international competitiveness."(ibid., 19). Johnson further asserts that a regulatory state like the US does not place emphasis on industrial structure, instead limiting itself to defining and monitoring the rules of the market process.

Following Johnson, a number of authors have stressed the state's crucial contribution to growth performance, for example in East Asian countries like Taiwan and South Korea. The seminal works are Amsden (1989), Wade (1990) and Evans (1995), and an overview is provided in Chang (2006). This literature generally addresses two main questions: 1) What kind of interventions resulted in the phenomenal growth rates in these countries, and 2) Under which conditions did the incumbents choose to adopt and implement this set of policies successfully? Fine (2006, 103ff.) uses these two guiding questions to divide the literature into an economic school focussing on the former question and a political school mainly concerned with the latter. Although authors of both schools would probably claim to have a broader research agenda, this distinction is useful for a brief summary of their main ideas.

6.1.1 Economic and Political Schools

Alice Amsden, whose work shall serve as an example of the economic school, posits that development is about increases in productivity that are potentially greatest in manufacturing. This is why developmental states like South Korea have subsidized the entry of entrepreneurs into the secondary sector at an early stage (Amsden, 1989, 2001). As the market process would not have led to diversification, due to a number of market failures, the policy makers deliberately had to "get prices wrong" (Amsden, 2001, 10), thereby setting incentives that facilitated manufacturing investment. For developing countries, the market failures most commonly identified in the literature are information and coordination externalities. The former relate to the uncertainty of entrepreneurs with regards to the profitability of new investments. They do not know the exact costs involved in the exercise, and thus cannot know whether it should be pursued or not. In case of failure, the costs are entirely borne by the entrepreneur, in case of success, the economy as a whole profits since the cost structure of the respective activity is now known and imitators will enter the industry and quickly erode any monopoly profits. Therefore the expected social value exceeds the private value and investment will be in short supply. The latter, coordination externalities, relate to the necessity of simultaneous, large-scale investments to make individual activities profitable (for example Rodrik, 2007, 104ff.).

Developmental states attempted to overcome these market failures through interventions in the form of developmental banking, subsidised credits in targeted sectors, and managed trade that combined import substitution and tariff protection with export subsidies. Crucially, support was always combined with policy standards (e.g. local content requirements) and performance standards. The latter, best exemplified by minimum export requirements, guaranteed efficient production, and a failure to comply with them resulted in a withdrawal of support. All contributions by the economic school identify an interventionist industrial policy at the heart of a set of policy interventions that led to industrial diversification and rapid economic growth, with macroeconomic, trade and welfare policies supporting the industrialisation strategy.

While the pursuit of industrial policy and trade policy, such as the import substitution strategy, was by no means geographically limited to East Asia, few other developing countries having implemented such policies can boast a comparable growth performance. Within the political school, authors such as Evans (1995) and Kohli (2004) attempt to understand why some states were so successful while others failed. The key issues under consideration are policy coherence and state capacity. Firstly, they relate to the state's capability to define and pursue narrow goals—industrialisation and rapid economic growth—that lead to a coherent development strategy and a coherent economic policy. Secondly, the successful implementation of policy in turn relies on a competent and capable bureaucracy, based on a meritocratic civil service regime, and a pilot agency that coordinates economic policy across all government agencies (e.g. the MITI in Japan, the Economic Planning Bureau in Korea).

Since the state is perceived as an actor in its own right analytically, both authors take into account the state's relation to society and classes. Evans coins the term "embedded autonomy" which captures the state's autonomy from particularistic interests, i.e. its ability to resist the pressure of influential groups with access to the corridors of power, and its simultaneous responsiveness to the needs of industry (Evans, 1995, 50). The concept of 'autonomy' specifically refers to the state's dominance over private capital, allowing it to withdraw support from a certain sector or company if that is perceived necessary for the economy as a whole. If it were merely a reflection of capitalist interests, it would not be able to prevent such 'rent-seeking' activities. On the other hand, 'embeddedness' describes the close cooperation and manifold ties between state and business that allow the state to elicit information from the private sector and to "orchestrate their activities" (Evans, 1995, 53). Kohli on the other hand asserts that successful developmental states usually pursue industrialisation and rapid economic growth in an elitist alliance with producer or capitalist groups. This alliance often comes at the expense of labour, which finds its demands suppressed by an authoritarian regime—notwithstanding those social policy initiatives that are perceived to be contributory to growth (Kohli, 2004, 10).

6.1.2 Social Actors and the Accumulation Regime

There are two critical omissions that Fine observes in the developmental state literature: an absence of the scrutiny of social actors and their interests, or class analysis, particularly visible in Evans' notion of state autonomy; and a lack of consideration of the structural features of an economy, the sectoral composition of its output and the specific system of accumulation in place - the "sectoral composition and level of investment, financed and coordinated through private and public institutions [...] specific to each country, reflecting its history and dynamic as well as its evolving class structure" (Fine, 2006, 115).

Kohli attempts to rectify the omission of social actors by emphasising the significance of the alliance between South Korea's capitalist class and the South Korean state under Park Chung Hee (in power from 1961 to 1979), in which the state played the dominant role. Under this regime, labour was tightly controlled and political mobilisation was suppressed (Kohli, 2004, 96ff.). Fine and Rustomjee agree with this description of the class nature of the Korean state, but they also show how pressure from below was influential in the land reform (Fine and Rustomjee, 1996, 46). The developmental state therefore needs to be situated in a conflictual context where policies invariably "have class biases either in their purpose or in their unintended outcomes. Some classes or groups become beneficiaries while others are alienated." (Cho and Kim, 1998, 130). Furthermore, state autonomy itself is a function of social and class conditions and not merely of bureaucratic competence. In a developmental context, it depends on the potential of resistance of the working class and peasants and of the old ruling class, presumably uninterested in change, and on whether a developmental alliance can be formed with capitalist groups (ibid., 131). Thus, conflicting class interests shape state institutions and policies and also determine the extent of state autonomy.

Viewed within the South African context, state capacity and particularly state autonomy will therefore inevitably rely on the power, influence and access of various groups to state institutions as well. When compared to the East Asian prototypes, the main difference that is evident is the higher degree of mobilisation of the working class—which has direct access to policy formulation via the inclusion of the unions in the governing alliance—and the historically stronger, more independent and outward-oriented capital groups that have grown in the mining sector. Both these groups and their interests and pursuit thereof will have to be taken into consideration when analysing questions of capacity and coherence in policy, where the latter stems to a large extent from state autonomy from particular interests.

With regards to the accumulation regime of South Korea, "the state's near-exclusive commitment to high growth coincided with the profit-maximizing needs of private entrepreneurs" (Kohli, 2004, 12f.). The domestically owned and diversified chaebols were mostly responsible for real accumulation, and government policy ensured domestic investment opportunities and their profitability in targeted sectors. At first this mainly applied to labour intensive sectors such as textiles, but in the 1970s the government also orchestrated a push into heavy industries such as steel and ship-building, which again served the interests of large-scale domestic capital and further marginalized other sections of business (Fine and Rustomjee 1996, 46, see also Cho and Kim 1998, 144).

The case of South Africa is quite different: historically, investment has been concentrated in mining and closely related downstream manufacturing. It has come from a small number of hugely influential conglomerates and from the state itself that long favoured a development path along these lines, particularly during the apartheid years. A developmental strategy of industrial diversification and less reliance on the mineral endowment thus represents a break with past patterns, and it requires influential and powerful actors in the country to change their strategies—a considerably more difficult challenge then the one confronting a state like South Korea in the 1960s and 1970s. Again, these structural preconditions have to be kept in mind when assessing any developmental—in our case industrial—policy initiatives.

To summarise, in this light neither state capacity and policy coherence nor economic policy choices can be analysed in isolation from the specific system of accumulation and the class relations in an economy. The latter shape institutions and policy choices and thus certainly help to explain the existence (or absence) of a coherent strategy and the expertise and capacity (or lack thereof) in different government agencies. Therefore, the following study of the South African developmental state, both as a broad concept and in a case study on industrial policy, will attempt to include these concepts and also shed light on social actors, their interests, the structure they create and how they shape the developmental regime.

6.1.3 A South African Developmental State

Based on a narrow interpretation of this literature, the definition of a developmental state is often limited to a list of interventionist economic policies, and industrial policies in particular, as well as an analysis of the state's capacity to implement them coherently. However a critical reading reveals as conducted above reveals that such an analysis must be placed within the context of a broader view of class relations and the accumulation regime within an economy. I will try to show that this analytical ambiguity is reflected in the controversial use of the concept and in studies on the South African development state thus far.

The Evolving Strategy of the ANC

In the mid-1990s the emerging economic strategy of the first African National Congress (ANC) government encouraged little debate on the notion of South Africa as a developmental regime. Too firmly was their strategy rooted in a discourse on macro-economic stabilisation that left little room for an activist state. The publication of GEAR (Growth, Employment and Redistribution) as a cornerstone of economic policy confirmed a narrow understanding of this stabilisation approach—fiscal restraint and inflation reduction accompanied by a liberalised trade regime. The adoption of GEAR and its consequences for the economy have been analysed above, in Chapter Two. At this point, I focus on the criticism of GEAR that emerged quickly within the ruling party and the recent strategic shifts that resulted from the criticism.

Not surprisingly, GEAR was met with stiff opposition from the ANC's alliance partners on the left—the trade union federation COSATU and the Communist Party of South Africa (SACP), exponents of which were later labelled 'ultra-leftist' by Mandela's presidential successor, Thabo Mbeki. The criticism never subsided, fuelled by a very mixed performance of the economy. While inflation and budget deficits came down, growth remained well below expectations. Contrary to the government's predictions, private and foreign direct investment did not pick up and massive job losses, particularly in manufacturing, led to an ever rising unemployment rate. As a result, social protests over delivery increased sharply, particularly after the second democratic election in 1999, and gave critics of GEAR more leverage (Ballard et al., 2006, 397).

In response, the ANC shifted its priorities, and the change became noticeable in more expansionary budgets after 2001. These were loudly trumpeted in the election campaign and the pre-election budget of 2004, which promised to halve unemployment and poverty in the country's second decade of democracy. A more activist state was supposed to increase public expenditure, particularly investment in infrastructure, and revitalise rather than privatise public enterprises, as well as further boost social and welfare spending (Daniel et al., 2005, xxiii).

While these changes are interpreted as a logical next step in government—successful macro-stabilisation followed by micro-economic reform and targeted intervention—in this case they also clearly signal a change in course. The ANC's key strategic documents indicate that it has now committed itself to building a developmental state. This state aims to mobilise society and gain a strong popular mandate in order to drive change and attain "sustained development based on high growth rates, restructuring of the economy and socio-economic inclusion" (African National Congress, 2007). The declared intention of this developmental state is to obtain the capacity to formulate the national agenda (e.g. a growth strategy) and implement policy throughout government spheres.

In terms of economic policy, this agenda has been most clearly laid out in the government-led Accelerated and Shared Growth Initiative (AsgiSA) which is supposed to remove the binding constraints that prevent the economy from achieving growth rates compatible with its ambitious socioeconomic goals. The most prominent interventions include increased infrastructure investments, an industrial policy with detailed sector strategies, the addressing of capacity issues within the public sector, skills development and the stabilisation of the exchange rate (The Presidency, 2006).

Since 2004, non-interest spending by the central government has increased annually by an average of more than 9%. The bulk of the money has gone into increased public investment, both by the government itself and by public enterprise, which was the fastest growing position, rising annually by almost 20% in real terms (Department of Finance, 2007, 46f.). In addition to roads and public transport infrastructure, this area also covers increased spending on social infrastructure, such as health facilities, schools, public housing, and access to electricity and water for poor communities. Social expenditure is thus geared towards increasing productivity levels. The government's vehement resistance against a monthly basic income grant, which would, according to various statements, establish a 'culture of dependency', is further indication of a 'productivist' social policy typical of developmental states. Despite increased spending, service delivery has not always kept the pace however, as many critics have pointed out and as the Treasury readily admits in its own assessment (Department of Finance, 2007, 49). Capacity problems within the relevant parts of the public sector—particularly the provincial departments of health and education—are responsible for poor delivery.

State-owned enterprises are considered key actors in the more interventionist strategy and have received budget boosts since 2004 that have allowed them to address infrastructure backlogs in electricity (by the electricity provider Eskom) and road and public transport infrastructure (by Transnet, which is responsible for South Africa's ports and railways). The state's attitude towards these public companies is quite telling in the context of strategic shifts in economic policy. Once a cornerstone of the apartheid regime's plan to achieve economic self-reliance, these businesses were partially privatised towards the end of the 1980s when a black dominated government became an increasingly likely prospect. Under the banner of GEAR, the ANC vowed to continue this policy, however, it preferred to label it 're-structuring' and aimed for the mobilisation of resources, increased efficiency, international investment and the diversification of ownership in the national economy through sales to black-owned companies (Southall, 2007a, 208). For various reasons, real progress has been slow, and in 2004 the minister of public enterprise, Alec Erwin, announced a "major investment and efficiency programme" for state-owned enterprises in keeping with the general shift to a more interventionist policy, along with a pledge to spend 165 billion Rand "to address chronic backlogs" (Southall, 2007a, 219). Quite characteristically, the state-owned enterprises are also supposed to be drivers of change and transformation, providing opportunities for aspiring black professionals through affirmative action hiring and black-owned companies in their procurement.

Another core aspect of the growth initiative AsgiSA is its pledge to implement sector strategies that provide targeted support for prioritised sectors. As a result, the cabinet adopted the National Industrial Policy Framework (NIPF) (Department of Trade and Industry, 2007a) in January 2007. It was released to the public in August 2007 and will be analysed in detail in the following section on industrial policy.

One last point worth mentioning here is the coordination and centralisation drive of the government under the auspices of President Thabo Mbeki, as it relates to the state's capacity to formulate and implement policy in a coherent way. Under Mbeki's reign, the Presidency became the coordinating and guiding unit within the government and steadily extended its influence over policy formulation. Additionally, departments were organised in clusters to align programmes and implementation (Makgetla, 2005, 12). Together with interventions to improve skill levels of civil servants and efficiency in service delivery, these initiatives clearly aim to replicate the capable bureaucracies that were characteristic of East Asian developmental states. While these efforts were positively received by cabinet ministers (ibid.), the concurrent centralisation of decision making within the ANC was far more controversial. It caused major discontent among ordinary ANC members and was an important reason Mbeki lost the party's presidency to his bitter rival, the trade union and communist backed Jacob Zuma, in December 2007.

Problems of Implementation?

In a first critical assessment of South Africa's attempts to become a more developmental state, a number of authors have pointed out stumbling blocks that could derail the project. Most prominently and in line with the emphasis of developmental state scholars, they point out limits in the state's capacity to implement policy, as well as a general lack of coherence in policy.

Capacity problems abound in large parts of the public sector and the resulting failures in service delivery are explicitly acknowledged by the government (The Presidency, 2006). They are most visible in the failure of provincial and national departments to spend allocated budgets and in the large number of unfilled positions in the higher management echelons of public administration (Hamlyn, 2007). They are however not uniform, neither across government agencies nor across regions. The National Treasury, at the heart of successful macroeconomic stabilisation efforts since 1994, is an oft-cited example for administrative excellence within government. It contrasts starkly with other departments that were not able to stamp their authority on government policy to such an extent—I will come back to this issue when assessing industrial policy below.

Nonetheless, the existence of capacity problems is not altogether surprising in light of South Africa's history. Public service delivery was extremely uneven during the apartheid years, and the notorious education policy led to a vast shortage of skilled workers. This shortage is most acutely felt in the public sector which not only aspires to become more efficient, but also more representative (Southall, 2007b, 6). If there is an equity/efficiency trade-off, this might be indicative of a broader dilemma for the ANC: Does its democratic tradition and its aim to transform South Africa into a truly democratic society stand at odds with the single-mindedness and coherence of the archetypal developmental state? In more controversial terms, is there a democracy/growth trade-off? Kohli emphasises this point: "[An] element of 'ruthlessness' or of coercion in its various forms has also been omnipresent in the most successful cases of rapid industrialization in the contemporary developing world. The normative implication then is to treat with suspicion claims that trade-offs are not necessary and that all good things can readily go together" (Kohli, 2004, 422). The broad-based alliance that governs South Africa certainly cannot and does not intend to pursue industrialisation and economic growth as its only policy goals. The racial transformation of the public sector is one example of this, and progressive labour laws are another.

Perhaps more importantly, the structure of South African capital bears little resemblance to that of East Asian countries. It was and continues to be shaped by the mining industry and big business, and therefore has a very different outlook. It is certainly more outward-oriented and therefore less inclined to favour domestic industrialisation (Makgetla, 2005, 6). While the ANC is aware of the powerful and antagonistic interests that pervade the South African socio-economic landscape, there seem to be different approaches to achieving policy coherence within the party. While the left argues for mass mobilisation of the working class and the poor and a strengthening of the party base to ensure hegemony for these forces (South African Communist Party, 2006, 29ff.), others strike a distinctly different chord. Alec Erwin, the minister of public enterprise and an influential member of Mbeki's cabinet, argues for the mobilisation of "a *multi-class* political force capable of designing and effecting a strong state" (emphasis added, Erwin, 2007). He asserts that, in the context of a globalising economy that constantly reduces policy space for nations while weakening local capital and the working class, national development can only be fostered by an alliance between these forces under the leadership of a strong state. Thus, there are different visions of the developmental state within the governing alliance, and the concept of development is vague enough to accommodate both those who aim to reduce the costs of doing business by eliminating binding constraints for investors and those who aim to alter the development trajectory of the South African economy by breaking the alliance between state and capital. While both of these camps want higher growth to tackle unemployment and poverty, their envisioned ways of achieving this goal are radically different.

The leadership struggle within the ANC, which saw leftist candidate Jacob Zuma's ascent to power, is indicative of the conflicting visions of a developmental state within the ANC. As a result of internal upheaval,

Mbeki and other key proponents of the '1996 class project' (a term the communist party SACP uses to describe the neo-liberal turn of the ANC that cumulated in the 1996 publication of GEAR) were relieved of their positions by the party base and replaced by a more left-leaning leadership. However, the battle is far from over and differing ideas and interests within the party will likely continue to be reflected in an incoherent policy. In this light, incoherence is better perceived as a result of conflicting class interests, as exposed in the above examples, than simply as a weakness of the state.

In the following case study on industrial policy, I try to illustrate South Africa's attempts to become a developmental state and 'the problems it has encountered along the way'. As I attempted to illustrate in the general discussion above, these problems are related to issues of capacity and coherence which cannot be fully grasped without considering the peculiar design of South Africa's accumulation regime.

6.2 Industrial Policy in a Developmental Regime

The analysis of industrial policy of course needs to be embedded in both a discussion of industrial development and the broader directions of economic policy. While this has been the focus of Chapter Two, I will recount these issues in the time period after 1994 below, with a particular focus on industrial policy measures implemented. This discussion will lead us to the recent shifts in industrial policy, expressed in the publication of the National Industrial Policy Framework NIPF in 2007, and to an evaluation of its content and hitherto implementation.

6.2.1 Industrial Policy after 1994

An interventionist industrial policy has undeniably formed the core of all East Asian developmental states. This means that an evolving range of sectors have been targeted over time and vigorously supported through an array of policy measures—from R&D support and subsidised credit to direct state involvement by public companies. South Africa's apartheid regime adhered to a comparable industrial policy when it supported and essentially built up industries such as iron and steel and later heavy chemicals. As was the case in East Asia, the ultimate aim of South Africa's policy was to preserve national security. However, while East Asian industrial policies successfully generated jobs and economic growth in the process, South African policy makers' focus on the white population and on economic and, more importantly, military self-sufficiency created different incentives. The resulting interventions—particularly the reinforcement of the minerals-energy core of the economy—were massive and continue to shape the South African economy.

After 1994, with macroeconomic stabilisation looming large in policy makers' minds, industrial policy and more specifically sector-specific interventions were not a priority area for the incoming government. Yet, this certainly was not due to a shortage of discussions on industrial policy within the ANC, its alliance partners and associated or sympathetic researchers. There were a number of research projects, but the discussions failed to produce a clear path forward in terms of industrial policy strategy, and the resulting ambiguities might be one reason for industrial policy's shadowy existence in the 1990s.

The most prominent among these works certainly was the report of the Industrial Strategy Project (ISP), a group of researchers affiliated with the biggest union federation COSATU, named "Improving Manufacturing Performance in South Africa" (Joffe et al., 1995). Its focus was on increasing the productivity of South African firms, eschewing a strategy based on cheap labour and instead focusing on moving up the value chain. The authors explicitly recognized that jobs thus created would in their majority be located at the upper end of the skills spectrum and that industrial policy alone would not solve the unemployment crisis. This view was also associated with a specific interpretation of the weaknesses of the manufacturing sector—resulting from a failed or exhausted import-substitution industrialisation strategy (Lewis et al., 2004, 154f.). In terms of policy recommendations, trade policy reform, skills creation and the support of technological upgrading and innovation (Joffe et al., 1995, 31) hinted at a supply-side oriented policy focus.

On the other hand, the work by Fine and Rustomjee (1996) interpreted South Africa's industrial history in a different light (see above). There are no easily applicable policy recommendations to draw from this strand of work, but "the MEC view tends to a more *dirigiste* approach to industrial policy, one inclined to a close interaction between the state and those relatively few firms that dominate the MEC core, interactions designed to strengthen their material linkages with the rest of the economy " (Lewis et al., 2004, 155).

Hirsch formulated this as a choice between support for "smaller businesses and pre-reform uncompetitive labour-absorbing sectors [or] policies designed to exploit existing comparative advantages and bigger projects" (Hirsch, 2005, 122). He also states that the actual outcome was more of an "unresolved compromise" (ibid.). This critical assessment from an inside perspective is widely shared in the literature and with policy makers. The Department of Trade and Industry initially focused on trade policy and supply side measures—with a myriad of support programmes for firms—in line with the priorities formulated in the Industrial Strategy Project report. Trade liberalisation was combined with a range of general—i.e. not sector-specific—supply side measures in order to boost international competitiveness and exports. These included export credit guarantees and support in market access, innovation, research and development. However, firms do not appear to have frequently taken advantage of these measures and this has limited their effectiveness (Kaplan, 2004, 626).

At the same time, there were also strong elements of continuity in the implementation of industrial policy which was historically tilted towards the MEC (Zalk, 2007). One of the most important supply side programmes, the Spatial Development Initiatives, and its flagship project, the Maputo Development Corridor, provide a telling example. The initiative intends to revitalise a long-neglected region of South Africa, Mpumalanga, by making it globally competitive. But the benefits of the improvement in infrastructure have been limited mostly to the anchor project—the huge aluminium smelters of Mozal that are extremely capital intensive and provide very few linkages with the regional economy (Soederbaum 2004, 160ff., see also Lewis et al. 2004, 171).

Another example is the Strategic Industrial Projects programme, implemented by the DTI between 2002 and 2005, providing tax relief for large investment projects. Again, these projects were mainly concentrated in heavy industry (Roberts, 2005, 25). The same is true for the lending of the Industrial Development Corporation (IDC), South Africa's main development bank and holding company. It has historically supported industries close to mining and continued this pattern throughout the 1990s. Continuity was particularly visible also in those fields of industrial policy that were not under the direct control of the DTI, such as infrastructure provision, electricity or arms procurement (Mohamed, 2007).

In contrast to these ambiguities, the commitment to trade liberalisation was strong. At first sight, this might seem surprising, but many in the incoming government viewed protective tariffs as support for a privileged group of white business and embraced a strategy of opening the economy to global competition (Lewis et al., 2004, 161). South Africa's offer to GATT in early 1994 was a joint effort by business, labour and the incoming government (institutionally situated in the 'National Economic Forum'), and was publicly endorsed by the then presumptive president Mandela. The country became a founding member of the WTO in 1995 and implemented a simplified tariff structure and an overall reduction of tariffs. At the same time, the expensive and—by many accounts—inefficient export support scheme GEIS (General Export Incentive Scheme) was abolished (Hirsch, 2005, 127ff.). This focus on trade policy also had institutional consequences, as the negotiation and administrative processes (including those related to later trade agreements with the Southern African Development Community and the European Union) tied up many of the resources available in the DTI, an institution already heavily taxed by internal restructuring processes (Makgetla, 2007; Mohamed, 2007).

One notable exception to this pattern—a successful sectoral support programme outside the confines of the MEC—is the automotive industry. The Motor Industry Development Programme (MIDP) managed to retain production in South Africa amidst a significant reduction of tariffs, helping producers achieve international competitiveness. Moreover, there are significant linkages to other sectors due to local sourcing incentives (Roberts, 2005, 28). Historically, producers in the local auto industry built a variety of vehicles (at high unit costs), predominantly for the protected domestic market. The imperatives of global trade reform and South Africa's commitment to liberalisation necessitated a reorientation and a move away from inward-oriented production patterns. The industry development programme, started in 1995, gradually reduced tariffs on fully built-up vehicles and at the same time introduced 'Import Rebate Credit Certificates' that could be earned by exporters of vehicles and components and allowed them the duty-free import of built-up vehicles and components (see for example Black, 2001, 782). The intention of course was to entice producers to reduce the variety of locally produced vehicles and focus on one or fewer models, manufactured at efficient scale and globally competitive costs. Although there is criticism, particularly from the point of view of domestic auto prices paid by South African consumers (there still is significant protection of the domestic market), the MIDP is generally regarded as a major success of industrial policy. The success of this sector, however, is exceptional and has not been repeated in other sectors where firms place little importance on the Department of Trade and Industry's strategies (Kaplan, 2004, 627). Perhaps characteristically, the MIDP was an outcome of research carried out within the union-aligned Industrial Strategy Project rather than an initiative of the DTI initially (Mohamed, 2007).

Not surprisingly, most assessments of industrial policy in the first decade of democracy are critical and find only limited success. As seen above, South Africa has certainly failed to significantly develop manufacturing capacities outside the MEC and limited pockets such as auto components. To a large extent, this view is shared by policy makers and also informs new policy priorities. Alan Hirsch, the former Chief Director of the DTI, states: "It is probably fair to say that government is haunted by the nagging feeling that we could have and should be doing more. Surely we know enough to be able to identify some key sectors that can grow faster with effective policies" (Hirsch, 2005, 160). This statement must be understood within the context of a gradual shift in emphasis occurring at the time—towards a more interventionist industrial policy that targets sectors explicitly and on a broader basis.

6.2.2 National Industrial Policy Framework

The industrial policy initiative NIPF must be examined within the broader context of the government's growth programme AsgiSA which—at the time it was implemented—already contained explicit references to this yet-to-be-published document. Just as AsgiSA provided a framework for the overall growth strategy, the NIPF lays out a vision for South Africa's industrial development and intends to be the point of reference for all stakeholders in the process. Most importantly, this includes other government agencies and private business. Through the publication of this document, the DTI seeks to achieve better coordination within government to provide the necessary coherence in industrial policy and to offer the private sector security about future policy directions.

The document begins with a critical assessment of industrial policy since 1994, admitting that, amongst other shortcomings, "sectoral programmes to restructure the industrial economy [...] were generally not of a sufficient scale to induce the necessary structural change." (Department of Trade and Industry, 2007a, 13). It further states that, in order to "facilitate diversification beyond our current reliance on traditional commodities and non-tradable services" (ibid., 6) and move towards tradable, labour-absorbing goods and services, South Africa cannot rely on market forces alone but has to implement an interventionist strategy based on an analysis of concrete constraints and opportunities. The DTI thus rejects the 'one-size-fits-all' approach of the Washington consensus and considers this the main lesson to be learnt from the successful development trajectory of the newly industrialised East Asian countries, thereby locating itself firmly within the discourse on developmental states.

In order to be successful, the DTI reckons that industrial policy interventions need to take place in a suitable macroeconomic, regulatory and infrastructural environment. With regards to the macroeconomy, this implies that fiscal, monetary and industrial policy need to better complement each other—a stable and competitive exchange rate is explicitly mentioned at this point. Furthermore, interventions are to take place on a sectoral level and on cross-cutting issues that concern the whole economy through Key Action Plans (KAPs) (Department of Trade and Industry, 2007b), and will always be preceded by consultation with business and other stakeholders in a so-called 'self-discovery process'. The Key Action Plans comprise detailed benchmarks to evaluate outcomes, name the stakeholders responsible for implementation and put specific time frames on expected completion. Although the NIPF itself does not intend to pick sectors (its focus lies on defining procedures), a number of priority sectoral groupings with potential are identified. The handful of priority sectors that will eventually be chosen for support every three years should mainly be found within these groupings. These are natural resource-based sectors, medium technology sectors, advanced manufacturing sectors, labour intensive sectors and tradable services (Department of Trade and Industry, 2007a, 19)—a broad selection by all measures.

The first round of action plans, which is intended for immediate implementation, focuses on the following four lead sectors: capital and transport equipment and metal fabrication; automotives and components; chemicals, plastics fabrication and pharmaceuticals; and forestry, pulp and paper and furniture (Department of Trade and Industry, 2007b). The metals sector provides 18% of manufacturing jobs in South Africa, nonetheless it has underperformed in the past. Providing mostly inputs to other industries, firms in the sector have certainly suffered from low investment levels in the economy, and particularly from the public sector and the mining industry. Additionally, and in common with the plastics sectors, the uncompetitive pricing of inputs is identified as the major constraint, and in both cases a review of tariffs on upstream products is suggested. With regard to steel and aluminium, the action plan in this sector also foresees a strengthening of the competition act to put more pressure on the dominant domestic producers with huge market power. The public infrastructure investment programmes, in particular the spending of state-owned enterprises, also come under scrutiny, as the DTI intends to commit relevant actors to a higher level of local content in their procurement. Policy in the automotives and components sector is driven by the Motor Industry Development Programme which expires in 2009. The DTI has committed itself to a continuation of sector support and announced the publication of a replacement programme that intends to help firms double production by 2020. Finally, the labour intensive forestry sector could provide jobs in poor rural communities. Technical and financial support should enable small growers to participate in the growth of the industry.

Apart from these sectors, the activities that have already been singled out in AsgiSA will continue to receive attention; among these are business process outsourcing, the tourism sector and biofuels; all three are characterised by their labour-intensity. In addition, the DTI intends to reserve some attention for the clothing and textiles sector, diamond beneficiation, agro-processing, film and television, and crafts; and will develop strategies or perspectives for mineral beneficiation, ICT services and products, creative industries, white goods, retail and other sectors.

The cross-cutting issues that are to be tackled immediately complement and often are a crucial part of the sectoral interventions. They include the improvement of the industrial financing system, the leveraging of public procurement, the reduction of intermediate input costs, and the improvement of research and development support, infrastructure and skills development. Industrial financing is to be expanded through the existing institutions—the DTI itself and the Industrial Development Corporation—and improved by more prioritisation, in line with overall sectoral priorities, and higher reciprocity. The massive increase in public investment that is currently under way should be carried out in a way that maximises opportunities for South African firms. While price and quality considerations must continue to inform procurement decisions, all government departments should include the domestic production perspective in their consideration. The reduction of input cost has already been mentioned in connection with the metals and plastics sector; the DTI's efforts in the field of infrastructure improvement and skills development mostly concentrate on aligning current initiatives of other departments with the sector priorities in the industrial policy strategy.

6.2.3 Capacity and Coherence

The public reception of the NIPF was decidedly mixed. While it drew applause from some quarters, it was met with skepticism and severe criticism in others. It is certainly too early to make a definite statement about the policy, however a review of recent developments and an interpretation of the policy's aims within the context of South Africa's growth trajectory permit a tentative assessment.

The publication of the NIPF has definitely put industrial policy back in the spotlight. First steps are being taken toward implementation and a comprehensive review of tariff protection for upstream industries is already under way. In timely coincidence, the Competition Tribunal has fined Arcelor Mittal Steel, South Africa's dominant steel producer, 700 million Rand for excessive pricing. The DTI also gave first broad indications of how support for the automotive industry will look when the original MIDP expires. The revised programme will be published in August 2008, but support has been pledged until 2020.

The MIDP and its successor programme can also serve to illustrate one of the major concerns—that of the department's capacity, or lack thereof. The review of the programme started in 2005, but publication of its results and the revised programme has been repeatedly postponed, much to the dismay of car producers and critics who have urged the government to provide clarity. Many interpret this as a sign that the DTI still faces severe capacity constraints. This is a long-standing problem to which the DTI itself cautiously admits: "[C]apacity to formulate and implement high-quality industrial policy interventions has been uneven across government departments" (Department of Trade and Industry, 2007a, 28). One reason for these capacity problems was the historical focus of the DTI on the administration of tariffs and, on the eve of democracy, on the export support programme GEIS. Its staff, redeployed to administer the taxing supply-side programmes that formed the core of industrial policy in the 1990s, struggled to fulfill this new role (Lewis et al. 2004, 175, Robbins 2007). Additionally, there were numerous processes of internal reorganisation which led to large fluctuations within the department and to a less than optimal retention of knowledge gained in the process of engaging with industry stakeholders (Morris et al. 2006, 207, Robbins 2007).

In addition to in-house capacity, the implementation of an industrial strategy requires close coordination across government agencies, in other words, the capacity of a nodal agency to drive policy. The sectoral and cross-cutting Key Action Plans invariably involve a number of different departments, agencies or state-owned enterprises that should play their part in implementation. Whether the DTI has the clout to be this agency in South Africa remains to be seen. It is an open secret that the National Treasury is less than convinced of the merits of an interventionist industrial policy. Its response to the publication of the NIPF has been lukewarm, and in his medium term budget policy speech before parliament in November 2007 finance minister Trevor Manuel told parliament that, in order to diversify its exports, South Africa would have "to ensure that competition is fostered through tariff simplification and reform." (Manuel, 2007, 6) The corresponding policy statement contains an explicit critique of high levels of protection in the auto and textiles industries without even mentioning the NIPF (Department of Finance, 2007, 22).

If there is a nodal agency with regards to economic policy in South Africa, it still seems to be the National Treasury that is at the heart of the economic policy making process (e.g. Mohamed, 2007, also Zalk, 2007). In another intervention that overlaps with the competency of the DTI, the Treasury hired an international advisory panel, comprised of mostly American-based economists, to identify the binding constraints that hamper the South African economy, and particularly its industry. The findings were published over a period of two years with the final report released on the Treasury's website in May 2008 (Hausmann, 2008). While they do not represent the policy positions of the Treasury, the findings nonetheless serve as an indicator for its overall policy preferences since they are concordant with its other publications and statements. Some of the recommendations of the panel are in line with the industrial strategy proposed by the DTI, notably the targeting of a more stable exchange rate, but also with regards to higher investment in public infrastructure. On the other hand, the authors are critical of sectoral targeting as proposed in the NIPF—they suggest to "[s]ubstitute or complement the current DTI policy of developing customized sector programs with a strategy based on an open-architecture approach with self-organization of relevant actors"(ibid.). Also, they call for a more wide-reaching simplification of the tariff regime and a reduction or elimination of tariffs on inputs. Lastly, the report is highly critical of initiatives to promote beneficiation, stating that, if viable, it should and would have happened already.

For now, the Treasury continues to subscribe to an economic policy vision that views sectoral targeting and tariffs with suspicion. From 'the other side' of the political spectrum, the unions put pressure on the government to implement a more interventionist strategy. In a strategy paper on industrial policy, COSATU asks for a "fundamental redirection of activities by all stakeholders, including the state, capital and even labour" (COSATU, 2006, 14). This redirection includes a more expansionary fiscal and monetary environment, more public ownership and a more protective trade policy, all under the mantle of a developmental state.

If coherence is one of the pillars of success of East Asian industrial policy, South Africa will in all likelihood fall short of meeting this criterion. Different players within the governing coalition and within cabinet adhere to differing strategic visions of industrial policy. The ascension of Jacob Zuma to President of the ANC and his likely taking over of the country's presidency after the general elections in 2009 might lead to a shift in policy priorities towards the vision expressed by COSATU. The union federation, the communist party and the ANC left are among his most vocal and influential supporters. For now, the more cautious stance of the Treasury holds sway, creating a significant amount of insecurity over future policy directions.

A similar argument could be made with regard to macroeconomic policy. The DTI is not alone in its call to alter monetary policy strategy in order to provide South African exporters with a more competitive exchange rate. However, the independent Reserve Bank's inflation targeting policy—causing high interest rates and an overvalued currency—is not under review. The liberalisation of the capital account, very much in the interest of mining conglomerates that rapidly internationalised since 1994 and saw investment opportunities mostly outside South Africa, is not under scrutiny—if anything there are calls for further liberalisation, for example by the panel engaged by the Treasury (Hausmann, 2008). So it is likely that interest rates will have to remain high to continuously attract short term capital inflows (Fine, 2008). And while state expenditure has indeed increased over the last few years, the Treasury remains cautious in its policy stance, budgeting for a surplus for the period from 2008 to 2010. So far there is no indication that industrial policy as laid out in the NIPF will also govern the decision making of these key economic policy institutions. This implies that a more conservative interpretation of the developmental state continues to hold sway in South Africa.

As mentioned above, the recent changing of the guard in the ANC could alter the balance of forces in government over time. In light of some of the policies the DTI promotes, this is probably a prerequisite for success. The first sector strategies target downstream industries such as plastics and they will inevitably have to tackle the monopoly power of upstream suppliers. The announced reduction of input tariffs will not suffice in this regard, and this might also be true for the strengthening of the Competition Act. Chang argues that a purely legalistic approach to competition policy is unsuitable because it is a long and costly process (Arcelor Mittal will of course appeal its fine in the Competition Appeal Court), which moreover does not achieve what South Africa needs most from its conglomerates: increased domestic investment. He advises a more hands-on approach, controlling outward investment and striking deals to increase domestic engagement (Chang, 1998, 68f.). What has happened so far is the opposite: South Africa experiences a net outflow of foreign direct investment and its economic policy facilitates further capital outflow (Fine, 2008).

This brings us back to the structural features of South African capital, which differs markedly from its counterparts in other aspiring developmental states. "Where the developmental states of Asia faced national capital groups that saw industrial growth as their main road to profit, key sectors of South African capital saw their future in mineral investments abroad" (Makgetla, 2005, 6). This point is also forcefully made by Fine, who claims that "conglomerates attached to the MEC [...] have otherwise demonstrated little or token commitment to the economic and social restructuring and expansion of the local economy other than in furnishing continuing and secure profitability to feed into their globalisation" (Fine, 2008). So far, the interests of mining and financial capital have been well served by economic policy—the immediate opening of capital markets in 1995 and the conservative monetary policy regime are obvious examples.

If the DTI is to achieve its objectives of industrial diversification and higher growth in tradable goods sectors, then macroeconomic policies will have to change as well—notably in the form of a more competitive exchange rate. This further implies a change in the financial system, gearing it to the needs of industry rather than those of international and domestic financial investors. The NIPF only tentatively addresses these issues and it indeed sounds rather ambitious. However, a changing of the growth trajectory of the South African economy will always be an ambitious project. A different policy outlook by the new ANC leadership might lead to bolder proposals and a more vigorous implementation in the future.

6.2.4 Competing Visions

The aim to transform South Africa into a developmental state is shared by all constituencies within the ANC. This goal therefore serves as a rallying point upon which all its members can agree. However, similarly to the strategic concept of the National Democratic Revolution, its interpretation is fiercely contested. While some merely consider the developmental state a competent state that can intervene in targeted areas to reduce the cost of doing business in South Africa, the left subscribes to a different interpretation, based on which a progressive developmental state would have to alter the capital-intensive growth trajectory of the South African economy and therefore clash with the entrenched interests of capital.

This case study on industrial policy has reaffirmed that there are indeed competing visions of the South African developmental state. While the National Industrial Policy Strategy sets itself the goal of diversifying the South African economy beyond its traditional reliance on commodities, this diversification will not be possible without a disruption of the dominance of upstream monopolies and a fundamental alteration of the macroeconomic framework. At the moment, the DTI does not have the clout to implement such measures. However, the recent change in ANC leadership could improve its chances to do so in future.

Finally, the case study also shows that, while concerns about the state's capabilities and the coherence of policy are justified, they cannot simply be interpreted as administrative weaknesses of the state. They are rather a result of conflicting class interests, reflected in the governing alliance and within government departments, and shaping its policies. The more fundamental issue at stake then is which groups can assert their interests and determine what kind of a developmental state South Africa eventually wants to be.

Chapter 7

Conclusion

This dissertation intended to answer to what extent linkages between sectors define South Africa's development trajectory, and how suitable its economic policy is to change its path to achieving a more diversified industrial sector that is less reliant on its mineral endowment and that is also more labour-absorbing. For this purpose, I provided a detailed overview of the history of the country's economic and particularly its industrial development. Building on the stylised facts established in that section, I implemented a model that aimed to take the mineral endowment and linkages between economic sectors into consideration. Lastly, an econometric exercise and a policy analysis assess the strength of linkages and issues of path dependence in policy formulation that explain the continued focus of the South African economy on sectors close to mining.

The historic overview has shown that it was indeed the country's mineral endowment, its abundant supply with gold, diamonds, coal, platinum and a host of other raw materials, that at first triggered and then continued to shape its development path. In the very beginning, manufacturing activity was started in reply to the needs of mines. Explosives, electricity, and a basic supply of consumer goods for mine workers were soon provided locally. At later stages, successive governments attempted to broaden the manufacturing base by employing import substitution policies, while those manufacturing sectors close to mining—basic metals and chemicals are the most important examples—also received strong government support. As a result, the South African economy inherited by the ANC when it came to power in 1994 was largely inward oriented. This was particularly true for manufacturing. The deficit accrued in these foreign-exchange consuming activities was financed mostly by the exports of minerals and of goods produced within the confines of the Minerals Energy Complex or MEC. In addition to inward orientation, this industrial structure was problematic for a second reason: despite a large supply of unskilled labour, South African manufacturing and industrial activities are very capital intensive, resulting in high unemployment. While the challenges were clear to the incoming government, the appropriate policy responses were less so. The discussions on the economic interventions focused on macroeconomic policy mostly, but were partly reflected in industrial policy as well. In the end, the ANC chose to liberalise its trade regime to foster an opening of the economy and increased competitiveness of manufacturing firms, simultaneously supporting them by a range of supply side programmes. However, at least in the early phases, the desired results—more diversification, job creation in manufacturing, an improved performance in international markets—were not accomplished. Quite to the contrary, the country experienced a more strongly accentuated development of capital-intensive sectors, while more jobs were lost in labour-intensive sectors such as textiles and clothing.

The simulation in Chapter 4—based on a New Economic Geography model of the vertical linkages type—takes two stylised facts from this historical development as its starting point: the role of a mineral endowment and the role of inter-sectoral linkages in the industrialisation process. I set up a three-regions model where only one region disposes of minerals that are used as an input in the production of one of its industrial sectors. All manufacturing sectors are linked with each other in an input-output framework. Other than that, they only use labour as an input in production. As is common in NEG models, there is an industrialised core region that concentrates economic production in the manufacturing sector within its confines. The driving force for this agglomeration (or, more precisely in a linkages framework, specialisation) are the forward and backward linkages at play. They allow firms to buy inputs more cheaply and to profit from a larger market for its output in the core region. On the other hand, higher economic activity in the modern sector drives up wages—the resulting wage gap with the peripheral regions acts as a countering force on complete specialisation. Of the two peripheral regions, one profits from the above-mentioned mineral endowment, most likely resulting in its specialisation in the respective sector.

From this initial point, a growth process is introduced which increases worldwide demand for manufacturing goods. The simulations show that this increase at first leads to further growth of manufacturing industries in the core—with the exception of the mining sector that heavily uses the mineral input—while the other two regions remain peripheral. Yet, at the same time, the wage gap widens, making it more and more attractive for some firms to go into business in the periphery. At one point, this resettling indeed occurs, its concrete manifestation depending on the strength of linkages in the respective sectors. Using an artificial input-output matrix with a mining sector, a strongly linked second sector close to mining and three very weakly linked labour-intensive sectors, the resettlement of industries takes place in the latter three sectors only, and they all move to the peripheral region without minerals, allowing it to profit from linkage effects itself and leading to its rapid development. The mineral-rich region (South Africa) continues to specialise entirely in the resource-heavy sectors and is eventually overtaken in terms of wage levels by the third region. With a more realistic input-output structure taken from South African data, the results are less clear-cut, but the overall picture remains the same: growth in the mineral-rich region is concentrated in sectors heavily linked to the mineral endowment (e.g. chemicals), while sectors more intensive in the use of other factors move to the third region. The simulation thus confirms on a theoretical level that it is indeed possible for a country to forego the opportunity of a more diversified and labour-intensive industrialisation path due to a specialisation in mining and closely related sectors—due to linkage effects and wage differences.

A simulation exercise is no substitute for empirical work, and thus Chapter 5 attempts to empirically assert to what extent linkages influence sectoral growth in South Africa and how growth shocks in a sector might pull other sectors along—or fail to do so. The method used is a version of the SVAR approach where sectoral performance is explained by its own and other sectors' past performances, and the latter are weighted according to linkage strength. Estimation points to a strong pulling power of the manufacturing sector as a whole which—due to linkage and spillover effects—has positive effects on the other sectors of the economy. This is in marked contrast to the MEC, which, despite sizeable linkages to the rest of the economy, does not provide comparable spillover effects. Looking at manufacturing sub-sectors, the effects are weaker, but a cautious interpretation points to a positive influence of the transport equipment and (to a lesser extent) the metals and metal products sector, while petroleum and chemicals, a very dominant and strong performer in the South African economy, has relatively weak positive spillover effects on other manufacturing subsectors. Growth in mining and closely related sectors thus diffuses only weakly to the rest of the economy, and particularly to those sectors that would provide more employment opportunities. This evidence could be read as a confirmation of the tendency towards path dependency established in the theoretical work or at least does not contradict it.

Lastly, in Chapter 6, the recent shifts in industrial policy came under scrutiny. Industrial policy and economic policy more broadly have to a large extent reinforced the lopsided development of the South African economy since 1994, despite the repeatedly stated aim of policy makers to change the economy's course. With the notable exception of the Motor Industry Development Programme that has helped the South African auto industry to become more competitive on a global level, industrial policy has failed to push the manufacturing sector towards more diversification. Particularly in the 1990s, institutions such as the Industrial Development Corporation, but also the broader macroeconomic and trade policy framework have favoured those sectors that have profited from policy support in the old regime as well: mining itself and the upstream users of the mineral endowment such as chemicals and basic metals. The latest initiative of the Department of Trade and Industry, the National Industrial Policy Framework, admits to these shortcomings and attempts to redirect policy interventions. The document puts a lot of emphasis on policy coordination of various government agencies, so that a consistent industrial policy in line with the DTI's goals can be pursued. While the attempt is laudable and the analysis it is based on confirms many of the findings of this study, a careful reading of the document, its reception in the country, and an analysis of the drivers of this policy and first initiatives that emerged from it lead to a cautious and rather skeptical assessment: it is questionable whether the DTI has the clout to implement the wide-ranging changes it envisions for the country's industrial policy strategy, and a number of indicators point toward a less radical change, leaving many of the key characteristics of policy as they were, and therefore implying more continuity in South Africa's industrial and economic policy regime.

The answer to my research question then is a nuanced one: linkages did play an important role in industrial development, yet they have often been reinforced by policy interventions that make it difficult to isolate their effect.

On a theoretical level, their importance in shaping the development path has been shown to be plausible, and empirically, the development of certain sectors is indeed strongly influenced by other sectors. As input-output linkages continue to matter today, so does industrial policy which shows a surprising amount of path dependency as well. Despite many assurances and honest attempts to change this fact, industrial policy is still geared to benefit the sectors close to the country's mineral endowment, and thus contributes to the continuity of South Africa's lopsided industrial development.

Bibliography

Abeysinghe, Tilak and Kristin Forbes (2005): *Trade Linkages and Output-Multiplier Effects: a Structural VAR Approach with a Focus on Asia.* In: Review of International Economics 13 (2): 356-375

Altman, Miriam (2001): *Employment Promotion in a Minerals Economy.* In: Journal of International Development, Vol. 13 (August): 691-709

Altman, Miriam (2005): *The state of employment.* In: State of the Nation - South Africa 2004 - 2005. Cape Town: HSRC Press: 423-454n, Miriam (2005): *The state of employment.* In: State of the Nation - South Africa 2004 - 2005. Cape Town: HSRC Press: 423-454

Amsden, Alice (1989): *Asia's Next Giant. South Korea and Late Industrialization.* Oxford: Oxford University Press

Amsden, Alice (2001): *The Rise of 'The Rest'. Challenges to the West from Late-Industrializing Economies.* New York: Oxford University Press

African National Congress (2007): *Building a National Democratic Society - Strategy and Tactics of the ANC.* Revised Draft (August). http://www.anc.org.za/ancdocs/policy/2007/conference/tactics.html (4.1.2008)

Auty, Richard M. (1993): *Sustaining Development in Mineral Economies. The Resource Curse Thesis.* London: Routledge

Baldwin, Richard/ Forslid, Rikard/ Martin, Philippe/ Ottaviano, Gianmarco/ Robert-Nicoud, Frederic (2003): *Economic Geography and Public Policy.* Princeton: Princeton University Press

Ballard, Richard/ Habib, Adam/ Valodia, Imraan (2006): *Social movements in South Africa: promoting crisis or creating stability?* In: Padayachee, Vishnu (ed.): The development decade? Economic and social change in South Africa, 1994-2004. Cape Town: HSRC Press: 397-412

Becker, Joachim (1993): *Von der De- zur Restabilisierung. Die westliche Politik gegenüber dem Südlichen Afrika.* In: Baiculescu, Michael/ Becker, Joachim (Ed.): Kap der kleinen Hoffnung. Das Südliche Afrika nach der Apartheid. Wien: Promedia: 8-23

Bhorat, Haroon/ Lundall, Paul/ Rospabe, Sandrine (2002): *The South African labour market in a globalizing world: Economic and legislative considerations.* Employment Paper 2002/32: International Labour Organization

Bhorat, Haroon/ Cassim, Rashad (2004): *The challenge of growth, employment and poverty in the South African economy since democracy: an exploratory review of selected issues.* In: Development Southern Africa Vol. 21 (March): 7-31

Black, Anthony (1991): *Manufacturing Development and the economic crisis: a reversion to primary production?* In: Gelb, Stephen: South Africa's Economic Crisis. Cape Town: David Philip: 156-174

Black, Anthony (2001): *Globalization and Restructuring in the South African Automotive Industry.* In: Journal of International Development, Vol. 13 (6): 779-796

Blanchard, Olivier/ Quah, Danny (1989): *The Dynamic Effects of Aggregate Demand and Supply Disturbances.* In: American Economic Review, Vol. 79 (4): 655-673

Brakman, Steven/ Garretsen, Harry (2006): *New economic geography: Closing the gap between theory and empirics.* In: Regional Science and Urban Economics, Vol. 36: 569-572

Brakman, Steven/ Garretsen, Harry (2007): *From theory to estimation and back: the empirical relevance of new economic geography.* In: Fingleton, Bernard (ed.): New Directions in Economic Geography. Cheltenham: Edward Elgar: 98-129

Chang, Ha-Joon (1994): *The Political Economy of Industrial Policy.* New York: St. Martin's Press

Chang, Ha-Joon (1998): *Evaluating the Current Industrial Policy of South Africa.* In: Transformation 36, 1998: 51-72

Chang, Ha-Joon (2006): *The East Asian Development Experience. The Miracle, the Crisis and the Future.* London: Zed Books

Cho, Hee-Yeon/ Kim, Eun Mee (1998): *State Autonomy and Its Social Conditions for Economic Development in South Korea and Taiwan.* In: Kim, Eun Mee (ed.): The Four Asian Tigers. London: Academic Press: 125-158

Clark, Nancy (1994): *Manufacturing Apartheid: State Corporations in South Africa.* New Haven: Yale University Press

COSATU (2006): *Industrial Strategy Document.* Document for the National Congress 2006 http://www.cosatu.org.za/cong2006/congress06/industry.pdf (24.6.2008)

Daniel, John/ Southall, Roger/ Lutchman, Jessica (2005): *Introduction: President Mbeki's second term: Opening the golden door?* In: Daniel, John et al. (Ed.): State of the Nation. South Africa 2004-2005. Cape Town: HSRC Press: xix-xlii

Davies, Rob/ van Seventer, Dirk Ernst (2004): *A three-gap and macrodecomposition analysis for South Africa, 1993 - 2002.* In: Development Southern Africa Vol. 21 (March): 133-153

Davis, Graham A. (1995): *Learning to Love the Dutch Disease: Evidence from the Mineral Economies.* In: World Development, Vol. 23 (10): 1765-1779

Department of Finance [The Treasury](1996): *Growth, Employment and Redistribution—A Macroeconomic Strategy.* Pretoria

Department of Finance [The Treasury](2004): *Medium Term Budget Policy Statement 2004.* Available at: www.finance.gov.za (16.8.2005)

Department of Finance [The Treasury](2007): *Medium Term Budget Policy Statement 2007.* Pretoria

Department of Trade and Industry (2007a): *National Industrial Policy Framework*. Pretoria: the dti

Department of Trade and Industry (2007b): *Industrial Policy Action Plan.* Pretoria: the dti

Dixit, Avinash/ Stiglitz, Joseph (1977): *Monopolistic Competition and Optimum Product Diversity.* In: The American Economic Review, Vol. 67: 297-308

Dobreva, Ralitza (2006): *Value Chains, Market Power and Competitiveness: Understanding the Performance of the Plastics Sector*. In: Roberts, Simon (ed.): Sustainable Manufacturing? The Case of South Africa and Ekurhuleni. Cape Town: Juta: 182-207

Edwards, Lawrence (2001): *Globalisation and the skill bias of occupational employment in South Africa.* In: South African Journal of Economics, Vol. 69 (1): 40-71

Ellison, Glen/ Glaeser, Edward (1997): *Geographic Concentration in U.S. Manufacturing Industries: A Dartboard Approach.* In: Journal of Political Economy, Vol. 105 (5): 889-927

Ellison, Glen/ Glaeser, Edward (1999): *The Geographic Concentration of Industry: Does Natural Advantage Explain Agglomeration?* In: American Economic Review, Vol. 89 (2): 311-316

Enders, Walter (1995): *Applied Econometric Time Series.* New York: Wiley

Epstein, Gerald (2002): *Employment-Oriented Central Bank Policy in an Integrated World Economy: A Reform Proposal for South Africa.* PERI Working Paper Series Nr. 39

Erwin, Alec (2007): *An effective developmental state needs a strong Alliance.* In: Umrabulo 30, November

Evans, Peter (1995): *Embedded Autonomy. States and Industrial Transformation.* Princeton: Princeton University Press

Fedderke, Johannes/ Szalontai, Gábor (2005): *Industry Concentration in South African Manufacturing: Trends and Consequences, 1972 - 1996.* World Bank Africa Region Working Paper Series No. 96

Feinstein, Charles (2005): *An Economic History of South Africa. Conquest, Discrimination and Development.* Cambridge: Cambridge University Press

Fine, Ben (2006): *The Developmental State and the Political Economy of Development.* In: Fine, Ben/ Jomo KS (ed.): The New Development Economics. London: Zed Books: 101-122

Fine, Ben (2008): *The Minerals-Energy Complex is Dead: Long Live the MEC?.* Paper presented to the Amandla Colloquium, Cape Town: http://www.amandlapublishers.co.za/component/option,com_docman/task,doc_download/gid,19/Itemid,163/ (25.6.2008)

Fine, Ben/ Rustomjee, Zavareh (1996): *The Political Economy of South Africa.* London: Hurst & Company

Forslid, Rikard/ Haaland, Jan I./ Midelfart Knarvik, Karen (2002): *A U-shaped Europe? A simulation study of industrial location.* In: Journal of International Economics, Vol. 57: 273-297

Fujita, Masahisa/ Krugman, Paul/ Venables, Anthony J. (2001): *The Spatial Economy. Cities, Regions, and International Trade.* Cambridge: MIT Press

Gelb, Stephen (1991): *South Africa's Economic Crisis: an Overview.* In: Gelb, Stephen: South Africa's Economic Crisis. Cape Town: David Philipp: 1 - 32

Gelb, Stephen (2003): *Inequality in South Africa: Nature, causes and responses.* Working Paper, The Edge Institute: Johannesburg

Gelb, Stephen (2005): *An overview of the South African economy.* In: State of the Nation. South Africa 2004-2005. Cape Town: HSRC Press: 367-400

Hamilton, James D. (1994): *Time Series Analysis.* New Jersey: Princeton University Press

Hamlyn, Michael (2007): *Manuel: State underspends by R5,3bn.* In: Mail&Guardian, 6 September 2007

Hausmann, Ricardo (2008): *Final recommendations of the International Panel on Growth.* Final Report of the International Advisory Panel, National Treasury: http://www.treasury.gov.za/publications/other/growth/default.aspx (24.6.2008)

Hausmann, Ricardo/ Klinger, Bailey (2006): *South Africa's Export Predicament.* CID Working Paper No. 129, August, Harvard University

Hausmann, Ricardo/ Rodrik, Dani (2006): *Doomed to Choose: Industrial Policy as Predicament.* Working Paper (First Draft), Harvard University: http://ksghome.harvard.edu/~drodrik/doomed.pdf (1.3.2007)

Head, Keith/ Mayer, Thierry (2004): *The Empirics of Agglomeration and Trade.* In: Henderson, Vernon/ Thisse, Jacques-Francois (ed.): Handbook of Regional and Urban Economics Vol. 4: Cities and Geography. Amsterdam: Elsevier: 2609-2669

Helper, Susan (2000): *Economists and Field Research: "You Can Observe a Lot by Watching".* In: American Economic Review, Vol. 90 (2): 228-232

Henderson, J. Vernon/ Shalizi, Zmarak/ Venables, Anthony (2001): *Geography and Development.* In: Journal of Economic Geography Vol. 1: 81-105

Hess, Simon (2005): *The concentration tendencies of SADC's manufacturing industries with regard to South Africa: 1970-1999.* Paper presented for the TIPS Forum 2005, http://www.tips.afrihost.com/ research/papers/pdfs/772.pdf (26.2.2007)

Hirsch, Alan (2005): *Season of Hope - Economic Reform under Mandela and Mbeki.* Scottsville: University of KwaZulu Natal Press

Hirschman, Albert O. (1966): *The Strategy of Economic Development.* New Haven: Yale University Press

Hirschman, Albert O. (1981): *A Generalized Linkage Approach to Development, with Special Reference to Staples.* In: Essays in Trespassing. Economics to Politics and Beyond. Cambridge: Cambridge University Press: 59-97

Iliffe, John (1999): *The South African economy, 1652-1997.* In: The Economic History Review Vol. 52 (1): 87-103

Imbs, Jean/ Wacziarg, Romain (2003): *Stages of Diversification.* In: American Economic Review Vol. 93 (1): 63-86

Joffe, Avril/ Kaplan, David/ Kaplinsky, Raphael/ Lewis, David (1995): *Improving Manufacturing Performance in South Africa: Report of the Industrial Strategy Project.* Cape Town: UCT Press

Johnson, Chalmers (1982): *MITI and the Japanese Miracle.* Stanford: Stanford University Press

Kahn, Brian (1991): *The Crisis of South Africa's Balance of Payments.* In: Gelb, Stephen (ed.): South Africa's Economic Crisis. Cape Town: David Phillip: 59-87

Kaplan, David (1991): *The South African capital goods sector and the economic crisis.* In: Gelb, Stephen (ed.): South Africa's Economic Crisis. Cape Town: David Phillip: 175-197

Kaplan, David (2003): *Manufacturing Performance and Policy in South Africa - A Review.* Paper prepared for the TIPS Forum 2003, http://www.tips.org.za/events/event_details/papers/forum2003/p_kaplan.pdf (31.1.2007)

Kaplan, David (2004): *Manufacturing in South Africa over the last decade: a review of industrial performance and policy.* In: Development Southern Africa, Vol. 21 (4): 623-644

Kennedy, Peter (2003): *A Guide to Econometrics.* 5th edition. Cambridge: The MIT Press

Kohli, Atul (2004): *State-directed development. Political Power and Industrialization in the Global Periphery.* New York: Cambridge University Press

Krugman, Paul (1991a): *Increasing Returns and Economic Geography.* In: The Journal of Political Economy, Vol. 99 (3): 483-499

Krugman, Paul (1991b): *Geography and Trade.* Cambridge: MIT Press

Krugman, Paul (1997): *Development, Geography, and Economic Theory.* Cambridge: MIT Press

Krugman, Paul/ Venables, Anthony (1995): *Globalization and the Inequality of Nations.* In: The Quarterly Journal of Economics, Vol. CX (4): 857-880

Le Roux, Pieter (1993): *The Mont Fleur Scenarios - What will South Africa be like in 2002?* Reprinted in: Deeper News, Global Business Network

Lewis, Jeffrey D. (2001): *Reform and Opportunity: The Changing Role and Patterns of Trade in South Africa and SADC.* World Bank: Africa Region Working Paper Series Nr. 14

Lewis, David/ Reed, Kabelo/ Teljeur, Ethel (2004): *South Africa: Economic Policy-Making and Implementation in Africa: A Study of Strategic Trade and Selective Industrial Policies.* In: Soludo, Charles/ Ogbu, Osita/ Chang, Ha-Joon (ed.): The Politics of Trade and Industrial Policy in Africa—Forced Consensus? Trenton: Africa World Press: 151-178

List, Friedrich (1950): *Das nationale System der Politischen Ökonomie.* Sechste Auflage. Jena: Gustav Fischer

Machaka, Johannes/ Roberts, Simon (2003): *The DTI's new 'Integrated Manufacturing Strategy'? Comparative Industrial Performance, Linkages and Technology.* In: South African Journal of Economics, Vol. 71 (4): 679-704

Makgetla, Neva (2005): *A developmental state for South Africa?* Discussion paper for Cosatu's 2005 Central Committee. http://www.cosatu.org.za/cc2005/Developmental.pdf (12.4.2007)

Manuel, Trevor (2007): *Medium Term Budget Policy Statement.* Speech by Minister of Finance. http://www.treasury.gov.za/documents/mtbps/2007/mtbps/speech.pdf (14.1.2008)

Marais, Hein (2001): *South Africa - Limits to Change. The Political Economy of Transition.* Cape Town: University of Cape Town Press

Marshall, Alfred (1938): *Principles of Economics.* London: Macmillan

Martin, Ron (1999): *The new 'geographical' turn in economics.* In: Cambridge Journal of Economics, Vol. 23: 65-91

Mbeki, Thabo (2007): *State of the Nation Address of the President of South Africa.* 9 February 2007, http://www.info.gov.za/speeches/2007/07020911001001.htm (20.2.2007)

McCarthy, Colin L. (1999): *Polarised Development in a SADC Free Trade Area.* In: South African Journal of Economics, Vol. 67 (4): 375-399

Morris, Mike/ Robbins, Glen/ Barnes, Justin (2006): *The role of government in fostering clusters: the South African automotive sector.* In: Padayachee, Vishnu (ed.): The Development Decade? Economic and social change in South Africa, 1994 - 2004. Cape Town: HSRC Press: 201-223

Myrdal, Gunnar (1957): *Economic Theory and Under-Developed Regions.* London: Duckworth

Naidoo, Kuben (2006): *Operationalising South Africa's move from macroeconomic stability to microeconomic reform.* In: Padayachee, Vishnu (ed.): The Development Decade? Economic and Social Change in South Africa, 1994-2004. Cape Town: HSRC Press: 108-125

Nattrass, Nicoli (1998): *South Africa: the economic restructuring agenda - a critique of the MERG report.* In: Third World Quarterly, Vol. 15 (2): 219-225

Nattrass, Nicoli (1998): *Globalisation and the South African Labour Market.* In: Trade and Industry Monitor, Volume 6 (July): 18-20

Neary, J. Peter (2001): *Of Hype and Hyperbolas: Introducing the New Economic Geography.* In: Journal of Economic Literature, Vol. 39: 536-561

Ocampo, José Antonio (2005): *The Quest for Dynamic Efficiency: Structural Dynamics and Economic Growth in Developing Countries.* In: Ocampo, José Antonio (ed.): Beyond Reforms—Structural Dynamics and Macroeconomic Vulnerability. Palo Alto: Stanford University Press: 3-43

Ottaviano, Gianmarco/ Thisse, Jacques-Francois (2004): *Agglomeration and Economic Geography.* In: Henderson, Vernon/ Thisse, Jacques-Francois (ed.): Handbook of Regional and Urban Economics Vol. 4: Cities and Geography. Amsterdam: Elsevier: 2563-2608

Ottaviano, Gianmarco/ Robert-Nicoud, Frédéric (2006): *The 'genome' of NEG models with vertical linkages: a positive and normative synthesis.* In: Journal of Economic Geography, Vol. 6: 113-139

Ottaviano, Gianmarco (2007): *Models of 'new economic geography': factor mobility vs. vertical linkages.* In: Fingleton, Bernard (ed.): New Directions in Economic Geography. Cheltenham: Edward Elgar: 53-69

Petersson, Lennart (2002): *The New Economic Geography and Industrial Location in SADC.* In: The South African Journal of Economics, Vol. 70 (8): 1222-1246

Porter, Michael (1990): *The Competitive Advantage of Nations.* London: Macmillan

Presidency (2006): *Accelerated and Shared Growth Initiative - South Africa.* http://www.info.gov.za/asgisa/asgisadoc.pdf (4.1.2008)

Puga, Diego/ Venables, Anthony (1996): *The Spread of Industry: Spatial Agglomeration in Economic Development.* In: Journal of the Japanese and International Economies, Vol. 10: 440-464

Puga, Diego/ Venables, Anthony (1999): *Agglomeration and Economic Development: Import Substitution vs. Trade Liberalisation.* In: The Economic Journal, Vol. 109: 292-311

Ramos, Joseph (1998): *A development strategy founded on natural resource-based production clusters.* In: CEPAL Review, Vol. 66: 105-127

Roberts, Simon (2001): *Globalization, Industrial Development and the Plastics Sector in South Africa.* In: Journal of International Development, Vol. 13: 797-810

Roberts, Simon (2005): *Industrial Development and industrial policy in South Africa - a ten year review.* Paper presented at 'South African Economic Policy under Democracy'-Conference at Stellenbosch University, October

Roberts, Simon (2006): *Encouraging Downstream Value-Added and Labour-Intensive Growth? The Case to the Metal Products Sector.* In: Sustainable Manufacturing? The Case of South Africa and Ekurhuleni. Cape Town: Juta: 159-181

Rodrik, Dani (2004): *Industrial Policy for the Twenty-First Century.* Centre for Economic Policy Research Discussion Paper 4767, http://ksghome.harvard.edu/~drodrik/UNIDOSep.pdf (2.2.2007)

Rodrik, Dani (2006): *Understanding South Africa's Economic Puzzles.* CID Working Paper No. 130. Harvard University

Rodrik, Dani (2007): *One Economics, Many Recipes.* Princeton: Princeton University Press

Rosenstein-Rodan, Paul (1943): *Problems of Industrialisation of Eastern and South-Eastern Europe.* In: The Economic Journal, Vol. 53: 202-211

Scheepers, CF (1982): *The International Trade Strategy of South Africa.* In: South African Journal of Economics 50 (1): 14-26

Schwank, Oliver (2008): *Limits to a Developmental Regime in South Africa—Industrial Policy Revisited.* In: Journal für Entwicklungspolitik 24 (2): 92-115

Schwank, Oliver/Wild, Michael (2008): *Testing for Linkages in Sectoral Development: An SVAR-Approach to South Africa.* Unpublished Manuscript

Seekings, Jeremy/ Nattrass, Nicoli (2005): *Class, Race and Inequality in South Africa.* Pietermaritzburg: University of KwaZulu-Natal Press

Seidman Makgetla, Neva (2004): *The Post-apartheid economy.* In: Review of African Political Economy 100: 263-281

Sims, Christopher (1980): *Macroeconomics and Reality.* In: Econometrica, Vol. 48 (1): 1-48

Soederbaum, Fredrik (2004): *The Political Economy of Regionalism: The Case of Southern Africa.* Basingstoke: Palgrave Macmillan

Southall, Roger (2007a): *The ANC, black economic empowerment and state-owned enterprises: a recycling of history?* In: Buhlungu, Sakhela et al. (ed.): State of the Nation South Africa 2007. Cape Town: HSRC Press: 201-225

Southall, Roger (2007b): *Introduction: The ANC state, more dysfunctional than developmental?* In: Buhlungu, Sakhela et al. (ed.): State of the Nation South Africa 2007. Cape Town: HSRC Press: 1-24

South Africa Foundation (1996): *Growth for All—An Economic Strategy For South Africa.* Johannesburg: SAF

South African Communist Party (2006): *Class Struggles and the post-1994 state in South Africa.* In: Bua Komanisi! Vol. 5 (1): 18-31

South African Reserve Bank (2005): *Annual Economic Report 2005.* www.reservebank.co.za/aer

Statistics South Africa (2006): *Final Supply and Use Tables, 2006: An input-output framework.* Pretoria: Statistics South Africa

Stone, Richard (1954): *Linear Expenditure Systems and Demand Analysis: An Application to the Pattern of British Demand.* In: The Economic Journal, Vol. 64: 511-527

Streeten, Paul (1959): *Unbalanced Growth.* In: Oxford Economic Papers XI (June): 167-190

Terreblanche, Sampie (2002): *A History of Inequality in South Africa 1652 - 2002* Scottsville: University of Natal Press

Tregenna, Fiona (2007): *Which Sectors can be Engines of Growth and Employment in South Africa? An Analysis of Manufacturing and Services.* Human Sciences Research Council Working Paper, Pretoria

Venables, Anthony (1996): *Equilibrium Locations of Vertically Linked Industries.* In: International Economic Review, Vol. 37 (2): 341-359

Wade, Robert (1990): *Governing the Market. Economic Theory and the Role of Government in East Asian Industrialization.* Princeton: Princeton University Press

Welsh, Frank (2000): *A History of South Africa.* London: HarperCollins Publishers

Yin, Robert K. (2003): *Case Study Research - Design and Methods (Third Edition).* Thousand Oaks: Sage Publications

Zellner, Arnold and Palm Franz C. (1974): *Time Series Analysis and Simultaneous Equation Econometric Models.* In: Journal of Econometrics 2: 17-54

Interviews

Booth, Mike (2007): Telephone Interview with author, Durban, 17 September 2007

Davies, Rob (2007): Telephone Interview with author, Johannesburg, 23 August 2007

Makgetla, Neva (2007): Personal Interview with author, Johannesburg, 15 August 2007

Mohamed, Seeraj (2007): Personal Interview with author, Johannesburg, 20 August 2007

Robbins, Glen (2007): Personal Interview with author, Durban, 7 August 2007

Zalk, Nimrod (2007): Personal Interview with author, Pretoria, 25 August 2007

Appendix

Simulation Parameters for Section 4.2.1

In the first simulation, the following parameter values are used: $\sigma = 5$, $\gamma = 0,94$, $T = 1,3$ (a low transport cost environment), and $\overline{Y} = 0,7$.

In terms of consumption shares, parameter values for μ_s are equal across all three countries and $0.098, 0.103, 0.109, 0.115, 0.12$ for industries 1 to 5.

The input-output matrix is defined as follows:

	MEC		*Non-MEC*		
	α_{1s}	α_{2s}	α_{3s}	α_{4s}	α_{5s}
α_{s1}	0,11	0,12	0,02	0,02	0,02
α_{s2}	0,1	0,1	0,02	0,02	0,02
α_{s3}	0,02	0,02	0,08	0,09	0,1
α_{s4}	0,02	0,02	0,07	0,09	0,09
α_{s5}	0,01	0,01	0,07	0,08	0,09

α_g, the share of the mineral resource in the production of the mining sector is set to $\alpha_g = 0,5$.

Simulation Parameters for Section 4.2.2

Parameter values used in this section are $\sigma = 5$, $\gamma = 0,94$, $T = 1,2$ and $\overline{Y} = 0,7$. Sensitivity analysis has been conducted for all of them. The value for σ, the elasticity of substitution, is a standard assumption in the NEG literature. Simulations show that the results hold for $3 < \sigma < 7$. For other values, the simulations yield non-real results. Sectoral growth outcomes are not affected by small changes in γ and T either, and both are again equivalent to the values assumed in related literature. Transport costs must of course remain sufficiently small, otherwise interior equilibria could no longer be expected.

Consumption shares μ_s are 0.05, 0.093, 0.099, 0.1, 0.102, 0.080, 0.085, 0.08, 0.08, 0.075 for the 10 industries and are equal across all regions.

The input-output matrix stems from the South African input-output matrix. Data are taken from the Quantec 'RSA and Global indicators' database and describe the intermediate outputs of mining and manufacturing sectors to other sectors for the year 2006 in 2000 Rand. The original matrix looks as described in the table A1 below.

	Min	*Food*	*Tex*	*Wood*	*Chem*	*NMM*	*Metals*	*ElecM*	*Trans*	*Furn*
Min	337	237	40	257	29200	3583	17264	45	409	6663
Food	23	15869	909	149	612	23	22	15	12	11
Tex	240	210	7966	208	551	42	170	113	1981	823
Wood	988	4476	299	21164	1190	457	595	419	464	3276
Chem	7151	5950	3617	6504	55637	1428	4895	3366	5327	2880
NMM	604	1300	87	62	703	2077	214	318	815	99
Metals	7836	3716	939	1945	4776	1432	51081	5742	13152	4834
ElecM	926	11	5	40	47	4	1118	6205	2159	110
Trans	2849	755	114	127	522	100	429	99	64784	77
Furn	61	87	233	488	297	25	187	497	30	1464

Table 1: Intermediate Inputs in Million Rand (A1)

Through normalisation, an identical structure with values suitable for the model is retained—see Table A2.

	Min	*Food*	*Tex*	*Wood*	*Chem*	*NMM*	*Metals*	*ElecM*	*Trans*	*Furn*
Min	0,002	0,001	0,000	0,001	0,145	0,018	0,086	0,000	0,002	0,033
Food	0,000	0,079	0,005	0,001	0,003	0,000	0,000	0,000	0,000	0,000
Tex	0,001	0,001	0,039	0,001	0,003	0,000	0,001	0,001	0,010	0,004
Wood	0,005	0,022	0,001	0,105	0,006	0,002	0,003	0,002	0,002	0,016
Chem	0,035	0,029	0,018	0,032	0,276	0,007	0,024	0,017	0,026	0,014
NMM	0,003	0,006	0,000	0,000	0,003	0,010	0,001	0,002	0,004	0,000
Metals	0,039	0,018	0,005	0,010	0,024	0,007	0,253	0,028	0,065	0,024
ElecM	0,005	0,000	0,000	0,000	0,000	0,000	0,006	0,031	0,011	0,001
Trans	0,014	0,004	0,001	0,001	0,003	0,000	0,002	0,000	0,321	0,000
Furn	0,000	0,000	0,001	0,002	0,001	0,000	0,001	0,002	0,000	0,007

Table 2: Normalised Intermediate Inputs (A2)

Again, α_g, the share of the mineral resource in the production of the mining sector is set to $\alpha_g = 0,5$

Data and Results for Chapter 5

Output performance The estimation is based on output development of the various sectors we analyzed in the different aggregations. Below, their output development is depicted for the period under consideration, 1970 to 2006.

The sectors are agriculture, mining, MEC manufacturing, manufacturing, and the tertiary sector. Data has been aggregated from the Quantec Database. The relatively stagnant development of mining in recent years is visible, yet overshadowed by the dynamic growth of MEC sectors.

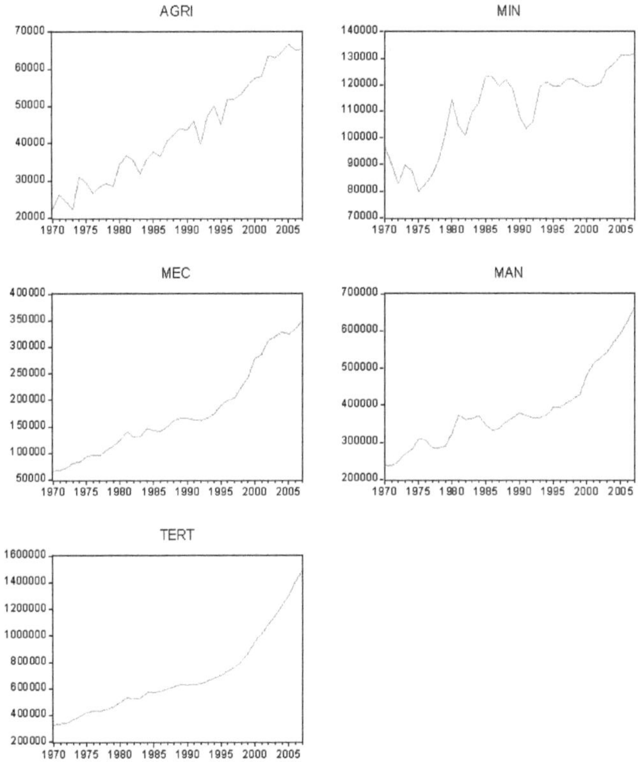

Figure 1: Development of output for 5 sectors

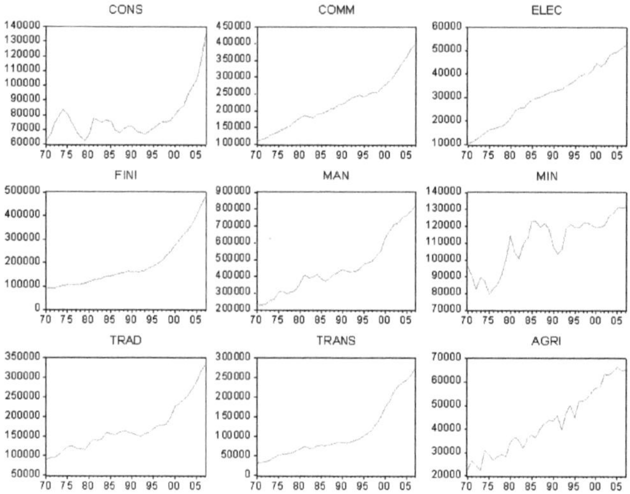

Figure 2: Development of output for the 9 2-digit sectors

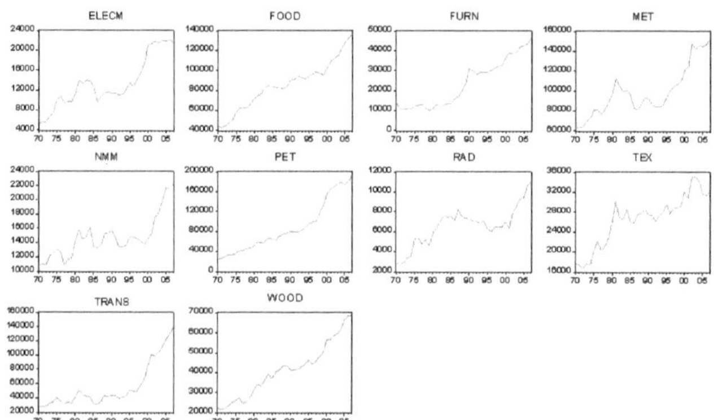

Figure 3: Development of output for the 10 3-digit sectors

Weighting matrices Linkages are modeled by using weighting matrices as explained in Chapter 5. The weighting matrices have been calculated for every year, to account for changes in the structure of the South African economy and thus of linkages between sectors over time. Below are three exemplary matrices for the year 2007—the most recent year used in the estimations. Matrices for other years are available upon request from the author. These linkages represent inputs from domestic sources - imported inputs have not been considered in order to better reflect impulses that might emanate from growth in one particular sector.

The tables have to be read in the following way: the share of intermediate input produced in one sector that is used in the other sectors of the economy is presented in the sector column. Intermediate input that is used in production within the sector is set to zero. Therefore, the columns all sum to one.

	Agri	Min	Man	Elec	Cons	Trad	TrSC	FinI	Comm
used in					*stemming from*				
Agri	0.000	0.002	0.085	0.022	0.012	0.029	0.031	0.011	0.088
Min	0.000	0.000	0.070	0.115	0.037	0.025	0.187	0.018	0.059
Man	0.974	0.696	0.000	0.405	0.001	0.461	0.237	0.273	0.401
Elec	0.000	0.247	0.018	0.000	0.143	0.010	0.007	0.020	0.001
Cons	0.000	0.019	0.184	0.011	0.000	0.036	0.017	0.050	0.010
Trad	0.017	0.001	0.140	0.131	0.216	0.000	0.242	0.312	0.035
TrSC	0.000	0.002	0.193	0.132	0.058	0.169	0.000	0.112	0.046
FinI	0.001	0.023	0.134	0.100	0.382	0.143	0.181	0.000	0.358
Comm	0.007	0.010	0.177	0.084	0.152	0.127	0.098	0.204	0.000

Table 3: Weighting matrix for 9 two-digit sectors, 2007

	Agri	Min	MEC	Man	Elec	Cons	Trad	TrSC	FinI	Comm
used in						*stemming from*				
Agri	0.000	0.002	0.060	0.059	0.022	0.012	0.029	0.031	0.011	0.088
Min	0.000	0.000	0.046	0.054	0.115	0.037	0.025	0.187	0.018	0.059
MEC	0.019	0.581	0.000	0.113	0.269	0.000	0.107	0.154	0.099	0.147
Man	0.955	0.115	0.424	0.000	0.136	0.001	0.355	0.083	0.175	0.254
Elec	0.000	0.247	0.007	0.020	0.000	0.143	0.010	0.007	0.020	0.001
Cons	0.000	0.019	0.129	0.132	0.011	0.000	0.036	0.017	0.050	0.010
Trad	0.017	0.001	0.052	0.163	0.131	0.216	0.000	0.242	0.312	0.035
TrSC	0.000	0.002	0.126	0.151	0.132	0.058	0.169	0.000	0.112	0.046
FinI	0.001	0.023	0.055	0.150	0.100	0.382	0.143	0.181	0.000	0.358
Comm	0.007	0.010	0.101	0.158	0.084	0.152	0.127	0.098	0.204	0.000

Table 4: Weighting matrix for 9 2-digit sectors including separated MEC, 2007

	Food	Tex	Wood	Pet	NMM	Met	ElecM	Rad	Trans	Furn
used in					*stemming from*					
Food	0.000	0.050	0.412	0.188	0.364	0.102	0.002	0.002	0.343	0.048
Tex	0.525	0.000	0.026	0.100	0.023	0.022	0.001	0.000	0.050	0.129
Wood	0.078	0.042	0.000	0.177	0.017	0.022	0.002	0.055	0.054	0.248
Pet	0.350	0.130	0.111	0.000	0.198	0.088	0.009	0.028	0.236	0.162
NMM	0.012	0.009	0.041	0.041	0.000	0.034	0.001	0.000	0.044	0.013
Met	0.012	0.037	0.055	0.144	0.061	0.000	0.254	0.095	0.194	0.103
ElecM	0.001	0.004	0.025	0.085	0.079	0.145	0.000	0.349	0.027	0.037
Rad	0.008	0.025	0.013	0.015	0.005	0.014	0.230	0.000	0.016	0.243
Trans	0.007	0.506	0.044	0.157	0.227	0.421	0.493	0.322	0.000	0.017
Furn	0.007	0.197	0.275	0.094	0.026	0.152	0.008	0.149	0.037	0.000

Table 5: Weighting matrix for 10 3-digit sectors, 2007

Forschungsergebnisse der Wirtschaftsuniversität Wien

Herausgeber: Wirtschaftsuniversität Wien –
vertreten durch a.o. Univ. Prof. Dr. Barbara Sporn

INFOS UND KONTAKT:

WU (Wirtschaftsuniversität Wien)
Department of Finance, Accounting and Statistics
Institute for Finance, Banking and Insurance
Heiligenstädter Straße 46-48, 1190 Wien
Tel.: 0043-1-313 36/4556
Fax: 0043-1-313 36/904556
valentine.wendling@wu.ac.at
www.wu.ac.at/finance

Band 1 Stefan Felder: Frequenzallokation in der Telekommunikation. Ökonomische Analyse der Vergabe von Frequenzen unter besonderer Berücksichtigung der UMTS-Auktionen. 2004.

Band 2 Thomas Haller: Marketing im liberalisierten Strommarkt. Kommunikation und Produktplanung im Privatkundenmarkt. 2005.

Band 3 Alexander Stremitzer: Agency Theory: Methodology, Analysis. A Structured Approach to Writing Contracts. 2005.

Band 4 Günther Sedlacek: Analyse der Studiendauer und des Studienabbruch-Risikos. Unter Verwendung der statistischen Methoden der Ereignisanalyse. 2004.

Band 5 Monika Knassmüller: Unternehmensleitbilder im Vergleich. Sinn- und Bedeutungsrahmen deutschsprachiger Unternehmensleitbilder – Versuch einer empirischen (Re-)Konstruktion. 2005.

Band 6 Matthias Fink: Erfolgsfaktor Selbstverpflichtung bei vertrauensbasierten Kooperationen. Mit einem empirischen Befund. 2005.

Band 7 Michael Gerhard Kraft: Ökonomie zwischen Wissenschaft und Ethik. Eine dogmenhistorische Untersuchung von Léon M.E. Walras bis Milton Friedman. 2005.

Band 8 Ingrid Zechmeister: Mental Health Care Financing in the Process of Change. Challenges and Approaches for Austria. 2005.

Band 9 Sarah Meisenberger: Strukturierte Organisationen und Wissen. 2005.

Band 10 Anne-Katrin Neyer: Multinational teams in the European Commission and the European Parliament. 2005.

Band 11 Birgit Trukeschitz: Im Dienst Sozialer Dienste. Ökonomische Analyse der Beschäftigung in sozialen Dienstleistungseinrichtungen des Nonprofit Sektors. 2006

Band 12 Marcus Kölling: Interkulturelles Wissensmanagement. Deutschland Ost und West. 2006.

Band 13 Ulrich Berger: The Economics of Two-way Interconnection. 2006.

Band 14 Susanne Guth: Interoperability of DRM Systems. Exchanging and Processing XML-based Rights Expressions. 2006.

Band 15 Bernhard Klement: Ökonomische Kriterien und Anreizmechanismen für eine effiziente Förderung von industrieller Forschung und Innovation. Mit einer empirischen Quantifizierung der Hebeleffekte von F&E-Förderinstrumenten in Österreich. 2006.

Band 16 Markus Imgrund: Wege aus der Insolvenz. Eine Analyse der Fortführung und Sanierung insolventer Klein- und Mittelbetriebe unter besonderer Berücksichtigung des Konfigurationsansatzes. 2007.

Band 17 Nicolas Knotzer: Product Recommendations in E-Commerce Retailing Applications. 2008.

Band 18 Astrid Dickinger: Perceived Quality of Mobile Services. A Segment-Specific Analysis. 2007.

Band 19 Nadine Wiedermann-Ondrej: Hybride Finanzierungsinstrumente in der nationalen und internationalen Besteuerung der USA. 2008.

Band 20 Helmut Sorger: Entscheidungsorientiertes Risikomanagement in der Industrieunternehmung. 2008.

Band 21 Martin Rietsch: Messung und Analyse des ökonomischen Wechselkursrisikos aus Unternehmenssicht: Ein stochastischer Simulationsansatz. 2008.

Band 22 Hans Christian Mantler: Makroökonomische Effizienz des Finanzsektors. Herleitung eines theoretischen Modells und Schätzung der Wachstumsimplikationen für die Marktwirtschaften und Transformationsökonomien Europas. 2008.

Band 23 Youri Tacoun: La théorie de la valeur de Christian von Ehrenfels. 2008.

Band 24 Monika Koller: Longitudinale Betrachtung der Kognitiven Dissonanz. Eine Tagebuchstudie zur Reiseentscheidung. 2008.

Band 25 Marcus Scheiblecker: The Austrian Business Cycle in the European Context. 2008.

Band 26 Aida Numic: Multinational Teams in European and American Companies. 2008.

Band 27 Ulrike Bauernfeind: User Satisfaction with Personalised Internet Applications. 2008.

Band 28 Reinhold Schodl: Systematische Analyse und Bewertung komplexer Supply Chain Prozesse bei dynamischer Festlegung des Auftragsentkopplungspunkts. 2008.

Band 29 Bianca Gusenbauer: Öffentlich-private Finanzierung von Infrastruktur in Entwicklungsländern und deren Beitrag zur Armutsreduktion. Fallstudien in Vietnam und auf den Philippinen. 2009.

Band 30 Elisabeth Salomon: Hybrides Management in sino-österreichischen Joint Ventures in China aus österreichischer Perspektive. 2009.

Band 31 Katharina Mader: Gender Budgeting: Ein emanzipatorisches, finanzpolitisches und demokratiepolitisches Instrument. 2009.

Band 32 Michael Weber: Die Generierung von Empfehlungen für zwischenbetriebliche Transaktionen als gesamtwirtschaftliche Infrastrukturleistung. 2010.

Band 33 Lisa Gimpl-Heersink: Joint Pricing and Inventory Control under Reference Price Effects. 2009.

Band 34 Erscheint nicht.

Band 35 Dagmar Kiefer: Multicultural Work in Five United Nations Organisations. An Austrian Perspective. 2009.

Band 36 Gottfried Gruber: Multichannel Management. A Normative Model Towards Optimality. 2009.

Band 37 Rainer Quante: Management of Stochastic Demand in Make-to-Stock Manufacturing. 2009.

Band 38 Franz F. Eiffe: Auf den Spuren von Amartya Sen. Zur theoriegeschichtlichen Genese des Capability-Ansatzes und seinem Beitrag zur Armutsanalyse in der EU. 2010.

www.ingramcontent.com/pod-product-compliance
Ingram Content Group UK Ltd.
Pitfield, Milton Keynes, MK11 3LW, UK
UKHW021832100926
8556IPUK00004B/298